T H E
COFFEY
FILES

T H E
COFFEY
FILES

ONE COP'S WAR AGAINST THE MOB

JOE COFFEY
AND
JERRY SCHMETTERER

ST. MARTIN'S PRESS
NEW YORK

DESIGN BY DIANE STEVENSON, SNAP-HAUS GRAPHICS

Library of Congress Cataloging-in-Publication Data

Coffey, Joseph J.
    The Coffey files: a man against the mob / Joseph Coffey and Jerry Schmetterer.
        p.   cm.
    "A Thomas Dunne book."
    ISBN 0-312-06934-0
    1. Coffey, Joseph J. 2. Police—New York (N.Y.)—Biography. 3. Detectives—New York (N.Y.)—Biography. 4. Mafia.
    I. Schmetterer, Jerry. II. Title.
    HV7911.C6A3 1992
    363.2′092—dc20
    [B]   91-35845
                                                                            CIP

First Edition: February 1992

10 9 8 7 6 5 4 3 2 1

To Joseph Coffey, Sr., My wife Pat, and children,
Kathleen, Steven, and Joseph
JC

To Emily
JS

ACKNOWLEDGMENTS

This book records the vivid memories of Detective Sergeant Joseph J. Coffey, Jr. It is based almost entirely on his recollection of events, how he was motivated by them, and how he affected their outcome. It depicts his role in the history of the New York Police Department's fight against crime. There were many people who urged us to put these memories into words. Time and again we turned to these friends and colleagues for their invaluable assistance. With special thanks to Detective Sergeant, NYPD Jim Mullaly (Ret.), for making the introduction of both of us to Tom Dunne. Dr. Sheldon Shuch contributed in ways that cannot be measured.

James Sullivan, former Chief of Detectives NYPD, Richard Esposito, Ed Fischer, Steve and Sharon Hittman, Patti Aronofsky, Doug Kahn and Stephen Mangione also contributed in words and deeds.

And thanks to Pete Wolverton; and to Tom Dunne for his encouragement and his cool, guiding, hand and his faith in both of us.

THE AUTHORS

CONTENTS

PREFACE

It was one of those things you register in the back of your mind to check out the next day. Then, when the next day comes, you can't remember who told you about it or how important it was. Reporters run into that a lot. Usually, because you're afraid you will miss a good story if you don't check it out, you start from scratch.

In this particular case I knew I had heard something about a big time hit man being busted as part of a Mafia drug ring. I was the police headquarters bureau chief for the New York *Daily News*. As part of my routine, every day, I called several contacts in the department who I knew would share information with me. It was a system that served both sides well. They knew I would give them a good write-up when they did something they wanted publicized. I mentioned, to one of them, my tip about the hit man. My contact told me she heard something like that. She suggested I speak to Joe Coffey.

"Joe Coffey? The Son of Sam Joe Coffey?" I asked. "Where is he these days?" My friend said Coffey was working in the chief of detectives' office. She said I'd be very interested in what he was doing.

It seemed I was always interested in what Joe Coffey was doing. My last contact with him was during the Son of Sam manhunt in 1977. Coffey was the detective sergeant coordinating the nighttime operations, which centered mostly around the borough of Queens. I was a reporter assigned to the paper's Queens bureau and trying every day to make contact with Coffey to find out if any progress had been made on the case the night before. Sometimes he was helpful. Most often the frustration that case was causing everyone was reflected in his "No comment" or "Why don't you ask Jimmy Breslin?"—a reference to the *News* columnist who received a personal message from the serial killer and was, daily, breaking the department's collective chops for the lack of progress. But I knew that if there was anything to know, Joe Coffey knew it. We had crossed paths many times before over the years. Joe was a favorite of many reporters. Some accused him of being a publicity hound.

I first heard about him in 1972. He was the young detective from District Attorney Hogan's office who connected a Little Italy thug named Vincent Rizzo to an international counterfeiting and robbery network. It was a complicated case that eventually involved the U.S. Justice Department and would leave loose ends and unexplained mysteries for the next two decades. The case became known as the Vatican Connection. It is one of the most spectacular detective stories of the twentieth century. Joe Coffey started it all.

We met again a couple of years later when a cop named Angel Poggi, on his very first night out of the Police Academy, walked into a booby trap set by the Puerto Rican terrorist group FALN. Coffey was a patrol sergeant. He was the first cop on the scene and held Poggi in his arms until

x

medics arrived. I was assigned to check out the report of an explosion the city desk heard over the police scanner. I got to the scene in time to see Sergeant Joe Coffey removing his blue police shirt, which had been stained with Angel Poggi's blood.

Coverage of terrorism took up a lot of my time over the next few years. In addition to the FALN, the Black Liberation Army was busy shooting police officers. My first genuine scoop involved the BLA. I learned that they were responsible for a $350,000 armed robbery of a Brooklyn department store. They needed the money to fund their war chest. Joe Coffey had a shoot-out on the Harlem River Drive with the BLA.

International groups like the Croatians and Omega 19 were also surfacing in New York in the early seventies, bombing airports and train stations. Detective Sergeant Joe Coffey was in the middle of that, too, as a supervisor in the Arson and Explosion Squad, the forerunner of the Anti-Terrorist Task Force. As a reporter I wanted to be where the big stories were. As a cop Joe Coffey, whether it was for the publicity or a genuine desire to serve the public, wanted the big cases. We both seemed to be having a run of good luck.

Then in 1976 David Berkowitz began his eighteen-month reign of terror. Every reporter wanted in on that story. And there was Joe Coffey once again in the middle of the action.

Now I was chasing him down again. I hoped he was in a better mood than he was during the "Sam" days, and I hoped he trusted me enough by now to let me in on this hit man story. I found him in a corner of the chief of detectives' office. He was in a good mood, and he gave me a great story.

The next day's paper had the headline "Cops Probing Mob Bust 500M Cocaine Ring." I reported that a special task force designated "Operation Rattle," because its mission was to "shake up organized crime," had broken up a ring that had smuggled cocaine worth $500 million from

South America and through Kennedy Airport in the past year. In the process a "senior mob hit man" named Marco "Tony Ugly" Mucciolo, 61, was arrested for two murders.

The article contained the first news of a handpicked squad of detectives that had been formed to investigate a rash of mob murders. Detective Sergeant Joe Coffey was commander of the special unit. I wanted to know more about the work those guys were doing. Coffey assured me the police department's attitude towards organized crime was changing. He said I would get a lot of good stories out of his office in the next few years. He was right.

JERRY SCHMETTERER
March 3, 1991

· I ·

THE COFFEY GANG

During the early days of 1978 the streets of New York ran red with Mafia blood. From January through March thirty Mafia hoodlums at all levels in the hierarchy of organized crime were murdered.

They had names like "Patty Mack" and "Sally Balls" and hung around with guys called "Tony Ugly" and "Matty the Horse." Their bodies were found twisted and jammed in the trunks of luxury cars in the parking lots of Kennedy and La Guardia airports.

Sometimes they were stuffed into plastic bags and discarded along dark roads in the Bronx and Brooklyn. Occasionally, depending on the personal style of the individual hit man, they were dismembered, mutilated, and strewn about local garbage dumps. Once in a while, the victim was gunned down or stabbed to death in public. Those bodies were left where they fell to deliver messages in Mafia code.

The city's tabloid press lovingly described every hit. Each 1 time a body was discovered, headlines screamed of blood feuds and brutal killings as Mafia families turned the sidewalks of New York into their private battlegrounds.

These murders were rarely solved. The New York police did not have the resources or the inclination to chase hit men who disappeared into the night to be protected by the Mafia code of silence. With a conspiratorial wink police officials told reporters the mob was doing the city a favor. "It's nothing but vermin killing vermin," they would say, asking not to have their name appear next to the quote.

Detectives would spend a few hours talking to the usual suspects, and the file would be put on the back burner. Attention could then be paid to crimes committed against honest citizens. Gangland rubouts were part of the folklore of America.

But in those early days of 1978 a shakeup was taking place on the upper floors of One Police Plaza, New York's Police Headquarters. A new police commissioner named Robert McGuire was in place. In his short time in office, he had already made it clear that he would push for changes in attitude and politics within the department.

Though never a cop himself, his father was a police deputy chief. McGuire grew up in a household that held firmly to the tradition of law and order and public service. He had been an assistant U.S. attorney and also served as a counsel for the Patrolmen's Benevolent Association, defending cops who got into trouble.

McGuire demanded excellence. Instead of apologizing for flaws in the department, he set about to repair them.

He chose as his chief of detectives a cop with a broad range of police experience named James Sullivan. A veteran of the uniformed Tactical Patrol Force, Sullivan had a master's degree in management and had commanded detectives in the Narcotics Division. He had also for a short time served as executive officer, second in command, of the Detective Division. The average cop thought Sullivan, a man with a broad Irish grin when he chose to show it, was as comfortable in the commissioner's boardroom as he was on the front lines of a riot. They believed that he presented a good image for the department.

Both Sullivan and McGuire resented the popular belief that organized crime could get away with murder. While both also knew the realities of the situation, they agreed the department should make some special effort—even a short term effort—to try to stem the organized lawlessness that was the Mafia's way of doing business in the early months of 1978.

Typical of their problem was the murder of Pasquale "Patty Mack" Macchiarole. His body was found stuffed into the trunk of his brand-new Cadillac on a gravel road alongside Rockaway Parkway in Brooklyn. He had been shot three times in the head with a .25 caliber pistol.

The precinct detectives went through their usual drill. They investigated the crime scene and, failing to find any obvious physical evidence that would finger the killer, filled out the proper forms. They told their supervisor it seemed to be a mob hit. The department's Organized Crime Control Bureau (OCCB), which investigated any crime that appeared to be the work of a gang, reported that "Patty Mack" was a capo in the Genovese crime family. The OCCB's records indicated he was in charge of a gambling and loan-sharking crew, and their experts theorized that "Patty Mack" had gotten caught skimming some profits and had to pay the ultimate penalty.

There was no real hope of solving the case through investigative procedure. Maybe someday an informant looking to save his own skin would squeal on the killer and explain why the hit was necessary. The case would be considered solved, even if no arrest was ever made.

Sullivan and McGuire were both very aware that unsolved Mafia homicides lowered the department's ratio of "cleared" cases. This made it appear that their detectives were not as good at solving homicides as they really were.

Sullivan told McGuire he had a plan. He thought it would   3 improve the homicide clearance rate while at the same time working toward changing the attitude of the police toward Mafia hits. He wanted to set up a special unit, working from his office on the thirteenth floor of police headquarters and reporting directly to him.

The unit would be called the Chief of Detectives' Organized Crime Homicide Task Force, specializing in solving murders attributed to organized crime. At the least, such a unit would give the impression that the department was trying to do something to destroy the myth of Mafia impunity. McGuire, thinking along similar lines, agreed with the concept. He would give the unit thirty days to see what it could do. He also agreed with Sullivan's idea of who should command such a unit.

On April 3, 1978, the chief of detectives placed a call to Detective Sergeant Joseph J. Coffey, executive officer of the Robbery Unit in the borough of Queens.

Sullivan had known Coffey since he was a captain on the elite Tactical Patrol Force and Coffey was a rookie under his command. Over the years the two had maintained a friendly relationship, although not often working directly together. Other cops remarked on the physical similarities between the two men, although Coffey at six-foot-four was about six inches taller.

Commissioner McGuire also knew Coffey. They first met when McGuire was an assistant U.S. attorney and they developed a social relationship, sharing a drink or two after work.

They met officially one night when McGuire was working for the Patrolmen's Benevolent Association. Both had responded to an incident in which a police officer shot and killed a New York City housing patrolman after the housing officer shot and killed the city cop's partner in a wild shoot-out on Lexington Avenue. Coffey was the highest-ranking detective on duty that night and was sent to the horrifying scene.

4   While technically on different sides of the investigation,

Coffey trying to decide if the cop had acted without justification, McGuire on the scene to protect the rights of the cop, their mutual respect helped bring some order to the chaos surrounding the incident. It was eventually ruled that the cop fired with due cause. The housing police were in civilian clothes and had started a drunken brawl with the cab driver, and the dead housing cop had shot the city patrolman when he responded to the brawl.

McGuire remembered the incident when he okayed Coffey for the new position.

"Joe, I have an interesting proposition for you," Sullivan said on the phone, "something I think you can sink your teeth into. Could you stop by my office on your way home?"

On the other end of the phone Joe Coffey was secretly pleased. He had been in the Queens Robbery Unit for a little more than eight months. He was sent there after heading up one of the units that captured the serial killer known as Son of Sam. While he enjoyed the duty—which often included leading shotgun-toting cops through barricaded doorways—it was not ideal for him. And he was a little bitter and disappointed that his work on the Son of Sam case had not resulted in a better reward. Homicide was his first love and the Mafia his favorite target. He did not run into either very often on the robbery beat. He had become constantly grumpy and was giving other cops a hard time.

"Chief, I'll be there forthwith," Coffey responded, using the police jargon for "immediately."

Within an hour he was in Sullivan's office listening to the plan for the establishment of the Homicide Task Force. "At first, while the chief was telling me about the idea, I was expecting him to offer me a spot as a detective assigned to the new unit. I was thrilled and I certainly would have agreed," Coffey remembers.

"Then the chief got very serious. 'Joe,' he said, 'the commissioner and I agree that with your background in District Attorney Hogan's racket squad and your organized crime and homicide experience, you should be the man to com-   5 mand this unit. You'll have my total support and the backing of the PC. We're going to give you thirty days and eight detectives to see what you can do.'"

April 3 was Coffey's fortieth birthday, and Chief Sullivan had handed him the best present he could imagine. But while he was intrigued by the offer, he managed to measure his response carefully.

"Chief," he responded, "I've been beaten down by department politics too many times to jump into something without first making sure my back is covered. I want this assignment, there's no way I could fool you about that, but I have to pick my own team. I want to select the eight detectives."

Sullivan was a little surprised by the request but understood Coffey had not built a record of success by being careless. "On what basis would you pick your men?" he asked.

"Loyalty," Coffey said bluntly. "We'll be stepping on a lot of toes in this assignment; a lot of noses are going to be out of joint. There will be enough pissed-off detectives and bosses around the city trying to sabotage me. I want to make sure I can trust my own men. If some jealous desk jockey or even some desperate hood is going to go after me, accuse me of corruption or dereliction of duty, I want to be sure he won't get any help from my own squad."

Sullivan too was a careful man and understood as well as Coffey the pitfalls of department politics. But he was also a skilled manager, so he asked why competence on the team wasn't the most important issue.

"I can teach competence. Loyalty is earned over years of sharing risks and rewards. I know the men I can trust. If I'm not working with them, this thing won't hold together even for thirty days," Coffey replied, hoping he wasn't letting the opportunity slip from his hands.

Sullivan considered the sergeant's words for a few moments, then nodded in agreement. "Okay, we'll give it a shot your way." He understood where Coffey had been and where he would have to go to make the assignment anything

6

more than window dressing. You've got a week to get your team together. Pick anyone you want. If any squad commander gives you a hard time tell him to call me."

Joe Coffey was the kid who had just been handed the keys to the candy store. He had been waiting for this assignment for more than thirty years.

During the fall of 1946, when Joe Coffey was eight years old, his family and many of their neighbors in the tenements that lined Third Avenue in the gritty shadow of the elevated subway were caught up in a dangerous struggle for control of the International Brotherhood of Teamsters Local 804. The local represented drivers of United Parcel Service, a company that delivered packages for most of the city's department stores, including the giant Macy's, Gimble's, and Saks Fifth Avenue. Joe's father and a few of the other drivers had founded the local.

Joseph Coffey, Sr., had grown up on the Lower East Side in the years around World War I. He lived in an area known as the Gashouse District and personified the Dead End Kids. In fact, a close friend in the those days was Huntz Hall, who achieved fame as one of the Bowery Boys, a group that could have very well been Joe's father's crowd.

Another of his group, Eddie McGrath, left the Lower East Side to become the boss of the city's Irish gangs.

In the 1920s, Joseph Coffey, Sr., supplemented his income by occasionally driving truckloads of Prohibition booze for the gangsters Dutch Schultz and Owney Madden.

But the Local 804 leadership group was as honest as it was tough. In the early forties their success in organizing UPS's employees made the local a lucrative target for New York's organized crime groups. The Mafia saw the local as an area of easy pickings with dues money and other funds set aside for workers' benefits waiting to be siphoned off. It was also seen as a mechanism for getting their hooks into the legitimate dealings of the department stores.

7

Joe, Sr., and his best friend, the union president, Lenny Geiger, began receiving regular visits from tough-talking labor racketeers offering favors. A typical request was for Geiger to okay the turning over of cash set aside for retirement funds to be used by the mob as collateral in a big construction deal. It would be worth big bucks to Geiger and anyone else he had to let in on the scam. Or they would be asked for a percentage of the dues paid by the drivers in exchange for allowing the trucks to go about their business undisturbed.

But Coffey and Geiger and the other officers refused the offers. At strategy meetings around the kitchen table, young Joe would listen in wonder as these honest men talked about the threats against them and described the characters who were attacking their honest way of life. He heard about trucks being set on fire, tires being slashed, and even drivers being beaten. He wondered about the cost of being honest and wondered if he could be as brave as his father and the others if he was ever put to the test.

One night Joe heard his father say he would refuse to even talk to an old friend of his, John "Cockeye" Dunn, a waterfront enforcer who thought because he was more willing to fight than work he deserved a share of the drivers' union dues. Dunn, who would eventually die in Sing Sing's electric chair, was known throughout the neighborhood for his cruelty to victims. Joe's admiration for his father grew as he realized he was not the least bit afraid of a monster like Dunn.

"I was totally fascinated by what was going on and knew instinctively that my father and his friends were fighting some kind of evil. I wanted to help them, but being a little kid I was usually told that if I wanted to be allowed to listen, I would have to keep my mouth shut," Joe remembers.

The kitchen of the Coffeys' third-floor railroad flat became Joe's college of criminal justice. His teachers were the union organizers who jammed into his mother's home planning their strategy to battle the labor racketeers. He was an eager student. He learned while still in grade school how an efficiently run organized crime gang could disrupt legitimate businessmen. The pressure of constant physical threats and the lure of big payoffs in return for a little larceny was sometimes impossible to resist.

He also learned that in those days of the union movement in New York City there was a thin line between being a legitimate union organizer and a labor racketeer. Sometimes the tactics of his father and Geiger were as tough and desperate as those of the out-and-out hoodlums. Their justification, they argued, if they threatened a truck driver in order to get him to sign on with the local, was that they had the good of the driver at heart. They were not organizing a local so that they could rape its pension fund for their own profit.

Then, on a chilly October night in 1946, Joe learned the real meaning of those threats. He was doing homework in the kitchen while his older sister, Pat, was babysitting their four-year-old brother. Suddenly they heard two loud bangs echo through the building's stark hallway.

"Somehow I knew they were shots. I can hear them today with the same clarity," Coffey says. "I also knew instinctively that my father was in trouble."

What he did next was also instinctive and is the single action that sets good cops apart from the rest of society. He ran towards the trouble. He charged out his apartment door and, three steps at a time, barreled towards the lobby of the building. As he bounded down the stairs, he feared most for his mother, pregnant with her fourth child, whose screams for help ricocheted through the tenement's winding stairwells.

The scene at the bottom of the stairs was permanently etched in Joe's memory. He saw his father bending over his distraught mother, whispering soothing words of comfort. With an eye for detail that would serve him well for the rest of his life, he noticed that the glass in the doorway behind his parents was shattered. The subway was going by on the

9

elevated tracks outside, but Joe thought he heard the door to the roof being slammed.

Frightened, and as near to sobbing as he would allow himself to be, Joe led his terrified mother back to their apartment. They were hardly inside before the senior Coffey, fighting to control his temper and not showing an ounce of fear in front of his children, phoned his friends and the police for help.

Later that night Lenny Geiger (who ten years later would be found dead in his car the evening before he was scheduled to testify before a Senate committee investigating organized crime's ties to unions) called the leadership of Local 804 together in the Coffey kitchen.

The police told Joe's parents they had been saved by an illusion caused by the single bare light bulb in the hallway. The harsh light made it appear that anyone on the stairs between the light and the door was actually standing just inside the door. The hidden assassin actually fired at the couple's image on the door. But it was close enough to frighten Joe's mother to the point of fear for her unborn baby.

Word of the attack spread quickly through the Irish neighborhoods of Manhattan. The Coffey phone was constantly ringing with information and offers of help. The word was that "Cockeye" Dunn was the shooter. More distressing was the news that Joe's uncle had fingered the Coffeys. The uncle was a close associate of mob bosses Meyer Lansky and Eddie McGrath. He had let Dunn know the Coffeys were out shopping and what time they would return.

Young Joe stood at the apartment door taking this all in. He was outraged that anyone could want to do this to his father. He did not understand the lure of money. He was confused to learn how many criminals there were and that they worked as hard at their illicit undertakings as honest men worked at their businesses. All his father and their friends wanted to do was earn an honest living. He was amazed that this actually offended some people.

Despite the ordeal, Joe's father stayed calm. He urged restraint, wanting to wait and see what might develop. But Mrs. Coffey saw things differently. She feared that any time wasted in going after the assassins would encourage them to try again. She did not expect the police to be of any help. Out of patience with the brave men in her kitchen, she took the only sensible course of action. She called the Coffeys' old friend, the kingpin gangster Eddie McGrath, who had of course already heard about the incident. Mrs. Coffey appealed to the hoodlum on the basis of their long-standing friendship to intercede with the gang putting the pressure on 804. In doing so, she told McGrath, he would be saving his friend's life.

About three days later, during the afternoon, when Mrs. Coffey and the toddler Edward were alone in the apartment—Joe and Pat were in school—she had a visitor. A McGrath henchman came by to say that his boss wanted her to know there was nothing more to worry about. The contract on her husband had been canceled. There would still be pressure on Local 804 to bend to the mob—after all, even Eddie McGrath could not understand why they resisted—but there would be no more gunplay.

That incident in the tenement hallway changed the life of Joe Coffey, Jr., forever. "I made up my mind that night that I would be an FBI agent—that I would find a way to help people like my father and Lenny Geiger stand up against organized crime."

He had learned a lot around his own kitchen table. Now the grade-school student began hunting down books. He read all he could find about the Italian Black Hand and the Mafia, the Jewish gangs, the Chinese Tongs, and Murder Incorporated. If the subject of a book was crime, Joe Coffey sought it out, read it from cover to cover, and read it again. He devoured the newspapers, searching for accounts of rub-outs and arrests, and he was the biggest fan of crime movies and radio programs. But, as much as the media often glamorized the life of a criminal, Joe never wavered from his desire to be on the right side of the law. His favorite stories were the ones that proved crime doesn't pay.

When he joined the police force in 1964 he was determined to use his career to bust the Mafia. It might have been a thought shared by many eager young cops: but how many of them had seen their fathers survive an attempted hit?

While working for the Manhattan district attorney's Rackets Bureau, he got his first taste of what a determined detective could do. There he investigated the criminal takeovers of legitimate businesses. He saw up close how mob tentacles snaked through people's everyday lives, from the restaurants they ate in to the churches where they prayed. He also helped solve such notorious cases as the barbershop assassination of Albert Anastasia and took part in the breaking up of the biggest loan-sharking and gambling ring in the nation. Now, five years after leaving the DA's office to track down terrorists and a serial killer, he was back on the beat he was born to walk.

Joe was very happy that evening sitting around his own kitchen table in the Long Island suburb of Levittown with his wife Pat and their three children, Kathleen, Steven, and Joseph III. He called his closest friends with the news and ignored their cynical remarks about the assignment's being window dressing to appease the press. Everyone was sure nothing could really be done in thirty days. They told him Sullivan and McGuire were playing a political card for Ed Koch, and after thirty days he would once again face the frustration that dogged his career. However, to Joe Coffey his new post as commanding officer of the Chief of Detectives' Organized Crime Homicide Task Force was a dream job.

The next day he began assembling his team. Using a desk set aside in a corner of Sullivan's headquarters office and surrounded by the statisticians and analysts whose work measured the effect, or lack of effect, of the chief's orders, he worked the telephone.

12

By late afternoon he had made eight calls and lined up the team he wanted. "We're going to have a gang of our own," Coffey told them, "and we're going to kick ass." As he knew they would, the eight detectives Joe enlisted for the Coffey Gang all jumped at the chance for a piece of the action—even for only thirty days. They all agreed to drop their current cases and report to One Police Plaza the following Monday morning.

The founding members of the Coffey Gang were detectives John O'Connell and Jerry Maroney from the 17th Homicide Zone, Jack Cahill and Dick Joyce from the 1st Homicide Zone, Joe Lyons from the 16th Homicide Zone, John McGlynn from the elite Major Case Squad, Frank McDarby from the tension-packed Anti-Terrorist Squad, and John Meyer from the Manhattan Burglary Squad.

Joe Coffey loved these men. Like him they had grown up on New York's tough streets and had lifelong contacts on both sides of the law, which proved invaluable over years of police work. Joe had spent countless hours with them sitting in dark cars on dangerous streets, chain smoking and trying to stay awake by drinking countless cups of coffee or, in his case, tea. He knocked down doors with them when they knew cold-blooded killers waited on the other side. Their loyalty to each other was similar to the family ties of the Mafia. But it was stronger and not in need of blood oaths and macho posturing. They were the Coffey Gang, ready to take on all comers—Mafioso, Westie, Chinese Tong, whatever.

Within a week of receiving Jim Sullivan's marching orders, Coffey had his gang gathered at headquarters. They were sitting around a big conference table. All were in their shirtsleeves. Some wore shoulder holsters, but most opted for the newer style of carrying their guns in ankle holsters. Joe's .38 caliber Smith & Wesson detective special was, as always, in a holster on his hip.

In the middle of the conference table was a pile of detective forms detailing more than twenty homicides that had

13

occurred since January 1. They were classified mob hits. Hidden among the police jargon and grotesque pictures of victims contained in that pile of paperwork, Joe Coffey believed, were the clues that would get his group rolling not only toward Sullivan's thirty-day deadline but toward a new attitude for police.

He locked the door to the conference room, and conversation came to an abrupt halt. The men sitting around the table were about to find out what they were there for. Joe reached into the pocket of his white button-down shirt and took out his ever-present pack of Marlboros. Purposely drawing out the moment for dramatic effect, he slowly lit the cigarette.

Carefully he circled the table and began the short speech he had mentally prepared while driving to police headquarters that morning. He told his gang, "I know as well as anyone here that we can't do much in thirty days. But I truly believe that if we show real progress, the deadline will come and go and no one will want to break us up. As far as I'm concerned, we're here to stay."

This particular group of detectives was used to hearing Coffey talk like that. They knew that through the force of his own will he had a unique ability to get the giant bureaucracy of the New York Police Department to bend. Coffey did not hesitate to break from tradition, to force issues within the department, or to serve notice on criminals from Wall Street to Mulberry Street that if he was on the job they shouldn't count on the old rules. It was an attitude that won him admiration from his peers but caused his superior officers to regard him as a pain in the ass—but one who got things done.

After reading all the reports, the group agreed on two things. First, despite what the newspapers were saying, this rash of murders was not the result of a Mafia gang war. Rather, they believed, the mob was taking advantage of the public hysteria by settling some old debts. The godfathers realized that the appearance of a gang war would discourage

1
4

any genuine effort by the police. They reasoned that the police brass would follow their old traditions and let "vermin kill vermin." They did not know about Joe Coffey's new assignment.

Secondly, the group decided to pick two cases that they thought could be solved quickly, in order to prove their effectiveness before the thirty-day deadline. They selected cases where there appeared to be a weak link. Either the victim was a fringe player dealing on the edges of organized crime whose associates might be more willing to talk than the colleagues of a "made" member of a family, or there were a lot of witnesses, honest citizens who might be willing to help the police.

Coffey chose two murders, both committed during the last week of March. The first involved Leo Ladenhauf, whose body was found stuffed into the trunk of his Oldsmobile in the parking lot of Kennedy Airport. He was a roofing contractor whom organized crime experts believed to be a loan shark involved with the roofers' union and construction industry—a classic fringe player. Coffey assigned Jerry Maroney and John O'Connell to find out who killed Ladenhauf.

The second case was the kind of gangland hit Hollywood loved to recreate. It involved the murder of Salvatore "Sally Balls" Briguglio.

Joe Coffey has always believed there is a special place in hell for Mafia killers. If these dead mafiosi can find some time in their torturous days to sit around telling war stories, "Sally Balls" has bragging rights to some of the most glorious claims to fame in Mafia history. He was the man the FBI believes abducted and murdered the notorious one-time head of the Teamsters Union, Jimmy Hoffa.

"Sally Balls" had the additional claim that he was set up for his own death by two Mafia superstars: Matty "Matty the Horse" Ianiello, the man who ran Times Square vice for the Genovese family, and Tony "Tony Pro" Provenzano, head of Teamsters Union Local 560, the only union local ever taken over by the federal government because it was so corrupt there was no other way to clean it up.

There were a lot of witnesses to the "Sally Balls" hit. It was carried out on a crowded Little Italy street at 10:30 in the evening, March 21, 1978. Coffey assigned Dick Joyce and John McGlynn to find a witness who would be willing to cooperate.

Coffey handed out a few more cases and ordered two pairs of detectives to begin a search of police files throughout the city to see if there was anything overlooked in any of the 1978 cases that could be helpful. Coffey himself would serve in a supervisory role, available to jump in and help any of the gang if they needed him.

Before dispatching the Chief of Detectives' Organized Crime Homicide Task Force on their first day of duty, Coffey made a short speech. He told them, "I know you guys are going to get a rough time from some precinct detective squad commanders. They are going to think we're stepping on their toes. They are right. But if they were doing their jobs, we wouldn't be necessary. We have a job to do and the police commissioner is behind us. No one else matters. If you have any trouble with anyone, anytime, don't put your own necks on the line. Reach out for me. I'll take the heat."

Within three weeks it was clear that Coffey had selected two good cases to run with. He was able to report to Jim Sullivan that the Ladenhauf hit was nearly solved and that it had a connection to the don of the Genovese family, Funzi Tieri. The Briguglio investigation offered greater potential. Coffey told Sullivan about the Jimmy Hoffa connection and the hopes of bringing down Provenzano and Ianiello. Progress was also being made on other cases as well. Sullivan heard Coffey out and told him to keep his gang working. Neither man mentioned the thirty-day deadline.

The Ladenhauf case was relatively simple to get a handle on. Maroney and O'Connell started their investigation by going out to the Ladenhauf house to speak to his family. They brought with them a subpoena ordering the dead man's son to appear before the grand jury assigned to the case.

Steven Ladenhauf was not happy to see the detectives and refused to let them into the house. O'Connell and Maroney left without pressing the issue. Instead they went over to the Ladenhauf contracting offices, where they learned that the last time Ladenhauf's employees had seen him he had left for an appointment with a Long Island restaurant owner named Peter Ranieri.

The two detectives drove out to Ranieri's restaurant. They found the restaurateur extremely nervous. Quickly he confirmed that Ladenhauf had come to see him to collect the $250,000 that Ranieri had borrowed to open the restaurant. With Ladenhauf were two shylocks, Michael Crimi and Bruce Kay. He said the three left together and that was the last time he saw Ladenhauf.

Back at headquarters Maroney and O'Connell reported that Ranieri was very nervous when talking to the detectives. He was afraid of being connected to a murder. They thought that Ranieri was hiding something but was too afraid of Kay and Crimi to talk.

Coffey told O'Connell to return to the restaurant and tell Ranieri that he was going to be charged with killing Ladenhauf. The motive would be that he could not pay the $250,000. "Give him a few days to think about whether he wants to work more closely with us," Coffey ordered.

"But first," he told his two detectives, "I want to meet this little shit, Steven Ladenhauf."

Coffey was seething over the fact that the young man had refused to see his detectives. If the Coffey Gang came calling, you had better pay attention. Otherwise they could not be any more effective than a village constable trying to take on Murder Incorporated.

The three cops returned to the Ladenhauf house. This time Joe Coffey rang the bell. Steven Ladenhauf opened the door but not the screen door in front of it.

Coffey's bulk filled the doorway. His anger was obvious as he announced, "I am Detective Sergeant Joseph Coffey and I have a subpoena for Steven Ladenhauf to appear before a grand jury investigating the murder of Leo Ladenhauf."

The younger man's reply did nothing to ease the tense situation. "You're a scumbag and you can shove that subpoena up your Irish ass," he told Coffey.

Before Ladenhauf could take another breath, Joe Coffey put into effect a police technique his colleagues over the years had come to call "Coffey's Martial Law." He smashed his huge fist through the screen door and into the face of Steven Ladenhauf. The young man hit the floor. Blood flowed from his nose down over his chin and onto the front of his shirt.

Coffey tossed the subpoena through the newly created hole in the screen door and without another word turned his back and walked away. O'Connell and Maroney approved of Joe's brutal act. They smiled at each other and followed their boss to their unmarked car.

Three days later Coffey and Jack Cahill were inspecting the facilities at one of the police department's best kept secrets—the "Bat Cave"—a deep underground garage adjacent to a Queens high school where the department's surveillance vehicles and equipment were stored and maintained. Joe always kept up-to-date on the latest electronic bugging devices. A tape recorder was as essential to his work as a nightstick was to a street patrolman.

The topic of the morning was a wiretap recording that an undercover agent working on a gunrunning case had brought in. The Bat Cave staff of technicians was having a good laugh over it. The agent was trying to get the gunrunning suspect, a soldier in the Genovese family, to admit on tape that he was in possession of a certain number of guns requested by the agent. A few days earlier the agent had purchased a stolen U.S. Army Colt .45 from the suspect. The soldier, however, was being cagey, trying to talk in code. It went like this:

Agent: Do you have the merchandise I ordered?

Soldier: Yeah, yeah, I got the 'tings.

The agent, knowing that " 'tings" would not hold up in court as "guns" and not wanting to use the word himself, which would have alerted the soldier's suspicion, pressed on.

Agent: Well did you get every item?

Soldier: Yeah, every 'ting. I got the twenty-two, the thirty-eight and the nine millimeter.

The word "millimeter" threw the Bat Cave crowd into hysterics. No juror could deny the soldier was talking about a gun. He had broken his own code.

But things got even funnier.

Soldier: Hold on a second, there's a fuckin' mouse in the room, I'm gonna shoot it. [A loud bang is heard on the tape.]

Agent: Did you get it?

Soldier: Nah, I woulda got it if I had that "big boy" I sold you the other day.

Agent: "Big boy?"

Soldier: "Yeah, the forty-five. I coulda shot the mouse and shot my aunt in the room downstairs at the same time."

Coffey joined in the laugh. He relished every instance of a wiseguy making a fool of himself. He considered mafiosi to be idiots, and as far as he was concerned they proved it time and time again. "The greenest detective in the worst squad in the city is smarter than any capo di tutti capi asshole," he would say.

Coffey was at the Bat Cave to line up wiretap equipment for the Briguglio investigation and to check out a new van that had been fitted with a periscope device. The periscope was hidden in what looked like an air conditioning unit on the roof. He was crawling around inside the van when his beeper went off.

He phoned headquarters and got a message to call O'Connell at Ranieri's restaurant.

"Joe," O'Connell said, "Ranieri is pissing in his pants. I told him he's going to have to talk to a grand jury about his role in the murder and he nearly passed out. He says Crimi is Funzi Tieri's nephew and will slice him in little pieces if he talks."

Funzi Tieri was the godfather of the Genovese crime family at the time, one of the most powerful gangsters in the country. Coffey's mind raced with the possibilities of connecting him to the Ladenhauf murder.

Up to this point all Coffey's gang really had on Ranieri was circumstantial. He was among the last to see Ladenhauf alive and he had a motive, the $250,000, but there was no physical evidence—no gun and no witnesses who saw the murder. However, the tactic of scaring the restaurateur was working. Joe decided to press harder.

"Tell Ranieri he's going to take the fall alone if he won't cooperate. Tell him we have no interest in messing with the nephew of Funzi Tieri as long as we can nail someone for the murder," Coffey told O'Connell.

Driving out of the Bat Cave into the bright light of the warm April day, Coffey told Jack Cahill to head for the office of the Queens district attorney, where an assistant DA was putting together the Ladenhauf case for presentation to the grand jury.

Cahill waited in the car while Coffey went upstairs to request a grand jury subpoena for Funzi Tieri. He did not really believe the old don had any knowledge of the Ladenhauf hit. From what he knew so far he did not believe it had anything to do with Mafia politics; it was more likely just a falling out of thieves. But because Crimi was throwing around his uncle's name, it gave Coffey a legitimate excuse to subpoena the old man and a chance to annoy the cranky hoodlum, who would certainly be angry with his nephew for causing a cop to visit his home.

Getting into the car, Joe told Cahill to stop at headquarters to pick up McGlynn and then "let's go visit Funzi."

About one hour later Coffey and McGlynn rang the bell at the front door of the Tieris' modest attached home in the pleasant middle-class area of Bay Ridge, Brooklyn.

"An elderly woman I took to be Mrs. Tieri answered the door, and I told her who I was. I said I wanted to see her husband. She was very gentle and polite and asked me to wait a minute. She closed the door in my face," Coffey remembers.

"A minute or two later Funzi himself opened the door and asked me to come in."

Funzi Tieri, in his late seventies at the time, was a diminutive man whose large, sharp nose and steely eyes gave him a hawklike appearance. A dangerous hawk to be sure.

The don led the cops to the front porch, and they sat on padded patio chairs facing out to the street, where Cahill sat in the unmarked police car.

"He was wearing a giant diamond pinky ring which I'm sure cost more than his house. I was laughing to myself over this image of a saintly grandfather enjoying his retirement. I knew his mistress lived right around the corner," Coffey says. The young woman was famous for singing the Star Spangled Banner at the opening of the annual feast of San Gennaro in Little Italy.

Mrs. Tieri brought a tray with a cup of dark Italian coffee for her husband and McGlynn and a cup of tea for Joe. He was flattered to realize they knew enough about him to know he did not drink coffee.

"Sergeant, what brings you to my home?" Tieri asked, as he placed his cup to his thin lips.

"It concerns the matter of a man named Michael Crimi who claims to be your nephew and I believe is involved in the murder of a loan shark named Leo Ladenhauf," Coffey replied, unconsciously adopting the formal pattern of speech Tieri favored.

"Oh yes, Mickey, he's the husband of my niece. A nice young man but maybe he talks too much. I am surprised to hear you believe he is involved in a murder," said the feeble Funzi, who had ordered hundreds of beatings and murders in a Mafia career that began when he was a teenager.

21

"Well, I do not doubt it. Since he is making a point of reminding other suspects that he's your nephew, I have a subpoena for you to appear at the grand jury on the case," countered Coffey, enjoying every moment of discomfort he was causing the old killer.

Tieri politely took the paperwork from Coffey.

"Thank you for your time. I'll be seeing you again," Joe said as he left the porch.

"You are welcome in my house any time," was Tieri's final remark.

Joe and McGlynn walked out the front door, down the steps of the front porch, and back to the car, where Cahill sat waiting. An ear-to-ear smile burst from his face. He had just broken the godfather's chops and was feeling great about it.

"Cahill," he said as he got into the car, "I love this job."

The following day the Queens district attorney was advised by Funzi Tieri's lawyer that his client was too ill to appear before a grand jury. That was okay as far as Coffey was concerned. The important thing was that Tieri made his displeasure known to his nephew.

And Coffey had one more trick up his sleeve for Ranieri.

The detectives had learned that he was a fanatic for attending his son's Little League games. For several Saturday afternoons, Coffey arranged for one of his detectives dressed like the typical mob thug—shirt unbuttoned to his waist, gold chains weighing down his neck, thick sunglasses—to sit in the stands at the Little League field.

The "hood" stood out like a sore thumb among the tennis shorts and T-shirts, and throughout the games he never even looked at the field. He just sat and stared at Ranieri.

The next time O'Connell and Maroney visited Crimi, Ranieri, and the strong-arm Kay, they reported a new level of cooperation. Crimi, it appeared, was no longer so sure of Genovese family backing. He and Kay began contradicting each other as to what they knew about Leo Ladenhauf.

Ranieri may have thought of himself as a wiseguy, but he was really a restaurant owner. He did not have the stomach to stand up to the kind of pressure being put on him. Thanks to Crimi's bragging and Coffey's stage direction, he thought he was the Mafia's next target. Only the law held out any hope of his surviving. Ranieri broke.

The district attorney provided the following description to the grand jury: Peter Ranieri wanted to open a fancy gourmet restaurant on Long Island and went to Leo Ladenhauf for a loan. He apparently was making the correct payments on the loan but Ladenhauf, the fringe player, was holding out the tribute money he had to pay Crimi, who was his connection with the Genovese family. Kay did Crimi's strong-arm work. Ladenhauf told them Ranieri wasn't paying, so he had nothing to give them.

Coffey's investigation concluded that there was a confrontation in Ranieri's restaurant on March 17. In front of Crimi, Kay, and another henchman named Caligieri, Ranieri said he had been paying Ladenhauf the required money. Ladenhauf, of course, said Ranieri was lying.

Crimi, Kay, Caligieri, and Ladenhauf then went to a nearby motel to sort things out. In the motel room Kay walked up behind Ladenhauf and shot him one time in the back of the head. Then the three mobsters stuffed Ladenhauf into the trunk of his car. Kay drove the car to Kennedy Airport and left it there to be discovered by a suspicious Port Authority cop four days later.

Only one obstacle remained in the way of Coffey's bringing Crimi and Kay to justice. The Queens DA's office seemed to be dragging its heels on moving toward pressing the grand jury for indictments.

Coffey had expected this resistance: "The Queens DA was traditionally linked to labor unions for political contributions. I was not surprised they weren't anxious to move against Crimi and Kay, who had links to the construction trades and the Teamsters," Coffey explains.

Finally, Coffey threatened to take the case to the "Twin Towers"—the World Trade Center office of New York State's special prosecutor, John Keenan.

The threat worked, and Crimi, Kay, and Caligieri were indicted for loan-sharking and murder. Ranieri agreed to testify against them.

Two weeks before the trial was supposed to begin Kay was murdered, his body found in the trunk of his car at La Guardia.

Without Kay, the shooter, the murder charges fell through. There was some disappointment, but Crimi and the others were nailed for loan-sharking. That took them off the streets for a little while. Joe felt that without his special unit the people of New York would not have had the good fortune of seeing Kay murdered, and Crimi would never have been indicted for anything, much less convicted.

The police department was pleased with the results of the Ladenhauf investigation and encouraged by the amount of information Coffey's gang was collecting along the way.

It was now well past the thirty-day deadline, and Sullivan gave no indication the task force would be disbanded.

After Ranieri agreed to cooperate, Coffey turned his attention to the Briguglio case.

The Mafia's need to murder "Sally Balls" Briguglio arose from the battle for power between former Teamsters Union President Jimmy Hoffa and Anthony "Tony Pro" Provenzano, head of Teamsters Local 560 in Union City, New Jersey, the most corrupt union local in the history of organized labor.

On July 30, 1975, Hoffa disappeared from the parking lot of the Machus Red Fox Restaurant in suburban Detroit, Michigan. The FBI established through sworn testimony that Hoffa was scheduled to meet with Provenzano that afternoon in an attempt to settle some of their differences—mainly who got what piece of the lucrative Teamsters pie.

It was also established that Briguglio, who was officially the business agent for Local 560, was seen in the same parking lot. An FBI search of the file cabinet in Briguglio's office revealed just what kind of duties he performed as Provenzano's business agent. In the cabinet was a pair of handcuffs, a pistol box, loan-sharking records, information linking the local to a mail fraud case in Florida, ammunition for a nine-millimeter pistol, and a target with Briguglio's fingerprints and several nine-millimeter holes. The business he conducted for Local 560 usually involved beating, murdering, and otherwise intimidating the many enemies of Tony Provenzano.

After a two-and-a-half-year investigation, the FBI concluded and shared with other law enforcement agencies that Briguglio picked Hoffa up ostensibly to drive him to the meeting with "Tony Pro." Instead he drove him to his death.

Provenzano's favorite way of conducting a hit was to have a friend or trusted associate of the victim lure him to a certain place and then have one of his men waiting as the executioner. It was Hoffa's stepson Chuckie O'Brien who drove him to the meeting with "Sally Balls." Hoffa knew Briguglio and had no reason not to trust him. In addition, other close associates were telling Hoffa that he should find some way of making peace with Provenzano if he ever wanted to get back into power. So he had no choice but to make that rendezvous in the Michigan parking lot where Briguglio was waiting.

Three years later Briguglio was in trouble over the murder of another New Jersey union official and was about to be indicted for a systematic pattern of kickbacks, extortion, and "sweetheart" deals on behalf of what the FBI called the Provenzano Organization, which was linked to the Genovese Mafia family.

"Tony Pro," who in March 1978 was also on trial for attempting to arrange kickbacks in connection with a $2 million Teamster loan for the renovation of a hotel, and the dons were worried that Briguglio would make a deal with the law in exchange for lenient treatment. They knew any deal would have to include information on the Hoffa hit and the Genovese link to the Teamsters.

Briguglio's time had run out. On March 21, 1978, his mentor "Tony Pro" and the powerful "Matty the Horse" Ianiello took "Sally Balls" out for a night on the town.

They started at a Little Italy social club named the Andrea Doria where they drank heavily. At around 9:00 P.M. they left for Benito's Restaurant on Mulberry Street where they ate and drank some more until 10:30 P.M.

The three left the restaurant together. As the door closed behind them "Tony Pro" took two steps to his right. "Matty the Horse" took two steps to his left. "Sally Balls," skilled assassin that he was, undoubtedly realized in those last moments of his life that he had just been set up.

But before his alcohol-laden brain could command his body to react, a car pulled up in front of him and four shots were fired. Each .45 caliber bullet struck the hit man in the chest. Staggering, he fell backward onto the sidewalk. As his blood spread along the street, one of the men from the car walked up to his heaving body and put a bullet into his brain. "Sally Balls" was taken out in the grand style he deserved, according to the lore and tradition of the Mafia. Teamsters Union Local 560 was going to need a new business agent.

A block away, two detectives from the New York Police Department's Intelligence Division, who were trailing Ianiello, witnessed the entire shooting.

Unfortunately, Coffey's detectives Dick Joyce and John McGlynn found a very cold trail of clues when they finally got to Mulberry Street about three weeks after "Sally Balls" was gunned down.

"The two Intelligence Division cops who witnessed the hit could have done two things that might have really helped us later," says Coffey. "They could have chased the killers or detained 'Tony Pro' and 'Matty the Horse' for questioning. They did neither."

What they did do was try to question other witnesses. But

people who encounter a murder on Mulberry Street at 10:30 at night are usually smart enough not to cooperate with the police.

"I would have loved to be in the place of those two cops, but they apparently just took it as vermin killing vermin and did nothing useful," Coffey reflects.

So Joyce and McGlynn had to start from scratch. The first thing they did was make appointments to talk to Ianiello and Provenzano. Joe went along for the interviews but got the same answer from both: "See my lawyer."

Next Coffey's gang set out to canvass the entire area again. Going back at 10:30 at night, the time of the shooting, they scoured the crowded sidewalks for four square blocks around Benito's. The hope was they would find someone who was usually on the street at that hour.

After about two weeks of returning to Little Italy every night, Joyce and McGlynn hit pay dirt. They stopped a Chinese teenager and asked him if he had seen anything unusual on the night of March 21. The young man, whose identity is being protected to this day, said he did know something about the murder.

He recalled that he was on Baxter Street, around the corner from Mulberry, returning home from his classes at St. John's University when a car skidding to a halt almost ran him down. Two men jumped out of that car and jumped into another waiting at the curb. Both cars then sped off. He said that he came face to face with one of the men.

"Would you recognize him again?" the detectives barked in unison.

"I'm not sure I would," the young student responded.

Neither McGlynn nor Joyce bothered asking why he had not come forward before. The formula for survival on the streets of New York did not include talking to the police about the Mafia hit you just witnessed. However, the detectives reported to Coffey that the teenager appeared to be willing to help.

He turned out to be very helpful. First from mug shots

provided by Coffey's gang he picked out a Genovese button man named Joseph Scarborough as the guy who almost knocked him over. Scarborough's description matched the one provided by the two Intelligence cops. Coffey believed Scarborough was the one who gave the coup de grace to "Sally Balls."

The young Chinese student also agreed to be hypnotized to help develop further descriptions. Under the spell of a police hypnotist he remembered the type and license plate of the second getaway car. It was a 1978 Lincoln Versailles that was eventually found in a small town in Georgia.

So now they had a description of a hit man and a motive for the murder. "Tony Pro" was afraid Briguglio was going to sing about Hoffa. Coffey took the information to the district attorney.

"The DA threw us a real curve ball here. He would not go with the kid's ID. He said it was too unreliable because he did not come forward right away. He said there was not enough evidence to seek indictments against the shooter or Provenzano," Coffey remembers.

"I was upset, but not too angry. After all, as far as the police department was concerned the homicide was solved and we could clear it from our records. We had solved two mob hits in a little over a month, we proved the effectiveness of the task force concept, and I was fulfilling a dream."

By the end of the summer of 1978 the Coffey Gang had become an integral part of the workings of the chief of detectives' office. They began to overcome some of the initial resistance of precinct detectives and some of the organized crime experts in the five New York City district attorneys' offices and in the department's Organized Crime Control Bureau. "We kept turning new informants and every day it seemed one of my men was testifying before one grand jury or another. We were even able to solve some very old homicides like the rubout of 'Crazy' Joey Gallo in 1972. Gallo was gunned down as he was celebrating his birthday over a plate of clams in Umberto's Clam House in Little Italy."

A button man named Joseph Lupurelli who took part in the hit turned informant. He laid the blame on his partners in crime, Carmine "Sonny Pinto" DiBiasi and Phil Gambino. Lupurelli said Matty Ianiello, who owned Umberto's, recommended it to Gallo to set him up for the hit. It was done as a favor to the Colombo family.

The Coffey Gang was even able to clear one of the most notorious rubouts in Mafia history from the department's unsolved files when they linked the 1957 murder of Albert "The Earthquake" Anastasia to a New Jersey hit man. "This was very important to the department's overall morale. We were actually beginning to change the perception that the Mafia could do anything they wanted and get away with it," states Coffey.

Coffey was also becoming somewhat of a police department ambassador of homicide information. He set up an information sharing network between his own gang and their counterparts in the FBI, the U.S. Attorney's Office, the Drug Enforcement Agency, and New York State's Organized Crime Task Force. Traditionally there was little spirit of cooperation among various agencies. Five years later these early contacts would play an instrumental role in bringing down the heads of New York's five crime families in an enormous case known as the "Ruling Commission."

On July 12, 1979, something else happened that would eventually play a major part in that case and haunt the godfathers of New York.

It was a warm, typical July day. There was a calm and peaceful feeling on the streets of the Ridgewood section of Brooklyn. The three- and four-story row houses, separated occasionally by an ancient wooden frame home, gave the neighborhood a deceptive feeling of small-town America that belied its connection to the surrounding city.

In the backyards of Ridgewood, Italian grandfathers, retired after years of back-breaking construction work, nurtured gardens of tomatoes, eggplant, and squash that rivaled the Sicilian fields of their youth. Some even found success with grapes that fed the family's personal wine cellars.

Joe and Mary's Italian Restaurant was a Ridgewood landmark known for its old-world home-style cooking. It was also a favorite dining spot for members of the Bonanno crime family. On that summer day in 1979 Carmine Galante, a Bonanno capo, decided to have lunch at one of the backyard tables at Joe and Mary's. He was joined by Cesare Bonventre, a cousin of Bonanno, and Baldo Amato, one of the Bonanno family's top earners. Both men had very close ties to the Sicilian Mafia. Although in the United States for many years, they still spoke in broken English with thick Italian accents.

Also present for lunch were two of Galante's closest associates, Leonardo Coppolla and Guiseppe Turano, owner of Joe and Mary's. Coppolla was a major drug dealer. Except for Turano, none of these men had ever done an honest day's work in their lives.

In this group only Galante enjoyed public notoriety. The press mistakenly believed he was the godfather of the Bonanno family, thanks mainly to the fact that the real godfather, Phil Rastelli, had been constantly in and out of jail since taking over the reins from Joe Bonanno himself. He wisely allowed Galante to get the publicity and take the heat from the other families when he tried to expand his drug business against their wishes.

Despite the fact that he had spent more than half of his sixty-eight years in prison, Galante made the most of his time on the outside. He was first arrested at age sixteen for stealing trinkets from a store counter. That sentence was suspended. When he was twenty he was charged with killing a police officer during a payroll robbery. Those charges were eventually dropped. Four months later he was caught fleeing the scene of a Brooklyn brewery robbery, and that time his luck ran out. He was sent to Sing Sing for twelve years. Behind the Big House walls he stayed in shape playing handball with other inmates who were under orders from

Galante henchmen not to win the game. Carmine did not like to lose.

In July of 1979 Galante had been out of the federal prison in Atlanta for three years after serving a fourteen-year term for drug conspiracy. The conviction grew out of his activities in Montreal, where he had established the Mafia in the early 1950s. In fact, Galante was somewhat of an international don, with hoodlums in Canada, France, and Italy following his orders. But because of his inclination to deal in drugs, he was never seriously considered to take the place of Joe Bonanno as don of the family.

Galante was the most brazen of all the city's capos. He spurned bodyguards, and his chauffeur, usually a job reserved for a loyal gunman, was his daughter Nina.

He had called the luncheon meeting to discuss his plans for expanding the Bonanno family's involvement in selling drugs on an international level. It was historically the Mafia's strategy to contract out most of its drug dealing operations. The godfathers like Bonanno, who in 1979 had already retired to Arizona, leaving his operations in the hands of Phil Rastelli, liked to give the impression that they would not dirty their hands with narcotics profits.

"They winked at drug dealing," Coffey says. "They wanted only their lowest-ranking soldiers involved in drug deals. Instead they allowed black organized crime gangs to deal in Harlem and Bedford-Stuyvesant, as long as they paid tribute to the Italian Mafia. So the upper-level mafiosi may not have been dealing directly, but they were raking in huge profits."

Galante, though, was bending the rules. He was personally setting up drug deals with Latin gangs. His own crew, the thieves and killers aligned with the Bonanno family that reported to him, was known to be running their own drug network. His greed regarding narcotics profits had finally put him in disfavor past the point of saving himself.

With Joe Bonanno himself enjoying the benefits of an Arizona retirement, the family was being run by Rastelli, who, while Galante was digging into his meal at Joe and Mary's, was taking his lunch at the Metropolitan Correction Center, the federal lockup adjacent to the Federal Court House in Manhattan. Rastelli was not only feeling the heat of the government at the time. He was also under pressure from the godfathers of the Gambino, Lucchese, Genovese, and Colombo families to do something about Galante's ambitions, before people began to believe the Mafia dealt drugs to school children.

This is how the godfathers decided to handle the annoying Carmine Galante: As Galante pushed away his empty plate at the table in Joe and Mary's backyard and placed his customary cigar to his lips, four Bonanno button men, including the father-and-son hit team of "Sonny Red" and Bruno Indelicato, swung open the small wooden door leading from the restaurant and entered the backyard. Without warning they opened fire with shotguns and automatic pistols. Galante never got to light his cigar.

In less than one minute their work was done. As they escaped in a car waiting outside the restaurant's entrance, Carmine Galante, Leonardo Coppolla, and Guiseppe Turano lay dead. They were blown off their chairs by the powerful blasts onto the patio's hard floor. Galante landed in the midst of Joe and Mary's prized tomato plants. John Turano, Guiseppe's son, who worked in the restaurant, was critically wounded as he ran to hide in a refrigerator. Cesare Bonventre and Baldo Amato, unhurt, ran from the death scene before police arrived.

Joe Coffey was off the day Galante was gunned down. He was at home when Jim Sullivan called, suggesting he travel to Joe and Mary's to see if he could be of any help to the precinct and OCCB detectives at the scene.

But before Joe and many of the other detectives arrived, the area around the restaurant was besieged by uniformed police; emergency medical technicians, who eventually saved John Turano's life; and the media. Reporters and photographers from the city's newspapers and television and radio stations were alerted originally by police scanner reports that four people had been shot in the restaurant. Knowing the neighborhood to be favored by the Bonanno family, the press rushed to the scene. Word that the powerful Carmine Galante had been hit was already thoroughly circulating throughout the city.

Several photographers, refused entrance to the crime scene, made their way to a nearby rooftop that overlooked the backyard dining area. The pictures they took have since served as the model of a mob rubout. There, lying among the scattered dishes and toppled dining table in the middle of the crushed and twisted tomato plants, was Carmine Galante, his shirt drenched in blood, his cigar grotesquely clenched firmly in his mouth.

By the time Coffey got to the backyard, Galante's body had been photographed by the police and removed from the scene. "But that didn't stop everyone from accusing me of putting that cigar in his mouth. The fact that the medical examiner determined he bit reflexively on the cigar when the shotgun blast hit him didn't discourage the rumor either. To this day there are people who believe I put that cigar in Galante's mouth to make him look ridiculous. It's not a bad idea, but I did not do it," Coffey swears.

Thirty-five minutes after the shooting, a scene was photographed by detectives from the Manhattan district attorney's office that changed forever the way law enforcement thought of the relationships between mob families.

Sitting in an apartment across the street from the Ravenite Social Club in Little Italy, Detective John Gurnee captured on videotape the image of "Sonny Red" and Bruno Indelicato being met in the street outside the club by Aniello Dellacroce, the underboss of the Gambinos, who reported only to Paul Castellano, the capo di tutti capi, the boss of all bosses in the American Mafia.

From the apartment, which was rented by the Manhattan district attorney's office for surveillance on the Ravenite, headquarters of the Gambinos, Bruno was photographed taking a pistol from his pocket and placing it under the front seat of the car. Then all three men embraced.

Gurnee was surprised at what he had seen: two Bonanno button men obviously being greeted with great warmth by the underboss of the Gambino family. The detective had no way of knowing at the time about the massacre at Joe and Mary's.

But when he found out later that evening, one of the first things he did was call Joe Coffey.

"Joe," he asked, "is it possible that Galante was hit by his own crew and it was sanctioned by the Gambinos?"

Coffey, by then fully briefed by his gang, which had been pressing their network of informants, replied that it was possible because of their anger over the drug dealing.

"Well, when you see what I've got on tape you're gonna believe it."

"When I saw the tape I reasoned that all the families must have been pissed off at Galante, but I didn't think they would order such a hit without Rastelli's okay. That would have gone against their code and would have resulted in just the kind of all-out gang war Jim Sullivan wanted me to prevent."

Coffey went to the Metropolitan Correction Center to find out who had been visiting Phil Rastelli. He learned that the day before the hit and the day after, Rastelli had meetings with capos of his own Bonanno family as well as high-level capos of the Gambino family.

"In my mind the scenario was clear. All five families wanted Galante hit, and Rastelli agreed to have his men do it. What surprised the hell out of me was the level of cooperation that allowed the Bonanno hit men to report back to the Gambino underboss, Dellacroce. This was a kind of cooperation not often seen."

34   Shortly after the shooting, an eyewitness gave one of the first detectives on the scene in Ridgewood a description of

the men she saw fleeing in a late-model Oldsmobile and the license plate of the car.

The car was found a few blocks away and fingerprints were lifted but did not connect with any on file at headquarters. Five years later this car, too, would play an important part in bringing the Ruling Commission, the leaders of all the city's Mafia families, to justice.

But the descriptions and the subsequent knowledge provided by Gurnee's tapes led Coffey to begin an all-out search for the Indelicatos and two men they were known to work with: Dominick Trinchera and Phil "Philly Lucky" Giacone. The Coffey Gang began meetings with all their reliable informants and set up their own surveillance on known Bonanno hangouts. After weeks of looking, though, it appeared that all four had vanished from the face of the earth. Dozens of hoodlums were called in for questioning but none had the nerve or personal motive to cooperate.

"There was a rumor that Bruno Indelicato was totally stoned out on cocaine and running through the streets bragging how he was going to be a don in the Gambino family because he hit Galante. There weren't even any rumors about Trinchera and Giacone."

In May 1981 a young boy walking his dog in a deserted area of Howard Beach, Queens, had trouble dragging the animal away from some kind of bone he found in the dirt.

Closer inspection revealed the bone to be the right arm of "Sonny Red" Indelicato, which had risen through the twenty inches of dirt piled on his body.

"A lot of young guys think the way to Mafia success is to carry out an important hit," Coffey says. "But the Galante case proves them wrong. All the shooters came to an untimely end, and Cesare Bonventre, who set up the hit, was murdered in 1984. So my homicide investigation was pretty much at a dead end."

"But once again," Coffey remembers telling Jim Sullivan, "we're learning things about the mob that we never believed possible before. Even when we don't make an arrest in a homicide we're building intelligence that I know will pay off someday."

Throughout his career Joe Coffey was always a hunch player. This was one hunch that one day would prove correct in a big way.

· II ·
THE
IRISH
MAFIA

In early spring 1979, Joe and Detective Jack Cahill were sitting in the bar of a trendy East Side restaurant, the kind of place cops go to when they are trying to get away from other cops, sharing some off-time waiting for word on indictments in the murder of "Sally Balls" Briguglio.

It appeared that the district attorney was not going to change his mind about not using the identities provided by the Chinese teenager to move for indictments against the hit men and Ianiello and Provenzano. The DA was concerned because the teenager had been hypnotized to get his evidence. That would not stand up in court. He also felt that Ianiello and Provenzano could not be considered accessories just because they were out with "Sally Balls." No amount of arguing from Coffey or Jim Sullivan could change the DA's mind.

Over the years Coffey was known as the kind of boss who

enjoyed sharing a cocktail or two with his men. He saw it as a way to keep morale up during frustrating times and to keep abreast of department rumors.

Joe Coffey led by example. He drove his men hard, but no one worked harder than he did. He expected them to be imaginative and to buck the system when they had to. He always stood behind them when they did. He thought the way to success was through honesty and hard work, and no one was more honest or hardworking than Joe Coffey.

He knew better than any of them that his style of police work resulted in more frustration than satisfaction. He had to bite his tongue when an archbishop in the Vatican slipped through the cracks of an indictment against an international ring of counterfeiters and forgers. He had to keep quiet when the green-eyed monster of jealousy that lurked behind every filing cabinet in Police Headquarters kept many of the men who gave a year of their lives to bringing Son of Sam to justice from getting credit. He was forced to watch as a murdering terrorist escaped being charged with eleven murders because a federal agent was more concerned with paperwork than justice.

Sitting at the bar he explained to Cahill how he realized that his own desire to make big cases often led to big problems for the department and frustration for him. But he had learned how to get satisfaction from preserving his own integrity. He maintained the inner knowledge that he did his job well, and, as importantly, the bad guys knew it.

In the Coffey Gang, Joe had assembled a group of cops who liked slapping cuffs on the bad guys. They did not share the department's joy in clearing cases just by knowing who the guilty participants were. It wasn't enough for them that they knew a hit man named "Joe the Blonde" had killed Albert Anastasia. They bemoaned the fact that the Mafia got "Sonny Red" Indelicato before they did. They were homicide detectives and they yearned for face-to-face confrontations with the killers.

The two cops were into major-league drinking when the

elderly bartender came over with two drinks in his hands. One of the reasons they had chosen that particular restaurant for their break was that Joe knew the bartender was an old-time friend of his father. He was once an agent for the Internal Revenue Service but had been waiting tables and mixing drinks since being busted for accepting bribes.

"Joe, see that guy over there," the bartender said as he put the drinks on the bar and tilted his wrinkled face towards a Runyonesque character sitting along the restaurant's back wall. "He sent these drinks over. His name is Butch Hammond. Says he knows your wife and wants to talk to you."

"I knew Hammond to be a half-assed trigger man and fringe player from Woodside where my wife grew up. I didn't see any harm in accepting his drink and hearing what he had to say. But I made sure Cahill sat with us," Joe says. "I did not want to be seen in public talking to a mutt like Hammond without a loyal friend to swear there was nothing corrupt going on. So Cahill watched my back."

Coffey and Cahill sat down with Hammond, who over the years had taken to talking like a gangster in the movies. With a conspiratorial whisper out of the side of his mouth he greeted Joe and shook Cahill's hand.

After some small talk, both cops, now a little high, were holding back their laughter over his Cagney imitation. Finally, Hammond leaned across the table and, with his face just inches from Coffey's and his eyes madly darting left and right, whispered, "Joe, did you hear about Tubby Walker's son Billy?"

No amount of booze ever slowed Coffey's encyclopedic memory. Instantly he fixed on Tubby Walker as a neighborhood guy in Woodside and a friend of Joe's wife Pat. Joe had played football and school-yard basketball with Walker and the rest of his crowd when he was dating Pat.

He couldn't imagine he would be interested in anything that involved Tubby Walker. With a look that implied "I hope you've got something more important to talk to me about than Tubby Walker," Joe told Hammond to "get to the point."

Hammond was used to being dismissed by people more important than he. He knew he'd better get Coffey's attention. "His boy was murdered, Joe. The scum on the West Side whacked Billy Walker. They whacked him for no reason at all," he whined.

The mention of the "scum on the West Side" fixed the cops' attention. Cahill noticed a change in Joe's attitude and leaned his head closer to the two men.

Hammond was now almost inaudible and obviously afraid to continue. He seemed almost sorry he started the conversation, but now Coffey was pressing.

Though he knew it was not true, he said to Hammond, "No one gets whacked for no reason at all, not even on the West Side. What was Billy Walker into?"

Hammond now relaxed a little. He sensed he had Coffey hooked. His risk at inviting two cops to have a drink would now pay off. He leaned back a little and lit a cigarette, letting it dangle from his lips like Nathan Detroit would have.

"I'm tellin' you, Joe, Billy was a legit kid. He smoked some dope and broke up some saloons but he wasn't into the rackets. He made a good living with the stagehands' union. That shithead McElroy whacked him over an argument about a pinball machine, for God's sake—they dumped him in the 79th Street boat basin. The fuckin' madman Jimmy McElroy did him. Do us a favor, go after him," Hammond pleaded.

Jimmy McElroy, Joe knew, was a member of a gang of Irish thugs and strong-arm men known as the "Westies" because they operated along Manhattan's West Side waterfront and the adjoining neighborhood known as Hell's Kitchen. They ruled the West Side by terror.

Their criminal family tree and their chain of command ran back to Owney Madden's gang in the 1920s. Today's Westies were the offspring of the men who had tried to kill

Joe's father, and he was being handed a chance to nail one of them for murder. Joe was hooked, but he was not entirely satisfied with Hammond's story. Hard guys like Tubby Walker and even wannabees like Hammond rarely went to the police for help.

"If you know who did it, why don't you guys take care of it?" Joe asked.

Hammond leaned back and lit another cigarette. Coffey, the chain smoker, also lit up. Cahill signaled for another round.

"There's no way we can handle this, Joe. McElroy is totally crazy. He kills for the fun of it and he's got 'Big Paulie' behind him," Hammond replied.

This was news, and Coffey and Cahill instantly sobered up. "Big Paulie" was Paul Castellano, godfather of the Gambino crime organization, the largest Mafia family in the country, counting hundreds of gunmen. More important, Paulie was capo di tutti capi—godfather of godfathers—the leader of all the Mafia gangs in the United States. Castellano was the number one target of the Coffey Gang.

The mention of Paul Castellano's link to a murder he might solve sent Joe's adrenaline pumping. The frustration brought on by past successes was forgotten. Another big case was in the making.

Gulping down the last of his drink, he tried not to reveal his excitement to Hammond. "Jack and I are on our way down to headquarters now anyway. I'll pull the file and see what I can do," he said.

It was news to Cahill that they were going back to the office. After a quick stop at the bar to say good-bye to the busted IRS agent, the two detectives headed south on Second Avenue towards One Police Plaza.

When they arrived at headquarters, Chief Sullivan was already gone for the day, so Coffey took some time to look up the homicide report filed on the Walker boy. He learned that the body had been found in Billy Walker's van in a lovers' lane along the 79th Street Boat Basin, a marina used by city dwellers fortunate enough to own small cabin cruisers and sailboats. There was also a handful of houseboats moored there permanently, an adventurous way to beat the city's high rents.

The first detectives on the scene had noted that it appeared Walker had been shot in the mouth or face. The entire back side of his head had been blown away by the exiting bullet.

Coffey was familiar with the work of James McElroy and his cronies Mickey Featherstone and Jimmy Coonan, who ran the Westies. They were known for two distinguishing characteristics: their viciousness and their stupidity.

Joe knew he was going to have to sell Sullivan on the idea of diverting some of the Coffey Gang's resources to go after McElroy. As he copied the Walker file, he mentally prepared for his conversation with the chief. He went over in his mind all he knew about the West Side Irish gang.

After Owney Madden formed the original gang, the Prohibition gangster needed a band of thugs to run illegal booze into his speakeasies, including the legendary Cotton Club. Joe's father even drove for Madden when he needed some extra cash to get the family through a difficult period.

In order to fight off the Mafia gangs of the twenties, Madden joined forces with Dutch Schultz. Their combined unit was known as the Arsenal Gang because it employed such heavily armed desperadoes as "Machine Gun" Campbell. The gang also included John "Cockeye" Dunn, who had botched the assassination attempt on Joe Coffey, Sr., that had convinced the young Joe to devote his life to bringing such killers to justice.

In the forties Eddie McGrath took over the Arsenal Gang and was considered the equal of such master criminals as Meyer Lansky, Vito Genovese, Lucky Luciano, and Carlo Gambino. Lansky, McGrath, and Gambino ran the New York mobs.

By the early sixties Lansky was forced out of the country, Gambino was in failing health, and McGrath had retired to

Florida. Before leaving, he turned the Irish gang, now called the West Side Irish, the Irish Mafia, or the Westies, over to Hughie Mulligan.

Mulligan was more of a character actor than a superstar on the level of Lansky, Gambino, or McGrath. Unfortunately for him, by the time he got control of the gang, New York's harbor was in the last of its glory days as a shipping and passenger port. As the port's business disappeared, so did the number of longshoremen and trucking contractors. They had provided a means for the gang to extort and steal money from businessmen who needed to move their wares off the piers and through the West Side streets leading to the garment center and the highways to Long Island and upstate New York. There were fewer trucks to hijack and fewer union men to exploit.

With the Mafia in control of the lucrative cargo routes, using Kennedy Airport as a hub, Mulligan's men were left to loan-sharking, bookmaking, extortion of the unions that serviced the Times Square theater district, and increasingly, whatever strong-arm work the Italian gangs would contract out to them.

An incident involving Mulligan is one of the best illustrations of why detectives hate to rely solely on planted listening devices for information.

In 1966, when Coffey was a plainclothes police officer working in the Rackets Bureau of the Manhattan district attorney's office, he was involved in the investigation of the Ruby Stein and Jiggs Forlano loan-sharking ring, which operated on Westie turf and paid tribute to Mulligan.

Mulligan was seen at a meeting with Stein, Forlano, and Mafia capo Carmine "The Snake" Persico in a restaurant on Third Avenue and 38th Street, four doors from the building where Joe Coffey, Sr., had survived the assassination attempt. Coffey was trailing Stein and Forlano, and as he watched the restaurant from a dingy bar across the street, he noticed numerous middle-aged, very straight-looking men milling about outside. One of the group, he realized, was Richard Condon, a detective who would eventually become police commissioner, but at the time was assigned to the department's Corruption Unit.

Coffey approached Condon and asked what all the cops were doing on the street. Condon, first demanding to know why Coffey was there, explained that his men were trailing Mulligan, who was heavily involved in bribing police officers.

Mulligan's involvement with Persico, Stein, and Forlano interested everyone. So it was decided to get court approval for a listening device in Mulligan's car.

Shortly thereafter the bug was planted and a surveillance plan was put into effect. A team of Condon's detectives would trail Mulligan everywhere he drove, recording his conversations as they were transmitted by the bug.

The morning the operation went into effect the running joke was that the detectives had better be careful in traffic because Mulligan was known to be a terrible driver. The humor, however, was lost on District Attorney Frank Hogan when his men had to report that the operation lasted less than one hour.

Minutes after leaving his garage Mulligan ran off the road and totaled his car, destroying the bug in the process.

The incident added to Mulligan's reputation as being more of a clown than a capo. The Westies were becoming a joke to organized crime and to the men whose responsibility it was to put them in jail. It bothered Joe Coffey that people were laughing at Mulligan and his gang rather than hating them for the monsters he knew them to be.

In 1968 Coffey arrested an up-and-coming West Side Irish mobster named Mickey Spillane for shaking down a West Side night club but could not convince Hogan to push the investigation further. Like his bosses before and since, Hogan told Joe, "Concentrate on the Italians."

Spillane, who would take over the gang when Mulligan died in 1974, pleaded guilty and served a short prison term. When he got out he started the gang on a new business.

With any kind of sophisticated criminal activity now totally taken over by the Mafia, Spillane hit on the idea of kidnapping Italian bookies and holding them for ransom to be paid by the appropriate Mafia family.

He got away with it a few times. The Mafia considered it nothing more than a nuisance and, wanting to keep the Westies around as their strong-arms, paid the money and shrugged it off.

But in an example of the senseless violence that had by this time become their trademark, Spillane killed a bookie named Ziccardi after the Gambino family paid the $100,000 ransom.

This was pushing their luck too far. Joe remembers being on patrol hunting Son of Sam on the evening of May 13, 1977, when a report of shots fired in a Queens housing complex came over his radio.

"Our orders were to respond to every call of shots being fired, but as we raced to the scene I remembered that Mickey Spillane lived in that neighborhood. I knew we were going to find his body in the street," Joe recalls.

It was indeed Spillane's corpse they found in the street outside his apartment house between two parked cars. He had been stabbed and shot in the lobby. He had staggered out to the street where he had been shot again. He had collapsed between the two cars and died.

Later the police would learn that he was lured to the lobby by a friend named Sonny Marini. There he was met by a Gambino soldier named Danny Grillo and two henchmen. The murder was contracted by Jimmy Coonan and Mickey Featherstone to the Gambino family.

The killers did not know and it did not make a difference that Spillane had just returned from a trip to Florida, where he had asked Eddie McGrath to appeal to the Gambinos to let him off the hook for his defiance of their code. McGrath, disgusted at what had become of his legendary gang, told Spillane some stories about how members of his gang like

4
5

"Cockeye" Dunn went to the electric chair like "men," and refused to call New York.

By the time Joe Coffey sat in Jim Sullivan's office to ask permission to go after James McElroy, all this information was fresh in his mind. He related his restaurant meeting with Hammond. He told Sullivan he had wanted to chase the Westies years before when he was a young detective in the Manhattan district attorney's office but because the gang was considered so low level, nothing more than street thugs, and because the only publicity came from busting Italian mobsters, he never got the okay.

"I know you brought me in here to go after the Italian gangs, but now it looks like there might be a provable homicide link between the Irish gang and Castellano. The West Side Irish are the most vicious, mad-dog killers in the city. This may be our chance to nail them," Coffey told the chief of detectives. He knew Sullivan was as proud of his own Irish heritage as he was of his. Both men were embarrassed by the way the Coonans and Featherstones and McElroys dragged their heritage through the streets.

Finally, Coffey threw his knockout punch: "These guys are direct descendants of the men who tried to kill my father," he reminded Sullivan.

"I don't really think Sullivan needed that much convincing. He wanted the Westies locked up as much as I did and, given the Coffey Gang's record of success, Sullivan was too smart a manager to hold us back. He told me to follow up the lead, the Castellano link," Coffey remembers, savoring the moment to this day.

Coffey assigned himself and detectives Frank McDarby, John McGlynn, and John Meyer to take on the Westies. One of the privileges of Coffey's position was that he could assign a detective to serve as his driver and aide-de-camp. Jack Cahill filled that spot and he would be good to have around if things got rough.

They realized from the start that the only way they were going to nail McElroy for the Walker murder was by finding a cooperative eyewitness. No bullet was recovered from the body, there was no murder weapon in police custody, and because McElroy had never been arrested there were no records of his fingerprints to match with prints taken from Walker's clothing. Without an eyewitness it could not even be established as evidence that McElroy and Walker were together the night of the murder.

So the cops hit the streets, going block by block along the West Side piers during the day asking people who could have been their brothers, cousins, or aunts if they knew anything about the death of Billy Walker. The follow-up question was if they knew Jimmy McElroy.

What they got back from these people was usually a blank stare indicating a total lack of understanding of the question. If they answered at all they said they never heard of anyone named McElroy. Some of the older dock workers offered a warning: "If I were you guys I'd steer clear of Jimmy McElroy."

They were told all kinds of stories about the viciousness of the Westies, and the people they spoke to wondered why all of a sudden the cops were taking such an interest in murder and mayhem on the West Side. Why, for instance, one wondered, was nothing ever done about the murders of Dennis Curley and Patty Dugan?

Curley and Dugan were involved in an incident that had become legend on the West Side. They were best friends who one day in 1975 got into an argument over a girl. Both were members of the Westies. They fought in the street outside the Market Diner, a favorite spot for longshoremen and truck drivers. Curley got the better of Dugan. Later Dugan went to Curley's house with a gun. He rang the downstairs doorbell and through the intercom asked Curley to come down to talk. When his friend came downstairs, Dugan shot him dead.

Jimmy Coonan, at the time leader of the Westies, was furious over the shooting. He liked Curley and considered him an important member of his mob. With the help of Edward "The Butcher" Commiskey he lured Dugan to the apartment house where Coonan's niece lived. In the young woman's apartment they took a steak knife and stabbed Dugan to death.

Commiskey, who was called "The Butcher" because he was taught that trade while serving time in Green Haven Prison, then proceeded to dismember Dugan. First he cut his penis off and put it in a jar. Next Coonan asked his niece for a bigger knife. They used it to cut off the victim's head. This they put in a green plastic trash bag.

Coonan loved Commiskey because he operated on the theory that without a body the police could not make a murder case against the killer. Commiskey also added the twist of freezing the hands of victims and then using their fingerprints at the scene of Westies' crimes in order to throw the police off the trail.

By the time their work in the kitchen was done, the parts of Patty Dugan's body filled six large plastic garbage bags. Five were dumped in the East River.

Coonan took the bag with Dugan's head and the bottle containing his penis and made a tour of Westie hangouts. He went into bar after bar and even stopped people on the street and showed off the body parts. "This is Patty Dugan's head. He killed Dennis Curley," he would say. "And this is Patty Dugan's prick," Coonan would add as he held up the jar for the bar to see.

The entire episode was pretty much ignored by the police. Commiskey was murdered in 1977 and Coonan continued to lead the Westies for another ten years.

Coffey loved hearing these stories and knew that someday he would catch up with Coonan, but he still needed something to tie McElroy to the Walker murder.

Detectives in the local precinct confirmed that "Big Paulie" Castellano was backing Coonan and his Westie cohorts. It burned Coffey that Castellano seemed to get more respect in this part of town than a detective sergeant in the New York Police Department.

Coffey decided that before they could go much further with the investigation they would need at least a picture of McElroy, and it would not hurt to get his prints.

They decided to stake out a bar called Hell's Kitchen on 43rd Street and Ninth Avenue, the heart of Westie territory, a place McElroy was known to favor. The three cops took up stations inside the bar with a good view of the entrance. Beginning around six o'clock each night they watched the parade of West Side characters walk in and tumble out of Hell's Kitchen.

On the third night, they saw McElroy walk in. He immediately spotted the three cops sitting in the back.

"So as soon as he got inside he made a big scene about needing cigarettes and turned to walk out again. By the time we were out of our seats he started running."

A young man in good physical condition, McElroy took off down Ninth Avenue with Coffey, McDarby, and Cahill in pursuit. But these were three cops who usually got their man, and after five or six blocks they grabbed the suspect, who continued struggling.

"We hit him in the head a few times but he wouldn't go down. He really was a tough kid. Then a precinct patrol car pulled up with its lights flashing, and two uniformed cops, one a woman, came at us with their guns drawn."

At the sight of the two cops McElroy began screaming for help. "They're robbin' me, they're robbin' me," he yelled.

"The two uniforms didn't know what to do. I don't think they thought three white men in business suits were mugging Jimmy McElroy. But finally, I got free of his swinging arms and was able to get my gold shield out. When I held it up the two cops backed off. Of course they didn't jump in to help. They knew McElroy and they would have to return to the neighborhood the next day."

Finally sensing his situation was hopeless, McElroy calmed down enough for McDarby to handcuff him while Cahill ran for the car. As was his style, Joe Coffey kept his gun in its holster.

Coffey eventually served more than twenty years as a uniformed cop and detective, pursuing many of the most violent criminals in the history of the NYPD, and fired his gun on only two occasions. The first time was when he was serving as a decoy cop, dressed like a woman, and a mugger attacked him. When the mugger managed to run away, Coffey fired a shot that missed by a mile but convinced the assailant to surrender. The next time he fired was in a wild shootout with the Black Liberation Army. Again he missed by a mile. He did use his pistol on two occasions to hit suspects over the head.

They took McElroy to the local precinct house, and Coffey left him with McDarby and Cahill to be fingerprinted and photographed.

"All the while McElroy was demanding to know what we had on him. He was screaming we had no right to bring him in. Of course he was right. This was an act of 'Coffey's Martial Law.'"

Coffey was headed out of the station house to get some coffee for his men and tea for himself when he heard a bloodcurdling scream.

"I raced back to the detectives' area. When I opened the door I saw McDarby holding McElroy by the neck about two feet off the ground. McElroy's face was turning blood red. He was clearly choking to death. Cahill was at the desk calmly filling out some forms. I asked Frank what the problem was."

"He wouldn't give me his wallet, Joe," McDarby answered as he lifted the wallet from McElroy's hip pocket.

After his picture was taken and he was fingerprinted, McElroy was allowed to return to the streets.

The following day Coffey returned to the hunt for witnesses. Billy Walker was a member of the Theatrical Workers Union, the Teamsters who worked on movies being shot on the streets of New York. Coffey decided that his coworkers might be more willing to talk about how he was killed than residents of Westie territory.

50

To a certain extent this hunch turned out to be correct. Coffey learned that on the night of the murder Walker and several other stagehands were partying around the Broadway and Times Square area and did stop for at least a while in the Hell's Kitchen Bar.

"They admitted drinking heavily and using cocaine and getting pretty rowdy," Coffey recalls. "But when it came to remembering when Walker disappeared from the group or what happened to him, they clammed up.

"Many of the stagehands were either loosely aligned with the Westies gang themselves or were related somehow to gang members. So there was no way they were going to give up McElroy. A couple of the older guys, however, admitted they were more afraid of Castellano, who they knew was backing the Westies. I figured I would have to speak to Big Paulie about this."

Around lunchtime the next day he and Frank McDarby drove out to the Veterans and Friends Social Club in the Bay Ridge section of Brooklyn which was, as every cop and reporter in New York knew, the headquarters of the capo di tutti capi, Paul "Big Paulie" Castellano.

Joe Coffey once told a reporter, "The Mafia is the biggest single shareholder in the American economy. They've become a second economy. They have more influence on the daily lives of all Americans than the government or Wall Street or even the Church. They can manipulate anything."

In 1978 Castellano was the CEO of that criminal corporation. In New York alone he ran loan-sharking, prostitution, pornography, drug dealing, gunrunning, extortion, bookmaking, and counterfeiting organizations and any other criminal enterprises that would add to the wealth of the Gambino clan.

If you wanted to unload your truck in the city's garment center or sell pictures of naked children in Times Square you had to pay tribute to a Castellano capo. If you opened a restaurant on the East Side or picked up a hooker in a Park Avenue hotel you put money in Paul Castellano's pocket. If you tried to do these things without giving "Big Paulie" his share, you put your life at risk. His negotiable currency was bullets. His executive staff was known for its ability to arrange a multimillion-dollar merger in a thirty-second conference in a Seventh Avenue alley.

Castellano savored his position and encouraged his image as a successful businessman. He was soft-spoken and gentlemanly in manner and read *The Wall Street Journal* every day. In fact, he invested much of his illicit earnings in legitimate businesses and watched the movements of those businesses with great interest.

But to Joe Coffey, Paul Castellano was a piece of trash lying in the street waiting for the sweeper to flush him down the sewer. He did not fear the godfather nor would he be intimidated by him.

"The gravy part of my assignment was getting the chance to sit face-to-face with scum like Castellano and Funzi Tieri and not have anyone think I was trying to make some kind of corrupt deal with them. Everyone on both sides of the law knew I was out to put him and the others like him behind bars."

Smiling and totally relaxed, Joe pushed past the doorman and opened the door to the storefront social club. The doorman, who saw him pull up in the unmarked car and made him for a cop right away, had already alerted the group inside.

A dozen button men were playing cards and nursing their midday Johnny Walker Red's and water. They appeared to be a peaceful group of unemployed laborers waiting around the union hall for their next job.

There was a moment of tension as the assembled hoods shot icy stares at Coffey standing in the doorway. There was no thought of interfering. These were men who did bloody work. They could sense fear in an adversary and knew how to exploit it. But Joe Coffey was not afraid. The message he sent out was, "I'm willing to be polite but I think you're all pieces of shit so don't push me."

The tension was broken when Joe Delmonico, one of Castellano's personal henchmen, put down his cards and rose to greet Joe. "Coffey, what do you want here?" he asked as he extended his handshake.

Joe ignored the offered hand and replied simply that he wanted "to sit down with Paul."

Delmonico told him to stay where he was and disappeared into the rear of the club.

For about five minutes Coffey stood alone just inside the doorway. Nobody offered him a drink, no card hands were played, not a word was uttered. Again, he was grateful McDarby and McGlynn were waiting in the car outside with Cahill. If things turned bad, he knew they would handle their end. They would watch his back.

He also knew that when word got out that he had been alone in Castellano's hangout for more than ten minutes, detectives from the Internal Affairs Division would be questioning his men about what went on. "Was Coffey putting the squeeze on Castellano?" they would ask. He knew many organized crime investigations, especially those involving drugs, never got off the ground because the detectives were afraid of being accused of corruption. When they did something unorthodox, like meeting face-to-face with the godfather, bells would go off in Internal Affairs. But Coffey knew McDarby, McGlynn, Cahill, and the rest of his gang would support him. That's why he had insisted on handpicking his team.

After what seemed like a prison stretch Delmonico returned.

"Mr. Castellano will see you tomorrow night," he said.

"I knew," Coffey remembers, "Castellano was in the back room and could have seen me then, but he needed to make the power play in front of his men. Since I was going to be asking him for a favor and wanted to maintain a decent relationship, I did not invoke Coffey's Martial Law and barge right into the back room.

"Instead, I said that would be fine and gave him my card

with the phone number at police headquarters."

That evening at home Joe related the visit to the social club to Pat and the kids. They loved to hear his stories. In a way it made up for the time his work took away from the family. Before going to bed, Steven reminded his father about a school basketball game the next night. "It starts at seven o'clock. I hope you can be there," Steven said. Joe promised his son he would try.

At eleven o'clock the next morning Coffey's direct phone line on his increasingly cluttered desk rang. It was Delmonico.

"Paulie says seven o'clock at Tomasso's," the thug said.

"I can't make it at seven," Joe answered. "My kid's got a basketball game. I'll send McDarby and McGlynn."

"No good, Joe. Paulie said he'd only meet with you and you alone."

For what seemed like the millionth time in his career, Coffey had to chose between something important to his family and his own mission in life. As usual he chose his work. He hoped Steven and Pat would continue to know that he loved them, thought of them always, and wished they would forgive him for the time he stayed away from them.

"Okay, tell Paulie I'll be there at seven," he told Delmonico.

At six thirty, Coffey, McDarby, and McGlynn drove up outside Tomasso's in Brooklyn. They circled the block twice, looking for any sign they might be walking into some kind of setup. When they agreed everything seemed to be okay, they parked, to the dismay of the doorman, right in front of the restaurant. It was the spot usually reserved for "Big Paulie."

At seven they were at the bar ordering drinks. Joe remembers the rest of the evening vividly:

"One minute later in walked Castellano surrounded by Delmonico and five mutts in Mafia uniforms—dark suits, open shirts, gold chains, shiny pointed shoes. Paulie, though, was wearing a tie and a white-on-white shirt. He looked like a legitimate businessman. Delmonico walked over and told me to come alone with him and Paulie. McDarby and McGlynn were joined at the bar by the five stooges.

"The restaurant had two private banquet rooms and the maitre d' led us to the smaller one. Inside a party of about ten people were having dinner. The maitre d' told them they would have to switch to the other room. Waiters cleaned up their tables and moved them. No one objected.

"Then Paulie and I were alone at a freshly made up table right in the middle of the room.

" 'Sergeant,' he said, 'I've heard a lot about you. I agreed to sit down with you because Funzi says you are a fair man.'

"For a moment I was surprised as hell. It was a shock to me that he and Funzi had talked about me. I was surprised that they talked at all. But I got right to business. I said, 'Paul, I'm here because a low-class vicious killer on the West Side named McElroy has been throwing your name around. He and the rest of his gang, including Jimmy Coonan and Mickey Featherstone, are killing legitimate people for no reason at all. People are afraid to talk up about it because they say they work for Big Paulie.'

"We talked for about half an hour. He actually admitted he knew Coonan and Featherstone but of course said he knew nothing about murders and did not believe legitimate people should be murdered for no reason. I believed him. It was part of the Mafia code that they tried to keep their savagery within the family. But he would not admit to knowing McElroy and would not commit to passing the word that he did not sanction the Westies' homicidal behavior.

"We pretty much ran out of things to say to each other, and after an awkward silence he started to tell me about a new house he was having built on Staten Island. He said that Pat and I—I was really surprised he knew my wife's name—were welcome there anytime and would be invited to the housewarming. He was feeling me out to see if I was corruptible. I said, 'Are you crazy? You think I want to be on Candid Camera?' He knew I meant the cameras the FBI and police intelligence would have trained on the house at all times.

"Finally he got up and I followed him out to the bar, where McGlynn and McDarby were bullshitting with the mob."

Coffey and Castellano, both six-foot-plus, both with the aura of powerful, successful men, caught the attention of the diners in the crowded restaurant. Conversation stopped as the two adversaries approached the bar.

Then the ever-present Delmonico grabbed his boss's arm. "Boss, this guy McDarby just told a great joke. You gotta hear it," he said, displaying his intimate relationship with the godfather for all to see.

"Frank, tell the boss your joke. Come on," he implored McDarby.

McDarby swallowed the last of his drink and walked in between his own boss and Castellano. In a friendly voice he repeated a joke about an Irish cop who came across a little black kid playing with a pile of dog shit in the street.

"'Son, what are you doing with that dog shit?' the Irish cop asks.

"'I'm making a statue of a cop,' the child responds.

"This angers the officer who demands, 'A cop, what kind of cop is that?'

"'It's an Italian cop. I'm making an Italian cop,' the boy answers."

At this point Castellano's face tightened. Did McDarby have the nerve to tell an anti-Italian joke to Paul Castellano, the most powerful Italian in America?

But quickly McDarby continued.

"So the Irish cop cracks up. He runs to the call box and calls his friend the Italian cop. Tells him to come over, he's got something to show him.

5   "When the Italian cop shows up, the kid repeats that he
6 is making a statue of an Italian cop. With smoke coming

out of his ears the Italian cop barks, 'An Italian cop? Why are you making an Italian cop?'

"'Because I didn't have enough shit to make an Irish cop.'"

The punchline delivered by McDarby threw the group at the bar, including Castellano and Coffey, into hysterics.

"Delmonico was laughing so hard tears were streaming from his eyes, and Paulie was also cracking up," Coffey remembers. "I don't think the five button men got it. With everyone laughing we took our cue and left."

Driving back to Manhattan, Coffey told his partners about his conversation with "Big Paulie." They discussed for the first time the idea that there seemed to be more cooperation between Mafia families than they previously had thought.

For instance, Funzi Tieri, head of the Genovese family, told the godfather of the Gambinos about his conversation with Joe Coffey about a murder case that involved a victim who wasn't even a family member, just as in the Briguglio homicide the Provenzano organization got the help of Genovese capo Matty Ianiello in setting up Briguglio. And now Paul Castellano admitted that the Gambinos knew Mickey Featherstone and Jimmy Coonan, heads of a gang that did little more than hijack trucks and bust heads. Coffey surmised correctly that Castellano was using the Westies to do strong-arm and contract killings.

All this cooperation was going on while the city was under the impression that a gang war raged. Coffey made a mental note to discuss this new trend with his old friend Ron Goldstock, who as an assistant district attorney specialized in organized crime matters.

As things turned out, Castellano did not pass the word that he was not protecting McElroy—so much for the Mafia code of killing only your own—but Coffey did come up with an eyewitness who finally agreed to cooperate.

He received a message at his desk one day to call a man about the "Billy Walker thing." The man turned out to be an older member of Local 817 of the Theatrical Workers

Union who admitted being out with Walker the night of the murder.

What he witnessed had made him sick, and he had been having nightmares ever since. He decided that the only way to feel better was to help nail the killer, no matter what the personal risk was. He was afraid he might be killed because of what he saw. The police, he reasoned, would protect him.

He identified McElroy from the picture McDarby had taken in the station house that night, and based on the eyewitness account and identification, McElroy was indicted and arrested for the murder of Billy Walker.

At the trial the witness testified that he and Walker and a few other coworkers spent the night of the murder, which was their payday, drinking and using cocaine, going from one West Side bar to another.

Toward the end of the evening, he testified, they found themselves playing pinball at a Hell's Kitchen bar.

He said that McElroy was in the bar drinking with another group and that he and Walker got into some kind of argument over a pinball game.

There was a little pushing and shoving, and Walker, a tough guy, held his own. Someone else broke it up, and McElroy stormed out of the bar.

Exhausted after his night of binging, Walker went outside to sleep it off in the back of his van. A little while later McElroy returned with a gun and found Walker asleep.

The eyewitness testified that without waking him, McElroy opened Walker's mouth and put the gun barrel in. With a bunch of stoned theatrical workers standing around, the witness said, McElroy pulled the trigger once. The shot blew off the back of Billy Walker's head.

It went down just as Coffey imagined. It was a case he couldn't have made without the eyewitness, who did a great job of describing the harrowing murder. Unfortunately he did too good a job. McElroy was acquitted of the murder of Billy Walker.

5
8   "We were stunned by the verdict and decided to interview

the jurors to see where we went wrong," Coffey says. "It turns out we lost to what we call the 'Perry Mason' syndrome. The witness seemed so well prepared and our case seemed so airtight that the jurors thought we had concocted it. The jury bought the defense argument that we coached the witness."

It was not the first time Joe Coffey had experienced a severe amount of frustration following months of hard police work. Sometimes the frustration was caused by the jealousy and narrow-mindedness of his colleagues, sometimes by the public's misunderstanding of police work.

The Coffey Gang was demoralized by the loss of McElroy. They were also starting to take some heat from their fellow cops and former bosses who would warn them they were throwing away good careers by chasing mutts like McElroy whom they couldn't put in jail anyway. In saloon bull sessions around Police Headquarters Joe found it more and more necessary to be a cheerleader.

He tried to emphasize the positive. The Walker case was solved, after all, according to police guidelines. They knew McElroy was the killer. The Chief of Detectives' Organized Crime Homicide Task Force was clearing almost one case a week. No one was talking about its being disbanded. In fact, it would operate for eight more years.

In addition, Ron Goldstock was increasingly fascinated by Coffey's theory that the different Mafia organizations were cooperating with each other on a grand scale. While following McElroy leads, Joe's men saw Westies delivering money to the East Harlem headquarters of the Genovese family don "Fat Tony" Salerno as well as to Roy DeMeo, one of Castellano's most important henchmen. Goldstock thought that pursuing the possibility that Mafia families operated under one umbrella might be a way to bring them all down at once.

In fact, the information gathered by the Coffey Gang was shared with investigators on all levels—city, state, and federal. They had turned over leads on more than thirty homicides, including that of Patty Dugan.

In less than two years after the creation of the Coffey Gang, Joe reported to the Police Department that in the area of cooperation with other agencies his men had accomplished the following: They had informed the FBI about mob figures active in New York and New Jersey in connection with the murder of "Sally Balls" Briguglio and the disappearance and apparent murder of Jimmy Hoffa. They had provided witnesses and information developed during the Ladenhauf homicide to the Internal Revenue Service with regard to a major case of labor racketeering and income tax evasion in progress. They had assisted the Drug Enforcement Agency in making twelve arrests of drug smugglers and seizing six kilos of 100 percent pure cocaine at Kennedy Airport, thanks to leads developed in the investigation of the murder of "Patty Mack" Macchiarole. They had used their knowledge of the murder of Mickey Spillane to aid the U.S. Secret Service and the Division of Alcohol, Tobacco and Firearms to make a major gunrunning and homicide arrest. They had developed an informant to work undercover for treasury agents; Alcohol, Tobacco and Firearms; and the NYPD's Organized Crime Control Bureau in an investigation of a series of homicides at Kennedy Airport that led to the arrest of fifty important mob figures. They had passed on information enabling the Secret Service to bust a counterfeiting ring.

By the end of 1981, the Coffey Gang had solved twenty-one gangland homicides and established an ongoing pattern of cooperation with the FBI, the Secret Service, and the U.S. Attorney's Office in the Eastern and Southern Districts of New York State.

A good example of how Joe's network of information helped other units was the raid on the Collins family. At the time of the McElroy trial, the Coffey Gang discovered that a family named Collins was operating a loan-sharking and gambling ring out of their West Side apartment.

Joe knew that detectives in the unit known as the Manhattan Detective Area were working a case that included a link to the Collins ring. He passed his information on to the Manhattan detectives and then joined them on a raid of the apartment. Inside, as he had suspected, they found evidence of extortion, gunrunning, loan-sharking and gambling.

Also in the apartment were Tom Collins, his wife, Flo, and their son Mickey.

Joe took the young man aside and offered him a deal. "Mickey," Joe told him, "fess up to possession of these items and we'll let your mother off the hook."

The young man did not hesitate before answering.

"Fuck my mother. She can take care of herself," he told Coffey. Tom, Mickey, and Flo Collins eventually received long prison terms.

"So you see why I wanted to press on with the Westies. They were scum and they all belonged in prison. At least the Italians confined their killing to matters of money. The Westies killed for the fun of it, and they did not even honor their own mothers.

"I would have been happy to devote all my time to pursuing them," Joe says.

But that was not possible. The Coffey Gang had become a victim of its own success. More and more they were being called on to take part in joint operations with other jurisdictions, and Sullivan never let them lose sight of the Mafia as their main objective.

In 1985, after Joe had retired in bitterness from the NYPD and joined Ron Goldstock's New York State Organized Crime Task Force, he attended a party for an old friend on Staten Island.

As he shared laughs and drinks with a group of men whom he had worked with for more than twenty years, an FBI agent he did not know very well grabbed him by the arm and eased him to a corner of the room.

"Joe, I always admired your work on the West Side Irish.

You really opened the door for everyone on that bunch of mutts. You'd probably like to know we've got an old friend of yours singing his brains out," the agent said.

"It's Mickey Featherstone, right?" Joe responded.

"That's right, how did you know? We've got him hidden away pretty good since he contacted Ira Block, the assistant U.S. attorney."

Coffey knew because it had been only a matter of time before Featherstone struck back at the men who framed him and sent him to prison for murder.

Featherstone was convicted in the murder of Michael Holly outside the Jacob Javits Convention Center on April 25, 1985.

Eyewitnesses had testified that it was Featherstone who screwed a silencer on a pistol and at high noon walked up behind Holly. The motive was the final settlement of an old feud in which Holly had been shot once before. In 1977 John Bokun, a Featherstone henchman, attacked Holly on Featherstone's orders as part of a struggle over a construction contract. Holly was hit in the leg, but Bokun was killed by a cop as he fled the scene.

Featherstone made it widely known that he believed Holly was cooperating with police in trying to nail him for that shooting in 1977.

Witnesses to the second shooting of William Holly said they were sure it was Featherstone and said they saw the killer flee in a brown station wagon registered to the Erie Transfer Company, where Featherstone worked.

Based on the eyewitness accounts, Featherstone was arrested and within a year was convicted and sentenced to at least twenty-five years in prison for murder.

Mickey Featherstone was no virgin when it came to being accused of murder. The Coffey Gang had him as a prime suspect in seven homicides and he had already served a prison sentence for manslaughter, but he was not going to allow himself to be framed and not strike back. He suspected Coonan had set him up, and he resented being dealt with in such a manner. If Coonan and McElroy wanted him out of the way so that they could control the Westies, he would have preferred to be murdered rather than be put in prison for life.

Featherstone was a supply room clerk in Vietnam who never saw a day of fighting but tried to explain away his murderous personality as battle fatigue. He decided to strike back. Not trusting the New York police, he called former Assistant U.S. Attorney Block, who interceded with the Manhattan DA.

They listened to Featherstone's story and agreed to let his wife Cissy wear a wire and try to trap the three men who Featherstone believed carried out the crime on the orders of Coonan: William Bokun, John's brother; Kevin Kelly; and William Shannon.

Cissy met with the men at the Ninth Avenue food festival, an annual event celebrating the ethnic diversity of the West Side, and on tape they admitted their roles.

The Manhattan district attorney was convinced that the Westies used a Broadway makeup man to make Bokun look like Featherstone. Shannon, they believed, drove the get-away car provided by Bokun, who, like Featherstone, worked for Erie Transfer and was the mastermind. Kelly helped with the plan. The disguise was so good it actually fooled the witnesses, who picked Featherstone out of a lineup.

Despite all the energy and interest the Coffey Gang invested in its 1979 investigation of the Westies, Joe never had a face-to-face confrontation with Featherstone. The one time the gang arrested him, Featherstone was a prisoner on Rikers Island, the city's largest jail, where suspects are held awaiting trial.

Nevertheless, Featherstone blamed Coffey for all the Westies' troubles. He would often repeat in saloon conversations how "that fucking Joe Coffey shoulda kept his nose out of the West Side" and how "Coffey was trying to ruin things with 'Big Paulie.'"

Shortly after Featherstone agreed to be a government witness, he told the FBI that when Joe left the NYPD he tried to get a position as head of security for the Javits Convention Center. "I went to 'Big Paulie' and stopped it," Featherstone bragged to anyone who would listen. The claim was a total lie.

At this time Featherstone was being held at the Metropolitan Correction Center. He was transported to the Manhattan district attorney's office every day for interviews with prosecutors and other law enforcement agencies. He talked for hours about the criminal exploits of his West Side crew.

Coffey was then heading up a New York State Organized Crime Task Force unit looking into mob control of the construction industry. He was asked to interview Featherstone to see if the stoolie could help tie any loose ends together.

"I remember Featherstone, who looked like a choirboy, sitting behind a table acting like he was king of the underworld. I knew him to be little more than a sadistic killer, but the assistant U.S. attorneys and the district attorney, basically a bunch of young kids, were fawning over him like he was Meyer Lansky," Joe says. "I asked him a few questions, just to get his opinion for the record—I really already knew most of what he could possibly tell us—and then I couldn't hold back any longer."

"Why did you tell the FBI that I tried to get the security job at the Javits Center?" Joe asked him.

"You did, you needed a job, didn't ya?" Featherstone muttered in response.

"You little prick, you know I never tried to get that job. You think anyone would believe I'd get myself mobbed up in an operation like the Javits Center?" Joe, his broad face now red with anger, bellowed.

Featherstone, clearly afraid that his nemesis was about to reach across the table and grab him by the neck, turned to Assistant U.S. Attorney Mary Lee Warren for help. The young woman quickly entered the fray, screaming at Joe to cool off and to stop badgering the killer.

"What are you, his mother or a prosecutor?" Coffey barked at the woman.

"That remark quieted the room down, and I got control of myself," Joe recalls. "I think they all realized that the story about the security job was a figment of Featherstone's imagination. I never went after the job. Not that there would have been anything illegal about it if I had. I just did not like the idea of his trying to be a big shot at my expense."

Featherstone eventually became one of the most celebrated canaries in mob history. He rolled over 100 percent on his old gang, telling the same tales of the brutal, senseless murders and the connections to Paul Castellano that had filled Joe Coffey's reports eight years earlier. He told about the murder of a man whose decapitated head was tossed into a furnace. He testified about Eddie Commiskey's penchant for cutting up bodies.

The government called seventy witnesses to back up Featherstone's testimony. One recalled the dismemberment of the gambler Ricky Tassiello, carried out in the bathroom of a West Side apartment. "Every time I looked in the bathroom he was getting shorter," the witness said.

Another time he testified that McElroy attacked a gangster named Bobby Lagville with Lagville's baseball bat and then ran him over with his car several times.

From the stand Featherstone called Joe Coffey "Joe Publicity" because he loved to make the Westies look bad in the press. Joe's love for seeing his name in print was a charge that shadowed him throughout his career. Behind the scenes Featherstone told FBI agents, jealous of Coffey's reputation as the man who had busted the Westies and trying to make a case against him, that Coffey could not be bribed.

He reported being called to a meeting in a Brooklyn restaurant in 1977 with Paul Castellano. He admitted he and Jimmy Coonan were afraid of going to the meeting, thinking Castellano might want to kill them because they had knocked off a couple of Italian bookies. They ordered a group of Westies to stand by in a West Side apartment with hand grenades and shotguns. If the two leaders did not return in two hours, the gang was to kill everybody in the restaurant.

What Castellano wanted to know was if the Westies had killed the notorious loan shark Charles "Ruby" Stein in 1977. "We want his black book; it has millions of dollars in shylock loans," Castellano said. The boys from the West Side denied having anything to do with Stein's murder.

Featherstone said Castellano told him and Coonan to stop acting like "wild cowboys—if anyone is going to be killed it has to be cleared with us."

"That meant we were with the Gambino family now," Featherstone testified in November 1987. Hearing about that bit of testimony, Coffey remembered his own meeting with Castellano and how surprised he was when "Big Paulie" admitted knowing Coonan and Featherstone.

"'Big Paulie' said he expected 10 percent of everything we made except for shylocking," Featherstone continued that day on the witness stand.

He told a nerve-wracking story of how the Westies were given a contract on Anthony Scotto, boss of the Brooklyn piers, in a dispute over jobs at the Javits Convention Center, and how it was called off minutes before it was to be carried out. "We were going to get $15,000 for the murder and $30,000 if we made the body disappear," he testified.

In the face of all this incriminating testimony, defense lawyers for the eight Westies on trial, including Coonan's wife Edna, could only argue that Featherstone was a "hopeless alcoholic" and "paranoid killer."

When Featherstone was finished with his operatic performance, Jimmy Coonan ended up with a sixty-five-year stretch that included time for the murder of Patty Dugan. Jimmy McElroy got his long-overdue reservation in a prison cell for sixty years. Six other Westie leaders were also sent to prison. Shannon, Bokun, and Kelly were sent away for conspiracy to commit murder. Featherstone is a free man and is being hidden through the Federal Witness Protection Program.

Coffey's investigation of the Westies was not the first time he found himself ahead of his time. When he was a young detective in the Manhattan district attorney's squad he got a hunch that paid off with some significant arrests within a year or two but because of bureaucratic resistance took ten years to come to complete fruition. It was a case that began on the streets of Little Italy and ended in the inner sanctum of the Vatican.

· III ·

COFFEY, JOE COFFEY

Detective Joseph J. Coffey sat ramrod straight in a hard-backed chair directly in front of the wide, highly polished desk of his boss Frank Hogan. He was more frightened than at any time in his career. At his left sat his immediate supervisor, Inspector Paul Vitrano, who was only slightly more relaxed.

It was February 12, 1972, and Coffey had served in the famed Rackets Bureau of Manhattan District Attorney Frank Hogan for five years. During that time he had built a reputation as a dogged, tough, incorruptible lawman. Though on the force for only eight years, he already had a reputation as a cop who would sink his teeth into a case and not loosen his grip until the bad guy was behind bars. It was a reputation not unlike Hogan's, and Coffey was proud to be thought of in the same vein.

Hogan was the undisputed czar of the New York State Criminal Justice System. While his authority covered only

New York County, the borough of Manhattan, his reputation and record of success had earned him national stature. Throughout the world of law enforcement he was known affectionately as "Mr. DA."

It was Hogan who plucked Police Officer Coffey from the ranks of the elite Tactical Patrol Force for duty in his detective team and took a fatherly interest in the young cop, guiding his career into the detective ranks.

Technically detectives assigned to work in the district attorney's office in each of the five boroughs were New York Police Department cops and were under the command of the chief of detectives. But in practice the DA called the shots, and in Hogan's case his clout outweighed the police commissioner's.

Cops call higher-ranking officials who help their careers "rabbis." A New York City cop could have no greater "rabbi" than Frank Hogan.

And that's why Joe Coffey was so scared. He was about to lie to "Mr. DA," about to gamble with his career because he had a hunch that had to be pursued.

Vitrano, the textbook image of a detective supervisor, did most of the talking. He and Coffey had agreed to tell Hogan a totally fabricated story in order to convince the district attorney to use his influence to get the police commissioner to agree to let Coffey follow a Mafia hoodlum to Munich, West Germany.

The New York Police Department had a hard-and-fast rule against such travel. The last time they had let a cop leave the country on an investigation was in 1909. That cop was Lieutenant Joseph Petrosino and he too was following a Mafia lead. They called it the Black Hand in those days. Petrosino's investigation began in the Little Italy section of Manhattan, and it ended in Sicily, where he was murdered by Black Hand assassins. That was enough for New York City police brass. They tried something once and it ended in disaster. Why try again?

The parallels between Coffey's current investigation and

69

the mission that led to Petrosino's death were too similar for Vitrano to expect out-of-the-country approval for Coffey.

Coffey had been trailing a Little Italy mobster named Vincent Rizzo for two weeks. Rizzo was a "made guy" in the Genovese crime family—he owed his allegiance to the family godfather, Vito Genovese, and he had at least one murder to his credit.

He was known as a big earner in the family, bringing in huge amounts of money through such criminal activities as extortion, drug dealing, counterfeiting and running a phony travel agency, which used forged and stolen airline tickets, for the mob.

Coffey's interest in Rizzo grew out of a case involving the attempted takeover of the New York Playboy Club by a group of mobsters. Until the DA's office broke up the racket, the mob had successfully extorted money from the management and, through blackmail, turned several of the "bunnies" who worked there into drug-using prostitutes whose earnings went directly to the Genovese family.

One of the key figures in that case did business with Rizzo. It was while following him that Coffey and his partner, Detective Larry Mullins, realized that Rizzo was more powerful and influential in the Mafia than they had previously believed.

They watched Rizzo's constant street corner meetings with known mob figures and his occasional dinners with higher-ups in the Gambino organization. Along with his connection to the Playboy Club scheme, documentation of Rizzo's daily activities enabled the cops to convince a judge to approve a wiretap on the telephones in his main hangout, a sleazy bar on the Lower East Side called Jimmy's Lounge. In addition, on several occasions Coffey went into the bar in the undercover role of a steamfitter stopping for a drink or two on his way home after a day of back-breaking manual labor.

On February 11, 1972, the cops, crowded in a steamy, smoke-filled basement room not far from Jimmy's Lounge, where the wiretap was being monitored, heard something that really surprised them. Vinnie Rizzo, the barely literate child of the New York slums, who spent his working day wheeling and dealing in the world of low-life strong-arm men and degenerate gamblers, was overheard speaking to Lufthansa Airlines and ordering an expensive package deal to Munich. Rizzo would be staying a week at the brand-new Palace Hotel overlooking the site of the 1972 Olympics, scheduled for that summer.

Besides its seeming out of character for Rizzo to make such a trip, Coffey was also intrigued by the fact that Rizzo booked the trip legitimately, not through the mob's phony travel agency of which he had a majority share. It appeared he did not want anything to go wrong with this trip.

Every instinct Coffey had developed as a cop, plus the knowledge that was an ingrained part of his streetwise upbringing in the tenement neighborhoods dominated by the Third Avenue El, told him that he had to find out what Rizzo was going to do in Munich.

Back at the DA's office he passed on the information to Vitrano, who was just as amazed. Neither man could guess a reason why a guy like Rizzo would step so far out of his comfortable corner of the underworld.

"One thing is for sure," Coffey told the inspector, "he's not going skiing. The only skiing this guy ever did was on the icy sidewalks of Avenue B when he ran from the truant officers."

Vitrano agreed with the assessment that it must be something big, something that would eventually end up in Frank Hogan's jurisdiction. But both men knew that they would never get permission to go Germany on just the hunch of an Irish cop. So they agreed to lie to Hogan.

The two concocted a story. They knew Rizzo had a history of being involved in arms deals with South American drug dealers. So it would not appear too farfetched, they decided, if they told Hogan that Rizzo had spoken on the phone about going to Munich to set up an arms deal for the Protestants in Northern Ireland. The weapons, they would argue, would probably be used against the IRA and other Catholic factions. Knowing Hogan's sympathies lay with the Irish Catholics, they thought that was their best chance of getting him to influence Police Commissioner Patrick Murphy to override the "Black Hand Rule."

Coffey knew that he was taking a big risk. If Hogan didn't care as much about Northern Ireland as he and Vitrano thought he did, they were back to square one. If he caught the lie, the two were headed for the night beat on the West Side piers.

Joe had reason to be scared as he sat in front of the imposing district attorney. But the DA seemed to buy the story and promised to speak to Commissioner Murphy. It was Friday and Hogan said he would try to have an answer by Monday. At any rate they had two weeks before Rizzo was booked to leave. In the meantime he suggested Coffey begin to liaison with the police in Munich.

Coffey assumed with his characteristic confidence that he would get permission. He wanted to time his trip so that he would arrive before Rizzo. That would give him the opportunity to install a listening device in the hoodlum's room and a tap on his telephone. In New York he knew both tasks would be routinely approved by a judge, based on just cause provided by investigators. He expected the same procedure in Germany. He would bring his notes and copies of the wiretap requests already used in the Rizzo investigation.

That evening, filled with energy, he raced home to Levittown, a suburb on Long Island famed for being the first mass tract development in the U.S.

He was not looking forward to telling Pat that he was going out of town for at least a week and maybe longer. For most of the time Rizzo was under surveillance in Manhattan, the wife of Joe's regular partner, Larry Mullins, had been ill. Coffey was forced to follow Rizzo around town by himself and stake him out for long hours. He was working as much as twenty hours a day and had not seen his children, Joseph, Steven, and Kathleen, for about a week.

It is times like these that strain relationships between cops and their wives, but Pat Coffey had always been understanding. In 1959, when Joe got out of the army, he returned to a job at Western Electric. The following year he and Pat married. One year later Kathleen was born. In 1962, hanging on to his childhood dream, Joe took the civil service test for New York City police officer. He passed, finishing near the top of a long list.

Almost immediately the department called to offer a place in the Police Academy. Since he was working at a job with great potential in the computer field, he declined. Another baby was on the way and he was concerned he would not be able to raise a family on a cop's salary. However, he asked to be kept on the list for the next round of hirings.

In 1964 the department called for the third time. This was his last opportunity. If he declined he would be taken off the list forever. He would never get the chance to avenge his father.

"I liked the computer business and I knew that someday it could be a financial bonanza, but I had not forgotten my boyhood dream. I still wanted to be a cop," Joe remembers.

He talked for hours with his young wife about what he should do and found her 100 percent supportive. She encouraged him to do what would make him most happy. "The family will be fine. Don't worry," she said.

So with Pat's support Joe Coffey quit a $12,000-a-year job with Western Electric and became a recruit in the New York Police Department for half the money.

Pat Coffey learned early that she was not going to see a lot of her police officer husband. She not only accepted that life but learned to find her own satisfaction in it. Joe often shared the details of a case with her, and she would not hesitate to offer an opinion. When he said he was following Vinnie Rizzo to Europe, she picked up on the same inconsistencies in Rizzo's behavior that her husband sensed and understood why it was necessary. She said she would help him pack when the time came and assured him the family would be fine while he was away.

"I never could have had the kind of career I had without Pat's help," Coffey says. "I was able to pursue leads and meet people at times when other cops were home with their families. It's not that I loved my family any less. I just seemed obsessed with my work. Even when I coached football and basketball in the Levittown community leagues, the other coaches knew I might show up late or not at all for the games. It bothered me to take the time from my kids, but I felt I was doing important work."

Coffey was restless all weekend and arrived at his office early Monday morning. About an hour later, Hogan summoned him and Vitrano to his office.

The DA told the two nervous cops that he agreed Rizzo should be followed to Munich. An arms deal to Northern Ireland was serious business and should be stopped if possible. He said he was surprised a punk like Rizzo had that kind of international connection but the possibility could not be overlooked. He approved sending one man to Munich.

"He told me that he could budget only $1,000 for the assignment and that I'd better come back with something worthwhile," Coffey remembers. "He probably knew I wanted to go so badly I would have paid for the trip myself. As far as results go? Well, I was always a hunch player and I was sure this was a solid one."

On February 24, two days before Rizzo, Coffey left for Munich. He had been working hard during the preceding days, researching German law regarding wiretaps and learning it was similar to New York's, requiring judicial approval based on police information. He also learned that Rizzo was the suspect in the extortion of a German citizen, a fact that made the Munich police even more anxious to help.

He hoped the eight-hour flight would give him a chance to catch up on the rest he had been missing, but once aboard the Lufthansa plane he remembered that he was afraid of flying. He had forgotten his fear during the exciting preparation for the trip, but once he sat down in the seat he began to sweat. He could not sleep on the flight, and no amount of airline booze made him forget he was flying thirty thousand feet above the cold Atlantic Ocean.

When he landed in Munich, Coffey was hung over, tired, and starting for the first time to feel some apprehension about his mission. He was not feeling much like the globe-trotting secret agent he was trying to portray.

"I was really exhausted, not in any shape to begin such an important investigation, but I figured I could get to my hotel, shower, and shave before hooking up with the local police," he remembers thinking.

His plan was dashed by the efficiency of the Munich Police Department. Two Munich detectives were waiting at the customs gate to meet him. Quickly they bypassed the lines and, within minutes of his arrival, were driving him to the police presidium (headquarters) in the center of the city. There, waiting for him with a big smile and a shot of cognac, was Klaus Peter, the detective who would work directly with him.

Peter explained he had arranged with the Palace Hotel for a room two doors from Rizzo's, where the cops could set up their own headquarters for the surveillance mission. Another room, two floors above, was reserved for Joe's use.

"The Munich police assigned sixteen detectives to Peter and me, and they were all highly polished pros. Their manner was much more professional than the cops I usually came across in the states," Coffey recalls.

The Munich police were very excited about working with the detective from New York. The Mafia to them was a legendary crime organization they believed to be more powerful than any police force. They had little contact with Mafia criminals, but were deeply interested in the efforts of their Italian, Dutch, and American colleagues who battled "La Cosa Nostra" on a regular basis.

Their enthusiasm rubbed off on Coffey. Some confidence and energy was just beginning to return to his tired body when Klaus Peter mentioned the major roadblock to proceeding any further.

"Of course you understand we're not sure we want to set up this eavesdropping device," Peter said.

"Why not! I thought you understood that was the basis of my trip. So far we've built our whole case on the wiretap evidence," Coffey responded.

For the next few minutes, Peter patiently explained that the Munich police had not conducted a wiretap since World War II, when they were controlled by the Nazi Gestapo. While the law was on the books and judges seemed willing to approve such measures, police departments in Germany were trying hard to live down the Gestapo image. Peter said they could discuss it with the Munich police commander the next day. The laws may have been similar to the United States codes, but the postwar attitudes were quite different.

As drained as Coffey was, he was determined not to let another day pass without the okay for the telephone wiretap and the listening device. He wanted to be sure it would be in place before Rizzo arrived in his room.

For hours the cops argued the case. Peter was sympathetic but very protective of his department's reputation. He explained that his men were experts in surveillance and routinely built solid cases without eavesdropping. But Coffey was adamant. He knew what he would have to take back to the states to build his case there. New York prosecutors wanted legally obtained tape recordings of criminals discussing their crimes. Juries in the United States loved the dramatic dialogue and occasional confessions such tapes produced. Several times Coffey bluffed that he would just pack the whole thing in if he could not get wiretaps.

Finally Klaus Peter agreed to let Coffey make his argument to Reinhard Rupprect, director of the department's criminal division and Peter's boss. Six months later Rupprect would become world famous as the man who led the German police against the Arab terrorists who attacked the Munich Olympic Village and murdered Israeli athletes.

Coffey found Rupprect very understanding. He also was concerned about the flow of illegal arms to Northern Ireland. His cop's instinct agreed with Coffey's that it had to be a big deal to flush a lowlife like Rizzo out of the protection of his own neighborhood. He agreed to pass the police request for a bug and wiretap on to the proper judicial authority.

In the states this is where Coffey would have expected resistance. American cops were always anxious to bug suspects. Judges took on the responsibility of protecting the suspect's rights and often refused the police requests. The Munich judge, however, spent only a few minutes reviewing the paperwork, and the electronic surveillance request was approved around midnight.

Coffey was exhausted. He turned down the Munich detectives' invitation to drink some beers at their favorite hangout and returned to his hotel, not far from the police presidium. Too tired to even call Pat, he collapsed on the bed with his clothes on and slept soundly until the hotel operator woke him up at 7:00 A.M.

By 9:00 he was at Klaus Peter's small office, chain-smoking and pacing. He was now bursting with energy, anxious to get up to the room the Palace Hotel had reserved for Rizzo to get the bug and the wiretap installed.

Peter showed up within a few minutes. He carried a small metal box which he handed to Coffey with the words, "I hate to see a good cop walking around naked. I thought you could use this."

Joe opened the box and took out the Walther PPK. He had left his own gun in New York rather than deal with the tangle of paperwork necessary to carry it onto the airplane and into a foreign country. Peter had noticed he was unarmed and thought he could do something to make his new American friend a little more comfortable. A fan of spy novels, Coffey recognized the weapon as the same one used by the fictional James Bond.

"The offer of the gun calmed me down a little. I realized Peter and his men knew what they were doing. I had been

7
7

embarrassed by the whining and begging I had to do to get the wiretap approval, and the Walther provided a laugh as I joked about being 007. It was a very important moment in the case because it proved the German cops had faith in me," Coffey remembers.

Continuing to make light of the emotional moment, Joe said, "What do expect me to do with this? I'll probably shoot myself in the foot."

The line brought a laugh from the group, and as Coffey slipped his belt through the holster's loop, he asked Peter if he could take a look at the surveillance equipment before they went over to the Palace.

"I might as well have asked him to see a heart-lung machine. He looked at me like I was from outer space," Coffey recalls.

Up to this point Peter had assumed Coffey had brought the necessary equipment with him. The Munich police, having never wiretapped a phone or bugged a room since the end of World War II, did not even have the equipment to do so.

Peter called Rupprect, the director of the criminal division, for advice. The solution was to meet with an American CIA agent with whom the Munich police had a discreet relationship.

Now feeling more and more like an international espionage agent, Joe met the spy for lunch at an American servicemen's club, very much like the ones he had spent time in thirteen years before while serving in the army in Germany as a cryptographer.

The CIA man was more than cooperative, offering not only the bug but a technician to install it. By early afternoon Coffey and a handful of Munich police officers, including a woman who was fluent in English, German, and Italian, were in Rizzo's room.

One of the first things a detective in the district attorney's office in New York learns is the art of eavesdropping. Coffey was much more comfortable around electronic bugging equipment than he was around high-tech weapons. "A good wiretap technician does more to put criminals behind bars than a dozen SWAT teams," he says.

He quickly realized, and was greatly surprised, that the gear provided by the CIA was outmoded, almost obsolete. The actual listening device was larger than what Coffey was used to working with. It had a very limited range and was operated by batteries that had to be changed regularly. Coffey told the technician to put the bug in the motor that ran the massage unit in the bed. Coffey realized that if Rizzo did his talking while enjoying a massage, the bug would be useless, but he decided it was the only centrally located spot that would hide the unit. The detective wondered to himself how the CIA managed to conduct any kind of sophisticated electronic surveillance with that kind of equipment. He assumed the KGB had better devices, and he knew the Manhattan DA did.

It was decided earlier to wiretap the phone by recording Rizzo's calls at the hotel switchboard, so that was no problem.

The next day, Sunday, February 27, Rizzo arrived in Munich. Coffey, his James Bond pistol on his hip, and two German detectives, followed the hood from the airport to the Palace Hotel. As Rizzo checked into his third-floor room, the cops went to the room two doors away, which was their monitoring post.

Rizzo unpacked quickly. Within minutes he was on the telephone, first calling the office of a man named Alfred Barg, the German director of a Swiss company. It was now late Sunday afternoon and the cops were not surprised there was no answer.

The next call was answered. Rizzo asked for a Mr. Ense. Rizzo had the wrong number, but the mention of Ense rang a bell with the Munich cops. Klaus Peter knew Wilfred Ense as a con man who was suspected in the robbery of U.S. Treasury Bonds and was a key figure in a ring that spread stolen stocks and bonds around Europe.

Rizzo had no luck on the telephone that evening and eventually went to bed without making a connection. So far, Coffey still had no idea why the street thug from Avenue A was in Munich, but the reputation of Ense was adding fuel to the fire.

Early the next morning Rizzo was dialing again. He tried first to reach a used-car salesman the Germans knew sold stolen cars to American servicemen. Then he got through to Alfred Barg.

It was a conversation difficult for the listening detectives to understand. Rizzo spoke no German; Barg apparently had little English. When Rizzo hung up, the cops played back their tape. After a few replays they agreed Rizzo was trying to collect $350,000 from Barg—money he owed to American criminals he had been involved in a stolen securities deal with. Rizzo demanded a meeting with Barg and Ense in his room at the Palace.

For the next two days Rizzo was on the phone repeatedly arguing with Barg and Ense. Once he left the hotel and went to Ense's office. Coffey got a kick out of Rizzo's attempt to threaten the Germans. He kept telling them what an important man he was in New York and gave them the names of several organized crime figures who would vouch for him and certify that he was authorized to collect the $350,000 debt.

But Barg and Ense were professional swindlers. They were expert at maneuvering events to their benefit and they were making Rizzo sweat. No amount of threatening seemed to speed up the process.

Finally, at a little past noon on Tuesday, Ense called Rizzo and agreed to come over with Barg. They would be there about 1:00 P.M. Rizzo said he would be waiting in the bar.

The cops down the hall were elated, but their instant celebration ceased when the CIA technician realized he had to change the batteries in the bug hidden in the massage unit. He had been counting on Rizzo's leaving for dinner, so the afternoon meeting caught him off guard.

When Rizzo, on his way to the bar, stepped into the elevator, the surveillance team swung into action. The CIA man raced for the bug, while others made sure they would have Rizzo and then Barg and Ense in their sight at all times. The team figured they had about fifteen minutes to get the battery changed. Coffey cursed the outdated equipment and set up position in the hallway, his eye on the elevator bank.

As the CIA man approached Rizzo's room, a hotel maid stepped out of the room directly across the hallway, a key in her hand. She clearly intended to enter Rizzo's room to make it up for the day. Coffey realized the problem. He had to think of a way to delay her so that the agent could get in to do his battery change.

He stepped into the monitoring room, which was now filling up with Munich detectives anxious to listen in on the expected meeting. He grabbed a glass from a room service cart and hurled it across the room. It shattered against the wall with a noise that rumbled across the third floor. Coffey stuck his head out of the door and screamed for the maid.

"Maid, we've got an emergency in here. Hurry, hurry!" he yelled.

The young woman withdrew her key from Rizzo's door and ran toward Joe. She had heard the noise and expected the worst. Once in the room, she looked around at a bunch of nervous men she immediately took to be cops and set to work cleaning up the broken glass. The CIA agent was finished in Rizzo's room about fifteen seconds before the maid returned.

By one o'clock Rizzo, Barg, and Ense were in the room, and Coffey and the Germans were listening. Their first order of business was to call room service for a bottle of Chivas Regal. After it arrived, each poured himself a drink and they settled in to talk business.

The three spoke in English. Barg's command of the language was obviously better than he first let on to Rizzo. Soon Coffey understood that Rizzo was trying to collect the money for a California wiseguy named Ricky Jacobs. Jacobs was in jail for running a crooked poker game at the Los Angeles Friar's Club. Coffey knew that several Hollywood stars had been fleeced by Jacobs.

Ense and Barg both denied they owed the money and started to recount all the details of their association with Jacobs. They spoke about meeting him in London with a man called Dr. Ledl.

Ense, who had consumed much of the Chivas Regal, said he helped Jacobs and Ledl work out a deal because Ledl could not speak English and Jacobs did not speak German.

"I learned they had a deal in Rome . . . with people in the Vatican, and Ledl needed counterfeit securities," Ense told Rizzo.

Ense was on a roll. He was doing all the talking. "Ricky made me ask him again and again, twenty times, is he quite sure that his people in Rome, in the Vatican, want counterfeit? And Dr. Ledl says, 'They want all the counterfeit securities they can get.'"

In the room, listening, the group of detectives sat stunned. Coffey had always felt he was on to something big, but this was beyond imagination. The group looked at each other; nothing was said. They were all cops; they were all Catholic; they did not have to be told they had just learned of a crime with enormous implications. Someone in the Vatican at least had attempted to acquire counterfeit securities from members of the American Mafia. At least $350,000 of the mob's profit was still unpaid, and that's why Rizzo was in Munich. Coffey realized the numbers involved must be staggering.

Ense continued blabbering. He told of two weeks spent in Rome with Ledl and a few other criminal connections setting up the deal. But Ense and Barg were totally drunk by then. They talked on, but it became more and more difficult to follow the trail they were trying to lay out. Clearly they were confusing the Vatican caper with some other enterprise he and Ledl worked on together.

Eventually Rizzo lost his patience. He really didn't care about what had happened between Ense, Barg, the mysterious Dr. Ledl, and his fellow hoodlum Ricky Jacobs. He was there to collect the $350,000. He was increasingly frustrated that his tough guy act was apparently not convincing Barg and Ense to reach for their wallets. In New York, it would be different. He had seen grown men wet their pants when Vinnie Rizzo showed up to collect a debt.

At one point Rizzo insisted, "I'm not interested in how much merchandise was involved; I'm only interested in the money that's coming to my people."

Rizzo apparently was in Munich only to collect the money due from the stolen securities deal. He did not want to be distracted by anything else—even news of a counterfeit securities deal inside the Vatican.

But to the delight of Coffey, Ense pretended not to hear and continued on about how Ricky Jacobs had promised him that the nine hundred thousand dollars' worth of merchandise was "qualified"—that it was Coca-Cola Bottling Company of Los Angeles merchandise.

Both Coffey and Rizzo knew that in mob jargon the word "qualified" meant that the merchandise (Coffey now understood it to be securities certificates) was not counterfeit, that it was genuine paper, stolen from either the company or legitimate dealers. Coffey thought that nine hundred thousand dollars of stolen Coca-Cola securities was an enormous haul.

Rizzo, now totally exasperated, said he would do Ense a favor and check whether they were real or counterfeit when he got back to New York. "But what has that got to do with this right now?" he demanded.

For almost two hours Ense and Rizzo argued, with Barg occasionally breaking in on behalf of Ense. The two con men were masterful at diverting Rizzo's attention. They pretended not to understand what Rizzo wanted, they claimed they wanted to pay what was owed but did not feel right giving it to Rizzo. They called him an errand boy which made him furious. By the end of the session, Rizzo still had not collected a penny, just promises. Coffey thought to himself that if the meeting were being held in a New York hotel room, Rizzo would have beaten up the two con men.

When Ense and Barg left and the recording machine stopped rolling, a heavy silence lingered in the air. Coffey had been chain-smoking through the entire meeting. He found himself breathing hard and sweating as he replayed the conversation in his mind. All the detectives were going through their notes, turning pages, searching back to the first mention of "Rome" and "Vatican."

Joe realized he needed some time to organize all this in his mind before calling New York. He and Peter had some lunch, carefully avoiding discussion about what they had just heard, so they would not add to the confusion. Then Coffey went to his room. It was early morning in New York but he gambled Vitrano would already be at the office. He called the Leonard Street number.

Vitrano was in, and without ceremony Coffey began pouring out the details of the Rizzo meeting. He was talking so fast and seemed so excited that Vitrano had to interrupt him to tell him to relax, to slow down. Then, as Vitrano began to comprehend the potential of what Coffey had overheard, he stopped the detective again.

"I want to get this on tape and I want to get Ron Goldstock in here," Vitrano said. Goldstock, at the time, was an assistant district attorney specializing in organized crime. He understood better than anyone in Hogan's office how the Mafia put together complicated deals involving millions of dollars.

For more than an hour Joe Coffey read his notes into the telephone and added his own interpretations. When he finished all three men were mentally exhausted.

"You did good, Joe. Get back here as soon as Rizzo leaves," Vitrano ordered.

Rizzo left the next morning after Ense agreed to open a

bank account in Munich into which he would deposit the money owed the American mob. Coffey was on a flight out that evening.

Aboard the plane he ran through the events of the past week. Again and again he read his notes. Who was this Ledl? How much money could possibly be involved? It had to be millions. Was the Coca-Cola company the only one hit? Ense had mentioned at least ten names, people in countries all over the world. Would he have to track them all down? And, most importantly, what was the Vatican Connection? Could these con men have actually gotten their hooks into the Vatican, or worse, could someone in the Vatican actually have been behind a scheme to steal and counterfeit American securities?

As the plane cruised towards New York, Coffey put away his notebook and shut off his overhead light. His fear of flying seemed trivial amid the events of the previous two days. In the darkened cabin he thought about his childhood.

The Coffeys were devout Catholics. His parents, Margaret and Joseph, Sr., children of immigrants from Ireland in the late nineteenth century, scrimped and saved to allow Joe and his brothers and sisters to attend parochial schools in their Manhattan neighborhood. Joe attended Xavier High School, a Catholic military academy, and later Fordham University, a Jesuit school. As a teenager he served as personal altar boy for the priest-philosopher Bishop Fulton J. Sheen, whose radio and television program and writings made him a national figure in the 1940s and 1950s.

Along with FBI agents, priests were among the heroes of Joe's youth. But when he was a senior in high school, something happened that began to change his attitude toward the church.

Joe's brother Edward had entered a seminary in Pennsylvania, and when he was eighteen years old, Joe and a neighborhood girlfriend went to visit.

"To my dismay and shock, we found almost all the priests

85

were obviously homosexual. There was nothing discreet about them. My brother was very upset because I was so annoyed. On the drive home I was almost in tears," Coffey remembers. Edward Coffey soon left the seminary, giving up his dream of becoming a priest.

Years later, when Joe first joined the district attorney's office, Hogan was wrapping up an investigation called the "phony cop case." It involved a blackmailer named Sherman Kaminsky who ran a ring of con artists and blackmailers who preyed on travelers at the city's bus and train depots.

Spotting people they believed to be homosexuals, one member of the team, called the "chicken," would convince the victim to go to a hotel room. Once they were there for a few minutes a second member of the team, who was called the "bull" and posed as a cop, would break in at the opportune moment and catch the pair having sex. The bull would threaten the pair with arrest and frighten the victim with tales of what prison inmates did to homosexuals. Eventually, of course, the bull would say he was willing to forget the whole thing for a price.

Before Hogan's men broke the ring, several well-known politicians, an admiral, and even a famous law enforcement official were snared by Kaminsky. But what bothered Coffey the most about the ring was that more than half of their victims were Catholic priests.

So the Joe Coffey flying back from Munich, Germany, in 1972 was quite a different person from the one who, as a teenager, attended to Bishop Sheen.

"It wasn't that I was no longer religious; I was. But I had learned that anything was possible. If I could believe that a priest could be a practicing homosexual, then I could believe he could be a con man and a swindler. And if he happened to work in the Vatican, well I could believe that too," says Coffey.

A car was waiting at Kennedy Airport to drive Joe back to Leonard Street. Much had happened since his telephone call to Vitrano and Goldstock. Most importantly, Vitrano had played Coffey's tape for the head of the New York office of the Justice Department's Organized Crime Strike Force.

The strike force people were immediately interested, but it was not the mention of the Vatican that had made them offer Vitrano all the money and manpower he needed. One of the things that sparked them was the mention of the Coca-Cola Bottling Company of Los Angeles stock. The Justice Department at the time was deeply involved through the FBI in investigating the manufacture and worldwide movement of more than fifty billion dollars' worth of counterfeit or stolen stocks and securities bearing the names of blue-chip companies. The strike force knew that Coca-Cola of Los Angeles had lost a large quantity of securities in the mail in 1970. Companies like Occidental Petroleum and Norton Simon also had reported large numbers of securities stolen and were part of the same investigation.

On several occasions the lost paper, even though it was eventually reported stolen, was used as collateral in million-dollar swindles all over the world. One scam almost bankrupted the government of Panama.

The other factor that caused the feds to jump in with both feet was the mention of Ricky Jacobs. They knew him to be one of the major American dealers in stolen and counterfeit securities, and whatever deal he touched they wanted to know about. Could Jacobs, Ense, Barg, and the others mentioned in Coffey's tapes be the masterminds behind these international scams? The tapes were the first solid lead the Justice Department had received.

William Aronwald, an assistant to the head of the strike force office, was assigned to coordinate the investigation with Vitrano and Coffey. For the time being, at least, neither he nor his bosses shared Coffey's interest in the possible involvement of the Vatican in an international swindle. Joe began to worry that the Vatican scam would be lost in the shuffle. He was afraid that the break they were handed when the Vatican was mentioned in that hotel room would not be pursued, and he decided to make sure the possibility of a Vatican investigation was discussed at every strategy meeting of the strike force. He began driving even his friends in the DA's office nuts with talk of the Vatican.

At Hogan's insistence Coffey was forced to take a few days off to spend with Pat and the kids. Within a week, however, he was back at work in the basement room where the wiretap on Jimmy's Lounge was still being operated.

Now much more of what Vincent Rizzo was talking about to his mob connections was understandable. The inclusion of the Justice Department in the investigation added a national scope that even Frank Hogan could not have initiated.

Using names and places from the Munich tapes, FBI agents were being dispatched all over the country. An FBI man named Dick Tamarro was assigned to work full-time with Coffey.

Rizzo's operations continued to amaze the New York cops assigned to tail him and listen in on his private conversations. He was constantly on the phone in Jimmy's Lounge calling upstate New York to order a shipment of counterfeit money, dispatching a hit man to California to collect a $25,000 debt, keeping his drug business going, and trying to figure a way to get that $350,000 still owed from the stolen securities deal. Ense and Barg continued to fend off Rizzo's threats.

Meanwhile Coffey's own level of frustration was rising as all the investigating activity around him seemed to bypass any further move on the Vatican. Even Hogan, who was so happy about being able to pass on the information from the Munich tapes that he never even asked about the gunrunning scheme, did not seem anxious to pursue the lead. Privately with Coffey he talked about the possibilities of the Vatican involvement in the counterfeit securities scam, but Joe worried that his mentor, like the feds, would be happy nailing the securities swindle ring and closing the books on Rizzo, Ense, Barg, and the others.

A few weeks after he returned from Munich, Joe learned

he had passed the NYPD sergeant's test. Police officers in New York have several career paths to choose from if they seek advancement in salary and responsibility. They can aim for the Detective Division, where promotion is based on achievement, but detective first grade is as high as they can go. That rank, while probably the most prestigious detective position in the world, does not pay as much as it is possible to earn by going up the civil service ranks of sergeant, lieutenant, and captain. Ranks above captain are appointed by the police commissioner.

But a detective runs a risk by taking the test for sergeant. If he passes, he must return to uniform patrol for at least six months and then hope for a rare opening for a detective sergeant to get back into the Detective Division.

Coffey wanted to take the chance. He needed the additional rank because he yearned for the authority to act more on his own instincts and hunches. He wanted to be able to command a detective squad, a position many in law enforcement believed to be the best job in the New York Police Department.

So Joe had mixed emotions about passing the test. He wanted the promotion, but he feared being transferred to uniform before the Vatican Connection was nailed.

For two months the FBI and New York police continued to run down leads produced by the Munich tapes and the subsequent surveillance of Rizzo and his now growing list of worldwide contacts. Coffey continued to be nagged by the realization that the Justice Department team was not interested in pursuing the Vatican lead. He continued to bother Hogan about it.

Alone in Hogan's office one evening, the district attorney counseled Joe not to worry so much. "Joe, let's take one thing at a time. The strike force is hot on the stolen securities case right now, and I think it is best not to distract them. I'm certain we'll get our shot at Rome," Hogan said.

In late April the wiretap in Jimmy's Lounge picked up a call from an Englishman named Tony Grant who said he was in New York and wanted to meet with Rizzo. Coffey's near photographic memory immediately clicked on. During the hours of recording in Munich the name Tony was often mentioned. He was called "The Englishman" and "The Tailor," but a last name was never used.

Coffey called a contact at Interpol and ran the name Tony Grant by him. The contact did not have to check his files. He told Coffey that Tony Grant was a well-known European swindler and forger with a record dating back to the 1930s. He often posed as a high-class tailor and dressed the part. He was most recently wanted in connection with swindling an elderly couple out of their life savings, which had been invested in precious jewels. As part of that scheme he used $20,000 in counterfeit U.S. currency.

Coffey was elated by the information. He knew the Tony on the tapes had to be this Tony Grant who was now in New York. Things were beginning to happen.

For three days, Coffey and Tamarro followed Grant around New York. The Englishman proved to be the pro his dossier described. He changed hotels every day and he never went directly to a meeting. It was a strain on the resources of both Hogan's office and the New York FBI to keep a tail on the slippery Grant, but it paid off when they overheard him make arrangements with Rizzo to fly together to Miami to set up a cocaine deal.

Grant would introduce Rizzo to a South American connection who would accept $60,000 in counterfeit money for a small supply of cocaine to get the relationship going. All parties hoped it would lead to a big-time drug network between the Genovese gang in Little Italy and Colombian dealers. It was agreed to let the deal go through in order to keep building a case against Rizzo. It was hoped that Grant could eventually lead the Justice Department and also the Secret Service (now involved because of the mention of counterfeit money) to the bigger stolen securities case.

Back in New York, Grant continued to do business with Rizzo's gang. On Mother's Day, 1972, he left for Argentina to continue to establish the new drug network. A Spanish-speaking detective from Frank Hogan's office and Coffey's regular partner, Larry Mullins, were on the same plane.

By now Rizzo's phone calls to Europe were showing his frustration with not being able to collect his money from Barg and Ense. But the two Germans continued to stall. On May 23 Rizzo decided he had to return to Munich. He took along a strong-arm man named Marty DeLorenzo. Coffey and Detective Mario Trapani were on the flight following Rizzo's. The Munich police were alerted to shadow the two thugs once they landed.

That same evening Rizzo met with Barg and Ense in Barg's home outside of Munich. There were no wiretaps installed, but it was later learned that Rizzo told them that DeLorenzo was the man to whom the $350,000 was owed, and he was in Munich to collect it in cash or blood. Rizzo said even he was afraid of DeLorenzo and that this was the end of the line. The money must be deposited the next day in the bank account set up for that purpose. Incredibly, facing the wrath of a Mafia enforcer, Barg and Ense continued to do business their way. Instead of money they convinced DeLorenzo to accept part of a phony Vermont vacation home deal as payment. DeLorenzo accepted.

Joe, convinced he would learn nothing more about the Vatican connection on that trip, decided he might be more useful back in New York on Tony Grant's trail. He returned to New York alone. Trapani would later report that Rizzo spent the rest of the week in Munich having an affair with a woman who worked in Alfred Barg's office.

The day Joe arrived back in New York he learned Tony Grant and a Genovese button man named Freddy Mayo, who usually ran the phony travel agency that was part of Rizzo's illegal empire, would be driving a shipment of cocaine into the city. It was decided to arrest them as soon as they hit city limits. Still suffering from jet lag, Joe and the others put a plan into place. Within eight hours Tony Grant was behind bars in the Tombs, the infamous city jail attached to the Manhattan Criminal Court building that in the past was the last stop for condemned criminals.

Freddy Mayo was also locked up. And punk that he was, he soon began spilling his guts about his mob relations. For a break on his sentence he was willing to help nail Rizzo for drug dealing, extortion, and other crimes he knew he had taken part in.

"What about Rome?" Coffey asked the sweating punk, not letting a chance to chase his Vatican hunch go by. "Did Rizzo ever mention Rome, or the Vatican?"

Joe Coffey had grilled enough low-life criminals to know that the vacant look in Freddy Mayo's eyes was his natural stare of noncomprehension. He knew nothing of any major deals Rizzo was involved in.

Tony Grant would not talk. He had been down this road before, and he expected Rizzo to get him a good lawyer and take care of his needs behind bars. For one week, then two, he refused to discuss the case with Coffey, Mullins, or Tamarro. Then Mullins got a call.

"Grant wants to talk to us," he shouted across the DA squad room to Coffey. "He's pissed at Rizzo for not sending him any cigarettes at the Tombs. He wants to help us nail him."

Both detectives rushed through the connecting hallway from the court building where their office was to Grant's cell block.

Grant was pacing around his cell. He was furious with Rizzo. The mafioso was ignoring his requests for cigarettes made through departing inmates. Grant was a chain-smoker and was suffering. Coffey, since he was also a heavy smoker, sympathized with the Englishman and knew his anger was genuine.

"You want Vinnie Rizzo. I'll give you Vinnie Rizzo," was the con man's greeting to Coffey and Mullins.

"Before we could sit down he began his spiel. We would have preferred to get it on tape, but we didn't want to interrupt him so we let him talk," Coffey remembers.

"He told us about the drug deal, how it got set up, who was behind it, and where the counterfeit money came from.

"Then he told us about the swindle that almost brought down Panama. Now he was getting into an area that interested me because I knew Barg and Ense had mentioned that in Munich. Then, and I'll never forget this moment, he said, 'And you must know about that deal in the Vatican. I'll tell you what Rizzo and Jacobs and that Austrian, Ledl, were trying to do.'

"All Grant wanted in return was a steady supply of cigarettes. He did not ask for a break on his sentence or for reduced charges. He was singing in order to get back at Rizzo for not doing the right thing. I wanted to kiss the old swindler," says Coffey.

Grant finally explained what the Vatican wanted with counterfeit securities. It was known, he explained, that the Vatican Bank was overextended and that certain officials of the bank sought help from bankers and investors with less than reputable backgrounds to help the bank get back on track.

Grant smoked and talked on and on. He was very willing to nail Rizzo. He was a crook from the old school. Once he agreed to tell Coffey what he knew, he kept his end of the bargain.

He implicated, Rizzo, Ense, Barg, Ricky Jacobs, and a host of other swindlers, con men, forgers, burglars, gigolos, and strong-arm types from all corners of the globe in schemes that ranged from ripping off wealthy retirees to flooding banks with counterfeit securities and creating vast resort developments with loans based on collateral of stolen and counterfeit securities.

"As for the Vatican," Grant said, "the word was that they were after about $900 million of counterfeit American corporate bonds. Everyone wanted a piece of that action. The Austrian, Ledl, made the deal. You'll have to get to him."

By the time Grant finished singing, Coffey and the Justice Department strike force team had plenty to nail Rizzo,

Jacobs, Barg, and Ense on, as well as a bunch of less important players, including the son of a former British defense minister.

In addition to the Coca-Cola of Los Angeles stock, the strike force could now connect Rizzo to stealing and counterfeiting the stocks of such companies as IBM, Norton Simon, Chrysler, AT & T, and General Electric. Rizzo had a portfolio that rivaled those of the greatest Wall Street investors. And he could always steal or forge more, when needed, to be used as collateral in a crooked deal.

Eventually charges against Rizzo would show that more than $18 million in blue-chip securities that had been stolen from the U.S. Postal Service, from messengers, and from people's homes had passed through his hands. The amount of counterfeit stocks and bonds was at least that much and probably very much more.

"The feds were very happy. They did not need to, and they did not want to, open the Vatican can of worms. I was arguing to continue the investigation, but I was a low-ranking member of that team even though I was the one who first brought the case to the Justice Department," Coffey remembers.

Coffey knew that eventually the Austrian, Dr. Ledl, would become a major figure in the case, but for the time being he was not anxious to return to Europe to track him down. During Joe's second trip to Munich, Pat had suffered a miscarriage. Joe did not learn about it until he returned home, and he was bothered by the fact that he was not there for his family when they needed him. He decided not to pursue Ledl unless he had a near 100 percent chance of getting something out of him regarding the Vatican.

As summer approached, the strike force began preparing their grand jury presentation against Rizzo. In August, Coffey's Interpol contact reported that a Dr. Leopold Ledl was under arrest in Vienna on a fraud charge and would certainly get a prison term.

This was great news. If Ledl was imprisoned, he might

be willing to talk about his connection in the Vatican in return for a deal not to prosecute him in the United States as part of the Rizzo ring.

Coffey began agitating for the chance to go after Ledl in Austria. He knew he was running out of time to nail the Vatican link. Word around the department was that the recently promoted sergeants would be sent to their new assignments in early 1973. Joe was sure that he would never get to Ledl once that happened, and he knew that no one else would try. He was losing sleep over the possibility that whoever violated the trust of Vatican office would get away with it.

Finally in mid-November he got the okay to travel to Vienna with Dick Tamarro to see what they could get out of Ledl. They were authorized to offer a deal of immunity to any charges he might face in the U.S.

During the last week of November, while their families were celebrating Thanksgiving, Detective Joe Coffey and Special Agent Dick Tamarro sat in the dank cellar interview room of a 150-year-old prison in Vienna. Across from them was Leopold Ledl, an international swindler accustomed to sharing the high society life of his victims. His stay in the Vienna prison had convinced him that he had to avoid extradition to America at any cost. He would do whatever was necessary to avoid this, even putting his life at risk by implicating some of the most important people in Rome in a counterfeit stock deal designed to shore up the weakened finances of the Vatican Bank, and even if one of those people was an archbishop in the Vatican.

The deal was made and Ledl talked.

"Ledl finally brought all the pieces together. He told us he had been approached by Cardinal Eugene Tisserant, dean of the Vatican's College of Cardinals, to buy $950 million in counterfeit U.S. corporate bonds. Ledl passed on the request to Rizzo," Coffey notes.

Ledl said that the deal had the total backing of Archbishop Paul Marcinkus, president of the Institute for Religious Works, known as the Vatican Bank.

Marcinkus's goal, Ledl told Coffey and Tamarro, was to use the counterfeits as collateral for loans. At first, Ledl said, he never spoke to Marcinkus directly—the cleric used emissaries and cover—but later he did have direct contact with the archbishop and eventually delivered $14.5 million in forged blue-chip securities to him. Ledl believed at least half of that amount was deposited in the Vatican Bank and a substantial amount was placed in the Bank of Italy and Banco Ambrosiano of Milan, Italy's largest private bank, which was headed by Roberto Calvi.

Rizzo, Ledl said, at first did not believe the Vatican could be involved in such a scheme and had been reluctant to put in an order for such a large amount of phony paper to be printed by the mob forgers. Ledl said he eventually showed Rizzo two typed requests, on Vatican letterhead, as proof of the Vatican contact.

Coffey and Tamarro left the interview stunned. All along they believed there was a Vatican connection, but neither man imagined it could be on such a high level.

"We walked around in a daze the rest of that day. We couldn't focus our attention on anything except what Ledl had said. We even unknowingly walked into a restaurant known as the most romantic in Vienna. When it dawned on us that all the people around us were young lovers, we looked at each other and cracked up. What we two very large cops must have looked like to the others in the restaurant we can only imagine. We hadn't even noticed the violinists playing behind us. But the incident broke the tension. Then we were ready to report back to New York.

"Our first order of business back in New York was to find out all we could about Marcinkus, who seemed to be the keystone of the whole operation," Coffey recalls. "What we discovered knocked our socks off."

96   Marcinkus was an American from Cicero, Illinois, affectionately known as "Il Gorilla" because of his burly, six-

four, 240-pound body. In 1972 he was one of the most powerful men in the Vatican, presiding over the Vatican Bank
and serving as the Pope's personal bodyguard and mayor of
Vatican City. He was a popular figure on Rome's golf
courses and a frequent guest at high society parties and
charity events.

Yet despite the public attention, an air of mystery surrounded the man because of his almost total control over
the finances of the bank. His secrecy regarding those dealings earned him the nickname "the Gnome of Rome," from
Zurich bankers.

With no formal education in finance or banking, it was
believed he owed his appointment to the bank position to his
friendship with Michele Sindona, the man known as "God's
Banker."

Sindona was an international financier who controlled
more than 140 companies around the globe. For many years
it was believed the Vatican bankers followed his lead very
closely, pouring millions of dollars in Vatican funds into his
ventures, not all of them eventually profitable. When the
Sindona empire finally collapsed, the Italian press reported
that the Vatican had lost more than $100 million.

Sindona, it appeared to some, used the Vatican Bank as
his personal slush fund to transfer funds secretly (and illegally) out of Italy and to launder illegally obtained cash and
counterfeit or stolen securities, sometimes at the behest of
the Sicilian and American Mafias.

In 1972 all of this was speculation, however—the instinctive beliefs and hunches of law enforcement agencies and
legitimate financial analysts and advisers. These groups
generally agreed that Marcinkus, at first, was duped by Sindona, but eventually had to know what was going on. Then,
instead of bringing the illegal dealings to a halt, he jumped
in with both feet, probably to avoid major scandal.

But if Joe Coffey was to have his way, major scandal was
about to come down on the Vatican anyway. He went to
Hogan and to the strike force and demanded that Marcinkus

be questioned with the aim of indicting him as a part of Rizzo's scheme to counterfeit and steal $950 million in American corporate securities.

Joe was on a personal crusade to nail Marcinkus. He was offended by the archbishop's alleged illegal activities not only because of his faith but because of the additional embarrassment of Marcinkus's having been an American. Skeptical as he was about the clergy, Coffey still loved the church. But the best thing to do with dirty laundry, he believed, was to air it. He had long talks with Hogan about pursuing the Marcinkus lead and found his boss in agreement.

Ron Goldstock, the assistant district attorney in charge of the case, also agreed, as did Vitrano and Tamarro. They also had the support of Bill Aronwald, who was coordinating the investigation for the Justice Department's strike force.

"We all saw it as our duty to follow any lead wherever it took us," says Coffey.

As in May, when he learned of Pat's miscarriage, Joe again returned home to some disturbing news after the Ledl trip. His son Steven had come in from playing one day over the Thanksgiving holiday and, as only a four-year-old would, decided to put his wet snowsuit in the oven to dry. When the suit caught fire, Steven pulled it out and, in panic, ran through the house dragging it behind him. Only quick action by his brother, Joseph III, who jumped on the suit and smothered the flames, saved the house from burning down.

The incident once again reminded Joe of the jeopardy cops often leave their families in for the sake of their jobs. "Here I was running around Europe trying to nail a Vatican official, who no one else seems interested in nailing, and my house almost burned down. I began to wonder if it was worth it."

He expressed his concern to Pat, who once again found the right combination of words and emotions to convince her husband he was doing right by his family. He had a calling as strong and demanding as that of any priest, to do what he did best: catch crooks.

Meanwhile the clerks at the grand jury chambers were being kept busy typing subpoenas based on information Tony Grant was giving. In an effort to save himself, each new suspect would invariably give up someone else, so the list of suspects continued to grow. Cops and FBI agents all over the country were serving subpoenas and making arrests based on the information.

Coffey had the pleasure of handing Rizzo his subpoena personally. During the first week of December 1972 he walked into Jimmy's Lounge and asked to see Rizzo. Coffey had been there before in his steamfitter's disguise but never had made direct contact with Rizzo.

"I had been following him and listening in on his conversations for almost a year. I knew when he went to the bathroom, when he made love, and when he ordered his henchmen to get tough with a late payer, but we never actually met until that day in Jimmy's Lounge," Coffey remembers.

"And I knew Rizzo to be an animal. I knew how brutal he was to his wife and kids. He once almost beat a young Puerto Rican kid to death with a bar stool. I knew he had no conscience and deserved no place in a lawful society. He was garbage."

On Rizzo's part, by that December day he knew he was being hounded by Hogan's man, Joe Coffey, and the feds. He was seeing his mob being rounded up, and he was getting reports from his own informants that his boys were singing like the cowards they were. But he had no idea that he had been under such intense surveillance for months. He had no idea that even the telephone in Jimmy's Lounge was being tapped. He could not imagine that as he had sat in the Palace Hotel in Munich and talked about collecting $350,000 owed from the stolen securities job and heard Enze talk about a caper in the Vatican, Joe Coffey had been down the hall recording every word for the benefit of a future grand jury.

Inside Jimmy's Lounge that day there was no doubt it was Joe Coffey who had come calling. Coffey fits the movie image of a cop. In his dark blue suit, a grin on his "map of Ireland" face and the subpoena clenched in his big fist, he asked the mob thug who stood in front of him, "Are you Vincent Rizzo?"

"That's me. You must be Coffey," Rizzo replied.

"I am Detective Joseph Coffey, and this is a subpoena ordering you to appear before a Manhattan grand jury."

Rizzo, who had been handed such paperwork on previous occasions, took the paper from Coffey.

"Yeah, yeah, big deal," he said. "Sit down for a minute. What do ya drink?"

"I wouldn't drink with you," Coffey growled as Rizzo pulled over an empty bar stool and snapped his fingers for the bartender to pour a shot of scotch.

"Come on, don't be such a tough guy. Things can be worked out," Rizzo countered, as he handed the shot to Coffey.

Joe took the glass, tipped it toward Rizzo as if offering a toast, and then turned it over and poured the scotch all over the bar. He turned and walked out the door.

Rizzo went berserk. He was not used to being treated that way. He had always been able to intimidate everyone. Even cops. As Coffey walked through the door Rizzo cursed after him. "You think you're hot shit now, but I'll get you! Count on it."

Before Coffey was back at Leonard Street, Rizzo had contacted a local drug dealer known to be an informant for the FBI. He told the dealer that Coffey had tried to shake him down for $50,000.

It wasn't until years later that Coffey learned that the FBI conducted a thorough investigation of the charge. Dick Tamarro was the agent assigned to look into every aspect of his friend's life to see if the allegation could be true. Nothing remotely incriminating was ever turned up, but Joe Coffey never forgave his colleagues for not letting him know he was under investigation.

"It doesn't matter that I was cleared. They were supposed to trust me over a low-life drug dealer. After a year of seeing what kind of cop I was, Dick Tamarro and the rest of them let me down. It hurts worse than if I'd been shot," Coffey says.

But in 1972 Coffey had no knowledge of that part of the investigation. He was occupied with trying to get permission to go after Marcinkus.

Rizzo and twenty-four members of his ring were quickly indicted in Manhattan for operating an international drug smuggling and counterfeiting ring. Right before Christmas he surrendered to Coffey at the Manhattan district attorney's office. With the city's press corps following, Coffey led Rizzo in handcuffs to the First Precinct and booked him on the charges. Later that day he was released on $25,000 bail.

Early in January, on the advice of their highly paid attorneys, Rizzo and his key henchmen pleaded guilty. Rizzo was sentenced on extortion, counterfeiting, and drug charges to a total of twenty-five years in prison. Because many of the charges were to be served concurrently, he could be back on the streets in less than ten years. Still being held over his head were the charges being presented to a federal grand jury by Aronwald and the strike force. It was during that case, Coffey hoped, that Barg, Ense, Ledl, and Marcinkus would also be brought to justice (the other Vatican official named by Ledl, Cardinal Tisserant, died in February 1972).

At first, in early 1973, Frank Hogan, trying to keep control of the case, appealed to Cardinal Terrance Cooke, head of the New York Archdiocese, to intercede with the Vatican and arrange for detectives to interview Marcinkus. Cooke did not take long to shoot the idea down. He told Hogan he saw no reason to believe any Vatican official was involved in a criminal act. He would not help.

As powerful as he was, Hogan was still a product of a political system. He could step on just so many toes before endangering his own position. Reluctantly, he realized he would have to count on Washington to investigate the Vatican connection.

The atmosphere in Washington at this time, however, was not conducive to chasing a big scandal. It was during the Watergate period, and Richard Nixon's administration was fighting for its life. Michele Sindona, Marcinkus's mentor, had been a supporter and adviser of Richard Nixon when Nixon was practicing law. It has been reported that Sindona offered a secret contribution of $1 million to Nixon's campaign fund, which was wisely refused but indicated the level of interest Sindona had in Nixon's success.

Aronwald's request to the attorney general's office for permission to travel to Rome to quiz Marcinkus was refused.

Hogan was furious. He considered the politics of his office a burden he had to bear in order to do the law enforcement work he savored. He was now ready to risk everything rather than see Marcinkus escape untouched by the investigation.

During his forty years in politics and law enforcement, Frank Hogan had developed an unequaled network of powerful connections from Capitol Hill to boardrooms of Wall Street. He began working his Rolodex as if he was a young lawyer running for office for the first time. He called in long-owed favors and put his personal reputation on the line with people who did not take such offers lightly.

And his efforts paid off. Washington finally agreed to send Aronwald, Tamarro, and Bill Lynch (head of the Organized Crime and Racketeering Section of the Department of Justice) to the Vatican. Joe Coffey was not allowed to go.

Hogan hit the roof: Coffey, he argued, was essential to the case. There would be no case without Joe Coffey. "You're only keeping him out because you don't want the tough questions asked!" Hogan screamed at anyone who would listen in Washington. But he was out of favors. This time, Mr. DA did not get his way. Joe Coffey, bursting with anger at the turn of fate, was left at home.

On April 23, 1973, Aronwald, Lynch, and Tamarro went to the Vatican City office of Archbishop Giovanni Benelli, the assistant secretary of state. Tamarro was forced to sit outside the office while Lynch and Aronwald spoke with Benelli and with Monsignor Martinez, an assessor in the secretary of state's office. Later Joe Coffey was allowed to read the report of the Vatican visit.

This is what he learned from that report.

Lynch presented the case to Benelli and Martinez. He outlined the evidence, mostly provided by Ledl, that $14.5 million in counterfeit bonds, forged by Rizzo's gang, had been delivered to Rome in July 1971.

Lynch told Benelli and Martinez that those bonds had been a sample to be shown to people in the Vatican, who eventually wanted $950 million in bonds. He said he was prepared to tell an American grand jury that Archbishop Marcinkus had been directly involved in the plot, as well as in other illegal dealings in association with Michele Sindona. In a veiled threat, Lynch indicated that no matter what transpired during his visit to Rome the information about the Vatican would make its way into indictments against Barg, Ense, and the others. Eventually it would become public record. Lynch showed Benelli the letter Ledl had provided to the doubting Rizzo as proof of the Vatican request for the $950 million. It was agreed the letter appeared to be genuine.

But Martinez refused to accept the letter or the word of the swindler Ledl as proof of Vatican involvement in an illegal deal. According to Lynch, Martinez refused to check a list of stolen and counterfeit securities against the Vatican's inventory on deposit in banks. He said such an investigation would be under the aegis of Archbishop Marcinkus.

The next day, with Tamarro once again forced to wait

outside, Lynch and Aronwald met with Marcinkus.

According to Lynch's report, Marcinkus listened patiently to the allegations against him and agreed to answer them.

He admitted a close relationship with Sindona, whom he considered a financial genius "well ahead of his time." But he said he had few financial dealings with him. He said he considered the charges against him serious but not based enough on fact that he would violate the Vatican Bank's confidentiality to defend himself. He implied that other Vatican officials jealous of his position of closeness to Pope Paul VI had conspired to implicate him.

He replied to all the specifics against him, falling back on the bank's need for secrecy when he could not satisfy Lynch and Aronwald. And then after about two hours he bid the two Americans good day.

Back in the states it was agreed on the highest levels that the case against Marcinkus could not be pursued further.

Coffey was crushed. To him Barg, Ense, Ledl, Grant, and even Rizzo were habitual, dime-a-dozen criminals whose place in the roster of organized crime would be quickly filled after their imprisonment or death. But Marcinkus was a different story. He was a man who held the trust of millions of Catholics. To let him get away with violating that trust was unthinkable to Coffey. Yet that is what happened.

Life in the DA's squad was becoming increasingly difficult for Joe Coffey. So, in May 1973, when the assignment came to join the 25th Precinct in East Harlem as a patrol sergeant, it was almost a relief.

Hogan was sorry to see his protégé go, but the department rule was a firm one. On his last day at Leonard Street, the DA called Joe into his office.

"I'm sorry the Vatican business ended the way it did," Hogan said, shrugging his shoulders in resignation, "and I'm sorry I won't be able to bring you back to my squad when your six months are up." Hogan had no opening for a detective sergeant. "But I do have a going away present for you," he said. He told Coffey he had arranged for him to join the Queens DA's squad as soon as possible.

So Coffey left for East Harlem feeling better than he had since reading Lynch's report. "In six months I'll be back with a crack unit chasing big cases," he thought.

Six weeks later he got a call from Vitrano saying the federal indictments were to be announced and he should be at the press conference.

On the morning of July 11, 1973, in the office of the U.S. attorney for the Southern District of New York, a press conference was held to detail the breaking up of a ring accused of trying to dump more than $18 million in stolen and counterfeit securities throughout the world. Sixteen men, including Vincent Rizzo, Winfried Ense, Alfred Barg, and Leopold Ledl were indicted.

Just prior to the press conference Bill Aronwald took Coffey aside. Relations had been strained between the two men since Aronwald's return from Rome. Coffey was convinced the prosecutor had engaged in a cover-up.

"I want you to stay away from the press. We do not want the Vatican mentioned," Aronwald warned.

"You're not my boss. I'll do what I want," Coffey replied.

Edwin M. Shaw, chief attorney of the federal Joint Organized Crime Strike Force, told the assembled press corps that the indicted persons had attempted to dispose of the fake securities in California, Panama, Italy, Belgium, and Switzerland. He said the forgeries were in the names of such companies as Pan American Airways, AT & T, and General Electric and that the ring dealt in securities stolen from Manufacturers Hanover Trust and Merrill Lynch, Pierce, Fenner & Smith.

Shaw also graciously explained how the investigation had started in Hogan's office, giving due credit to Coffey and to Assistant District Attorney Ron Goldstock.

And because mention was made of the Vatican in the indictments, mostly in reviews of conversations between the defendants, Shaw made sure to emphasize that the twenty-page indictment contained no criminal charges against anyone connected with the Vatican.

Following the official press conference Coffey fielded a question from a *Wall Street Journal* reporter who asked about the involvement of the Munich police. Coffey explained they had provided invaluable surveillance and logistical help.

The next day several newspaper accounts did focus on the meager mentions of the Vatican in the indictments. In the New York *Daily News*, reporter Ellen Fleysher wrote that "two of the defendants reportedly told other ring members that they could dispose of $14.5 million in fake blue-chip bonds through a source within the Vatican."

The Wall Street Journal quoted a source as saying that "a man of the cloth was suspected of being the fence within the Vatican."

"Aronwald thought I was the source of that quote and he was pissed off," Coffey says. "I wasn't. The reporter used my name with a quote about the Munich police involvement, and I stood by that.

"But Aronwald was fit to be tied. He threatened to ruin my career and make me sorry I ever spoke to the press. He said now he was going to have to subpoena the sixteen Munich cops I worked with.

"Of course it was nonsense. He didn't need those cops for his case. But he stayed mad at me. I told him to take a hike. He didn't run my life."

So that was the end of it. Vinnie Rizzo got more jail time, eventually serving about twelve years. When he got out he was never able to return to his powerful position in the Genovese family because of suspicions that he had turned informant.

Ledl, thanks to the deal he made with Coffey and Tamarro, was never indicted. Barg and Ense got slaps on the wrist. Tony Grant, because of the help he provided in nailing Rizzo, was allowed to return to England, where he vanished into the underworld.

But to best understand the final results of the investigation that began when Joe Coffey got the hunch to follow Vinnie Rizzo to Munich, one has to let about ten years pass.

Thanks probably to the toes he stepped on, especially Aronwald's, in pursuit of Marcinkus, it took Joe Coffey two years to get off patrol in Harlem and back to detective work. In 1979, when Pope John Paul II arrived in New York as part of a tour of the United States, Joe, a prominent detective in the department, was assigned as bodyguard.

Leading the Pope's team of bodyguards was Archbishop Marcinkus, whose power and clout in the Vatican had not diminished following the death of Pope Paul VI.

Directly after the pope's arrival in Manhattan, a group of New York dignitaries including Police Commissioner Robert McGuire was gathered to meet him. When McGuire stepped forward to kiss the Pope's ring, Marcinkus stepped in front of him. "No cops," he demanded and pushed McGuire aside.

Later McGuire asked Ellen Fleysher, the former reporter who was now the department's deputy commissioner for public information, who the rude cleric was. "Ask Joe Coffey," Fleysher said. "He can tell you all about him."

The incident rekindled the fire in Joe. He decided to collaborate on a book about the case with author Richard Hammer.

"It was clear as we worked on the book that many people were going to try to stop its publication," Coffey remembers. Church officials refused to cooperate. They sent the police department's Catholic chaplain to persuade McGuire to prohibit Coffey from taking part in the book. But McGuire remembered Marcinkus. He backed Coffey.

Even a former New York City mayor, Robert F. Wagner, who once served as the U.S. Ambassador to the Vatican, got into the act. Representing Marcinkus, he threatened to sue the publisher.

As Coffey and Hammer worked on the book in early 1982, the Italian police finally began to pull together their own investigation of the crimes of Michele Sindona and Roberto Calvi.

Their biggest break came in March 1980 with the conviction in the United States of Michele Sindona, "God's Banker," on sixty-five counts of fraud and perjury. It was found that he had siphoned $45 million in funds from the Franklin National Bank in New York. Bankers claimed at the time that the Vatican Bank had secretly lent Sindona $30 million to help save the Franklin. In jail Sindona bragged that Marcinkus "earned at least $200 million from me."

In March 1986 Michele Sindona was murdered in a jail cell in Italy by someone who put cyanide in his food.

In the summer of 1982 the Italian government accused the Vatican Bank and its president, Archbishop Paul C. Marcinkus, of looting $1.2 billion from Italy's largest private bank, Banco Ambrosiano of Milan.

In June 1982 Roberto Calvi, who was the head of Banco Ambrosiano a decade earlier when Leopold Ledl said he was collecting counterfeit securities for delivery to Marcinkus, was found hanging from the scaffolding of Blackfriar's Bridge over the Thames River in the heart of London's financial district.

The Vatican Bank has repaid about $250 million to the Central Bank of Italy but admits no wrongdoing. In 1987 Italian authorities issued a warrant for the arrest of Marcinkus. Had not the courts ruled that he enjoyed immunity as a Vatican employee, he would have been indicted and stood trial along with thirty-five others on charges of bankruptcy fraud.

In 1990 the archbishop voluntarily resigned from Vatican duty to take a parish post in his native Cicero, Illinois.

· IV ·

THE
FIGHT

Coffey's assignment to protect Pope John Paul II was not the first time he was entrusted with someone's life. As a detective in the DA's office he would often find himself babysitting a mob stoolie or, less often but more significantly, an honest civilian who had agreed to cooperate in an investigation. Then there are those special occasions that even an active, risk-taking policeman like Joe Coffey can never forget.

Once near the end of his career with the New York Police Department, he was placed on special assignment to help protect the first lady, Nancy Reagan. She was in New York to take part in a cultural event at Lincoln Center. Also present was Britain's Prince Charles.

The pressure of having two high security-threat personalities moving around the city at the same time overloaded the State Department, Secret Service, and NYPD intelligence units. Coffey and a few other crack detectives were temporarily placed under the command of Captain Frank Bolz, the prominent commander and founder of the Hostage Negotiations Team. Their assignment was to protect the perimeter of the dining and dancing area set up in a huge tent behind Lincoln Center.

"Everyone was wearing tuxedos and beautiful gowns. It was really a glamorous crowd, great dancers, smooth talkers—the jet set! All the cops were really impressed and were afraid of doing something wrong," Coffey remembers. "Even Frank Bolz, who has a real outgoing personality, was on his best behavior. He was serious as could be."

Then something happened that scared the breath out of Bolz, a man who had faced down countless desperate characters. Joe Coffey asked Nancy Reagan to dance.

"I don't know what came over me. Here comes perhaps the most famous woman in the world. She's wearing this fabulous glittering gown and she walks right up to me and asks if I'm a New York police officer."

Coffey thinks it took him about ten seconds to compose an answer. Then the best he could come up with was, "Yes I am."

"Well, my husband is a great admirer of police officers," Mrs. Reagan responded.

"I was completely tongue-tied, couldn't get a word out of my mouth. Then, all of a sudden, the band started playing—some kind of fox-trot—and I asked if she would like to dance."

The wife of the president of the United States said she would be honored to dance with Detective Sergeant Joe Coffey. In a flash the six-foot-four Coffey was walking towards the dance floor arm in arm with the diminutive first lady.

"Across the room I could see Bolz having a conniption. He was shaking his head—no, no—but I was in another world. It was great," says Coffey.

"She felt like a doll. I'm no Fred Astaire but she really knew how to dance and we glided across the floor for about a minute. She told me how the president always supported the work of police officers and how important he thought they were to our society. I don't remember what I said. I felt like an awkward schoolboy dancing with a movie star, which really wasn't far from the truth."

To the relief of Bolz, the dance did not last long. The Secret Service men let it go on for about two minutes. Then one walked up to Mrs. Reagan and whispered that they would appreciate it if she sat down. Coffey got a dirty look from the agent, but it could not put a damper on the glow of the moment.

"Bolz was waiting for me with a drink. He was trying to be mad, but all the New York cops thought it was a fantastic thing. It's still one of our favorite stories. It's one of the great things about being a cop in New York. How else would a guy like me get to dance with the first lady?

"A cop sees the best of the best, the worst of the best, the worst of the worst, and the best of the worst. We see everything. We don't make much money, but being a cop is a wonderful job."

When he retired from the New York Police Department in 1985, with the arrests of more than 200 major crime figures throughout the United States, Europe, and South America to his credit, Coffey made a farewell speech to his friends. He concluded the speech by saying: "I want to thank the New York Police Department for giving me a ringside seat to the greatest show on earth."

In March 1971 Coffey literally was ordered to take a ringside seat—in Madison Square Garden for the first heavyweight championship fight between Joe Frazier and Muhammad Ali. Frazier's life depended on it.

Four days before the fight Joe got a call from Frazier's manager, the brilliant, colorful fight game character, Yank Durham. Coffey and Durham had known each other for a few years. They first met when District Attorney Hogan's office was conducting an investigation of a fixed championship fight between a tough pug from Jersey City named

Frankie De Paula and the world-class light heavyweight, Bob Foster.

It was eventually determined that De Paula, who had no chance of winning against the likes of Foster, had taken a dive at 2:17 of the first round. Coffey's investigation resulted in an indictment against James "Jimmy Nap" Napoli, a capo in the Genovese crime family.

Coffey also arrested De Paula, who was eventually murdered in the hallway of his Jersey City apartment house because the mob thought he was singing to the cops.

"I really felt sorry for De Paula. He had more muscles than brains, but he was a pretty nice kid. The mob used him and then murdered him when they thought he was standing up for himself. In reality, he had refused to help us at all. He was more of a stand-up guy than most of the capo di tutti asshole types we brought in for questioning in that case," Coffey believes.

Coffey was also able to determine that Foster knew nothing about the fix. During the course of his investigation he and some important figures in the fight business, even some who walked on the other side of the law, developed a mutual respect.

Durham was one of the legitimate fight people, so when he called for help, Coffey was inclined to believe him and offer what help he could.

Durham explained that the Frazier team, training in Pennsylvania, had been receiving threatening telephone calls and letters from a splinter group of the Southern Christian Leadership Conference, the organization once headed by Rev. Martin Luther King, Jr. The callers accused heavyweight champion Frazier of being an "Uncle Tom" and of taking part in a fight that was being financed by white money. They said the fight would benefit only the white community and warned that Frazier would be killed before he stepped in the ring.

At first Durham did not take the threats seriously. Such letters and calls to prominent athletes were common. In

112

1971 two militant black groups, the Black Panthers and the Black Liberation Army, were active and used every opportunity to spread their doctrine. Then Durham's car disappeared from a lot at the Franklin Motor Inn in Philadelphia, where the Frazier camp was headquartered. Two days later a car belonging to Cloverlay, the corporation which backed Frazier, was vandalized. Finally, Durham got a call from a contact in Ali's camp—Yank actually had represented both fighters in negotiating their $2.5 million purses—who said Ali had received some threats that also included Frazier.

Durham decided it was better to be safe than sorry. After getting little help from the Philadelphia Police Department, he called Joe Coffey.

Coffey remembers getting Durham's phone call as he made a brief stop at the district attorney's Detective Squad office on Leonard Street. Coffey wasn't spending much time at the office. More often, he was hunched over in the basement of a West Side building monitoring taps on the telephones of Ruby Stein and Jiggs Forlano, the two biggest loan sharks in the country.

He explained to Durham that he might not be able to take on the Frazier problem personally but would pass on Durham's concerns to his boss, Inspector Paul Vitrano, and recommend a unit be assigned to protect "Smokin' Joe" when he arrived in New York.

Vitrano was willing to go along with the idea; but District Attorney Hogan's support was needed because normally the police department's Intelligence Division, in 1971 known as the Bureau of Special Services Intelligence (BOSSI), would be assigned to such a task. They would be jealous of the opportunity to run such a high-profile mission. But it was Coffey who had gotten the call from Durham, not an Intelligence Division detective.

Durham spoke to Hogan. He told him he had gotten little help from the Philadelphia police when he first brought the threats to their attention. He also said he did not trust the Madison Square Garden private security police to handle the entire operation. He said he wanted a real cop. He said he wanted Joe Coffey on the case.

It didn't matter to Yank Durham, but Coffey was still just a detective third grade, not the necessary rank to oversee this kind of task. Once again, Coffey found Hogan in his corner as the DA okayed the bodyguard plan and Vitrano freed twelve detectives to work with him. But Coffey was told he would still be responsible for the Stein-Forlano case. Frank Hogan had been after Ruby Stein for a long time and would not be happy if he slipped through this current trap. Coffey assured Vitrano he could juggle both balls for the few days Frazier would be in town. Vitrano told him he'd better.

The assignment excited Coffey, thirty-three years old at the time. He was an athlete himself, a standout football player in college and for an army team during a two-year stint in Germany. He was also a fanatic New York Yankee fan. Now he would have the chance to meet, up close and personally, "Smokin' Joe" Frazier and probably even the enigmatic Muhammad Ali, whose camp would have to be included in the heightened security arrangements.

Using the phone in Vitrano's office, Coffey called over to the wiretap location and began shuffling schedules. He wanted to put together his best team. Coffey made sure his regular partner, Larry Mullins, was included in the group. Next he called Pat in Levittown and asked her to pack a bag for him, explaining he would be handling security for Frazier but leaving out the information about the threats. Coffey told his wife it was a routine assignment that he was lucky to get. It was already Friday afternoon, Frazier was to drive into New York the next day, and the fight was scheduled for Tuesday. Four frantic days lay ahead.

By Friday evening, while seven-year-old Joseph Coffey spread the word among his disbelieving second-grade classmates at the Northside School in Levittown that his father was protecting Joe Frazier, the men who would do the job were gathered on Leonard Street.

Joe explained how the case had come under their jurisdiction and detailed Durham's fears. Coffey had had his own experience with black militants and agreed with the others that the controversial Ali seemed a more likely target of some splinter group than the withdrawn family man, Frazier.

Joe believed that it was under the threat of death by Muslims that Sonny Liston dumped his second fight with Ali; but he knew that Durham and the Muslims maintained good relations, and finally it was agreed to discount them as the foe. Coffey bought into Durham's theory about the SCLC. Officially, the group had protested the promotional arrangements of the fight, which excluded black firms from sharing in the major money. They had picketed Cloverlay's office in Philadelphia and had had a public confrontation with Durham.

Durham's own sources in the SCLC and the Philadelphia Police indicated there were members, fueled by the militant rhetoric of the times, who were fed up with peaceful picketing and were pressing for more immediate action.

Finally, Coffey had a source of his own in the Philadelphia Police who confided that one of the threatening phone calls had been "trapped," that is, traced back to the SCLC headquarters in Atlanta. Because they could not be sure who had actually made the call, and because of strained relations between the Philly cops and the city's black community, that information was kept under tight wraps. For Coffey there was no doubt that the death threats had to be treated seriously.

It was agreed that there was little time to solve this problem through investigation and arrest. The emphasis would have to be on physical protection of the fighters. Ali had his own highly competent contingent of Muslim bodyguards from Chicago, so the Hogan men would concentrate on Frazier. Joe Aquafreda, the head of Madison Square Garden Security, was brought into the team and a plan was worked out.

Early the next morning, as Frazier and his entourage began their drive from Philadelphia, the Coffey plan went into effect.

It was widely known through the media that Frazier planned to stay at the City Squire Hotel on the West Side, just uptown from Madison Square Garden. The area around the hotel was abuzz with fight activity. For days fans had been hanging around in front of the hotel, and much of the media also registered there to be near any fight-related developments. Coffey reasoned that an assassin would have little difficulty hiding among the crowd. He had no intention of letting Frazier near that hotel.

Instead, arrangements had been made for the fighter and his immediate inner circle—Durham, Frazier's private security man Tom Paine, his chauffeur Les Perlman—and Coffey's team to check into the Hotel Pierre. "The Pierre, with its old world charm and old money clientele, was about the last hotel where you'd expect to find a black heavyweight contender from Philadelphia," Coffey reasoned. "I thought it would be a perfect place to hide, and it turned out to be the single element that made the whole plan work."

By eleven o'clock Saturday morning, Coffey, Mullins, and Detective Mario Trapani were waiting in an unmarked car on the New Jersey side of the Lincoln Tunnel. They did not expect the two cars carrying the Frazier people to arrive for at least another hour, and they used the extra time to check out the tunnel entrance. Frazier would have to stop to pay the toll, and that would give a sniper time to line up a shot.

The one-hour wait became almost four hours because a mix-up in messages had made Durham think Coffey wanted him at the tunnel at 3:00 P.M. It was an anxious wait, and the three cops began thinking something might have happened along the turnpike from Philadelphia. Finally, the three DA squad cops spotted Frazier's gold Cadillac limousine turning down the long curving approach to the toll booths, and Coffey got out to motion them over. The second Frazier car, carrying sparring partners, pulled up behind the Cadillac.

Coffey, taking immediate charge, ordered Frazier into the back seat, where Durham, a look of doom clouding his broad face, a cigar chomped tightly in his jaw, sat next to a reporter named David Wolf, who was close to Frazier and had been let in on the plan. Coffey slid in next to Tom Paine and told Les Perlman to follow Mullins through the tunnel.

As soon as they hit the New York side, Coffey told Perlman to head to the Pierre, while the second entourage car, as previously planned, continued to the City Squire. Now, two more cars filled with Coffey's men, shotguns cradled in their laps, picked up the route. As Mullins turned away, in order to circle around and check the back end of the route, another car of detectives would protect the front.

The security team kept in contact by walkie-talkie. They were using a radio frequency reserved for special intelligence operations. Joe thought it was unlikely an assassination squad would be able to monitor the frequency. It was unknown even to the city's aggressive press photographers who regularly monitored police activity.

As they pulled up to the Pierre's Fifth Avenue entrance, detectives were already waiting with room keys, and the staff quickly took the small amount of baggage from the Cadillac's trunk. It was a procession rarely seen in the staid hotel. The hotel doormen in their French gendarme costumes stood staring at the gold Cadillac with the leopard-skin roof.

Frazier wore a fur coat, a big floppy hat, and gray tweed knickers, which were a style of the day but probably never before seen in the deep-carpeted, gold-trimmed lobby of the Pierre, where a black guest was a rare enough sight in 1971. The fighter carried his ever-present guitar case, as did Perlman and the four white men in dark business suits who surrounded the Frazier party. The only difference was that Frazier and Perlman actually had guitars in their cases, whereas the white detectives were carrying shotguns in theirs.

The atmosphere of subdued elegance in the Pierre's lobby began to change as word spread that Frazier had arrived at the hotel. Coffey did not want a scene. Up to now he was satisfied that the Pierre ploy was working, and he did not want to risk word leaking to the street that the fighter was there. So he ushered his group rudely through the lobby and into an elevator, while the Pierre management took care of registration at the front desk.

The hotel's management was totally cooperative, although Coffey sensed they wished he had picked another hotel. Within five minutes Frazier was in a suite on the twelfth floor, which had been virtually given over to the fight entourage.

Before Frazier could sit down, Mullins and Trapani went over the two-bedroom suite. They checked for bugs under pillows, behind the toilets, in the curtains, and of course on the telephone itself. They made sure that the window shades and curtains were drawn and that all the locks in the room worked. Only then did they proclaim the room "clean."

Coffey was about to have his first real conversation with Frazier since picking him up at the Lincoln Tunnel, when Durham walked in complaining about the "goddamn whorehouse these jerk-off New York cops picked to stick us in." Durham and the other men who lived and worked with Frazier were rough-and-tumble characters who had risen from meager backgrounds to earn fame and fortune in the bloodspilling world of prize fighting. They did not usually choose hotels that filled their rooms with magnificent displays of freshly cut flowers.

Durham thought the atmosphere would soften his fighter's hard edge. For his part Frazier said that the lilac scent was hurting his nose. "This place smells like a fucking whorehouse. Get these flowers and shit out of here," Durham barked at Coffey. Quickly the hotel bellboy and the shotgun-toting detectives were carrying vases of flowers into the hallway for disposal.

There was no doubt Durham would get what he wanted. The fight promoters were picking up the entire tab for the Pierre and other expenses related to the security. No expense was spared to keep Frazier comfortable. Over the next four days Coffey would see an almost nonstop supply of room service steaks and drinks flow into the room.

To Coffey, Mullins, and the other detectives, whose salaries at the time were less than $15,000 a year, the experience provided an intimate look into the lifestyle of the wealthy. Coffey, who at the time worked weekends for $50 a day as a waiter and bartender for a Long Island caterer, related more to the room service waiters bringing the food in than to the fight crowd eating it. The cops bemoaned the fact that Durham had gone through official channels to ask Coffey for security help. If one of the cops had been approached unofficially, they could have "moonlighted" the security detail. That is, they could have done it while off duty, charging as much as $500 a day each for their highly skilled services. "Make sure Durham has your home phone number the next time he needs help," the cops kidded Joe.

By early Saturday evening everyone had settled in, and Frazier had changed from his furs and knickers into a rubberized sweat suit. He asked Coffey where he could go to run a few laps, just to work out some of the tension. Coffey pointed to the suite's living room. "I do not want you leaving this room until the weigh-in tomorrow," Coffey told the heavyweight. A tense silence fell over the room. This was the first security demand that might affect not only the boxer's physical well-being but also, more important at this time in the training schedule, his mental attitude.

"I knew the order to stay in the room did not sit well with Frazier, and I saw Durham bite harder into his cigar, but neither man complained. Frazier went into the living room and started running in place," Coffey remembers. "I had feared this moment and now it passed without incident. I was beginning to gain a great deal of respect for Joe Frazier."

That evening, Coffey and Frazier sat together watching television, and a lifelong friendship was born. Muhammad Ali was being interviewed on every sports report and his "spiel" included denouncing Frazier as an "Uncle Tom" and "white man's slave." He promised to destroy Frazier in the ring. While in later years it would be realized that Ali was a showman, saying what he thought he needed to say to build interest in his fights, in March 1971 much of white America looked on him as a violent revolutionary and the Muslims as a group determined to subvert society.

Coffey had been on investigations into black revolutionary groups and had testified in court against the Black Panthers. He had also learned a lot about the Black Muslim movement in America. He knew Ali's Muslim beliefs were antiviolence and were rooted in deep moral convictions. He knew Muslims did a lot of work in their own communities to combat drug use and prostitution. But he was still amazed about how senselessly virulent Ali could appear in public, and he carefully watched Frazier's reactions.

"If I had had any money to bet, I would have bet it all on Frazier. He was the underdog even though he was champion, but as we watched television or read newspaper stories about the fight, I saw his determination to win build. I thought to myself, 'This man is not going to allow himself to lose.'"

Into the night, the detective and the heavyweight contender talked about their families and religion, with Frazier constantly getting out of his chair to stretch or run in place. Several times during the evening, he spoke on the telephone to his wife and five children back in Philadelphia.

Sunday morning the security team woke to the throbbing of loud rock music as Frazier did his "road work" in the suite's living room, and various sparring partners and hangers-on began showing up for breakfast. Joe was staying in an adjoining suite, and his first duty for the morning was to relieve the cops who had patrolled the corridor and outside the hotel all night. Next he called over to the Stein-Forlano wiretap room where several detectives were doing double duty in order to spring enough help for the Frazier detail. Everything was going well; the wiretap team informed Joe that Stein was betting heavily on Ali. "If Ruby could see the determination I've been seeing in Frazier, he'd lay off some of that action," Coffey told his wiretap man.

When he got to the suite, Coffey found an agitated Yank Durham. "Joe, *The New York Times* is on to our problem," Durham shouted.

A *Times* sports columnist had picked up on the fact that Frazier was not at the City Squire Hotel. He connected it to some rumors about the Muslims threatening Frazier and to the old story about Sonny Liston's dive. He was now pursuing a story that Frazier was in hiding because his life was in danger.

Durham's main concern about the story was that it would disrupt Frazier's concentration. Coffey, by now, felt very close to the boxer and did not share Durham's concern. But to ease the manager's anxiety, he took Frazier aside and explained that deep down his detective unit did not think an attack was a real possibility. Instead a decision had been made to provide a high level of security and they were going to stick with it. "I told him to concentrate on his job and that I would concentrate on mine, and that would insure a positive outcome for both of us," Coffey remembers. "Of course if I screwed up my job, 'Smokin' Joe' would never get a chance to do his."

After his talk with Frazier, Coffey and Mullins and Durham went to Madison Square Garden to meet with Aquafreda, Coffey's NYPD supervisors, and the uniform brass who would be controlling the overall security operation the night of the fight. It was decided that 280 New York City cops would be assigned to the Garden to augment the sports facility's own 240-person private security force. Aquafreda also agreed to employ for the night 150 off-duty NYPD detectives who would be placed undercover throughout the enormous arena. Coffey's team of twelve detectives would be joined by seven of Aquafreda's best men, once they entered the Garden. *The New York Times* and the rest of the media would be told that all the extra police presence was due to the discovery of a rash of counterfeit $150 tickets.

Following the meeting, evidence turned up for the first time that an assassin might indeed be stalking Joe Frazier. As they drove away from the Garden's 33rd Street entrance, Mullins noticed a green 1970 Plymouth pull out behind them. As he turned north on Eighth Avenue, the Plymouth also turned and seemed to get in the lane directly behind them. Mullins alerted Coffey to his suspicion. For a few blocks Coffey watched the Plymouth follow them up Eighth Avenue. As they approached 42nd Street, Coffey ordered Mullins to turn left and head west, away from the direction of the Pierre. The Plymouth stayed with them. The Plymouth was close enough for Coffey to spot two white men in the front seat. "Head for the tunnel and lose these guys," Coffey ordered Mullins.

Coffey and Mullins had both been taught the art of tailing and shaking a tail by two legendary NYPD wheelmen, Tony Procino and John O'Donnell. Mullins was as good at that particular game as Joe Frazier was at his. He knew he needed to accomplish two things. First, he had to make the men tailing him believe he did not know he was being followed and was headed in a direction that would lead the assassin to the target. Second, as their confidence grew that they had accomplished a successful tail, Mullins had to give them the slip. When he made his move he had to leave them in the dust with no ability to regain their tail.

Mullins headed for the Lincoln Tunnel at seventy miles per hour. The tail remained two cars behind the detectives' undercover car as Mullins approached the tunnel entrance. Then just as he was about to go underground, Mullins swung his car around, knocking over dozens of orange rubber traffic cones. Mullins completed a U-turn and with tires squealing was once again headed east away from the tunnel. The tail, caught totally by surprise, was forced to continue on to

New Jersey. The key to a clean escape would depend on whether or not the tail had a second or even third car sweeping the front and rear of Coffey's car. So Mullins still did not head directly back to the Pierre. First, he turned south back toward the Garden, then west again, and finally, after Coffey was certain there were no sweep cars still on their tail, returned to the Pierre.

Throughout the incident, Durham sat in the back of the car biting through his ever-present cigar. He was becoming a nervous wreck. Coffey suggested to him that he should not let Frazier see him that way. Durham followed Coffey's advice and stopped for a drink before returning to the hotel.

Coffey entered the suite with a heightened concern for Frazier. By this time he had come to like the fighter very much. The entire security team had fallen for the man's quiet charm and were feeling even more protective because they all felt like they were helping a friend.

Having a black friend was a new experience for most of these cops. Like Coffey they had all come from white, middle-class backgrounds, from white urban neighborhoods where blacks were looked upon as threats to law-abiding, clean-living citizens. Though they may not have had any more money or education than the blacks in the ghetto neighborhoods, they were brought up feeling superior to and suspicious of blacks.

When they joined the Police Department in the 1950s and 1960s, they found relatively few blacks on the force. Few blacks were assigned to the prestige units like the DA's squad, and they were rarely teamed with white partners. The general attitude among the police force was that blacks were the enemy of a lawful society. Most cops were rooting for Joe Frazier because they were frightened by Ali when he hooted that Frazier was an "Uncle Tom." Ali and his rigid Muslims, cops believed, were a threat to white America.

Joe Coffey was a product of that system, and his work against the violent Black Panthers had served to reinforce many of those ingrained feelings. He once was described as a "fascist" by a reporter because after a raid on a Black Panthers headquarters, Coffey ordered poster of Che Guevara taken off the walls. But he remembers beginning to doubt, for the first time, his willingness to follow the company line.

"We were so impressed with Frazier as a man that we forgot what color he was. His professionalism and his regard for his family gave us a look at a black man that we normally did not have the opportunity to see. Protecting Joe Frazier made a better man out of me, and I know it had the same effect on several other members of the security force," Coffey says.

Coffey low-keyed the car incident. He thought the two white men who followed them were probably reporters but decided to use his beat-up 1963 Oldsmobile for any further trips away from the Pierre.

There was a lot of eating and drinking in the Frazier suite that day. Detectives from the Stein-Forlano wiretap stopped over, and higher-ranking officers from headquarters came in to meet Frazier and have a drink. "In the DA's squad we loved assignments when the food and booze flowed. Durham was picking up the tab and money was no object. The joke about our squad back then was that we only drank *on* duty," Coffey says.

Saturday night a story in the *Times* pretty much nailed the death threat angle. While it did not mention where Frazier was holed up, it indicated he was being kept under heavy guard. Joe knew the *Times* reporter and decided to call him to find out how much was really known.

Coffey had maintained a sophisticated relationship with the press in New York. He knew that by calling the reporter he would confirm the story, but he also understood he would be giving the reporter enough to do his follow-up story without causing any kind of pressure that might hinder the security setup.

Sunday morning, Vitrano was on the phone with Coffey

1
2
4

before Frazier was even awake. There had been more threats. A local radio station received an anonymous call threatening that Frazier would be dead an hour before fight time. The Garden was getting bomb threats. Vitrano sent more detectives up to Coffey's suite.

A little after ten that morning, two limousines arrived at the Pierre to take the Frazier group downtown to Madison Square Garden for the weigh-in. Surrounded by detectives prepared to put themselves between him and an assassin, Frazier left the hotel for the first time in two days. The limos drove right into the arena, stopping about 100 feet from the weigh-in scales.

Now the champ and his opponent were surrounded by people: New York State Boxing Commission officials, the entourages from both fight camps, and of course the press. Coffey's men stood in a circle around their fighter except for the moments he was on the scale and getting his blood pressure and other cursory physical checks.

When they returned to the hotel, Frazier slept while the cops played cards and drank much of the scotch that seemed in endless supply.

Monday, fight day, tension grew among Coffey and his men. The assassins were running out of time to strike. The detectives spent the day pacing the room and drinking coffee. Frazier remained the calmest in the group. At 7:30 P.M., with three hours to go before round one, the Frazier group left the hotel and drove directly into Madison Square Garden. By this time the arena was crawling with uniformed cops and detectives, including more from Hogan's office and off-duty detectives from dozens of different NYPD units.

Detective Toby Fennell, Frank Hogan's personal bodyguard, was assigned to conduct a security sweep of Frazier's dressing room. Inch by inch he went over the room, which contained only two lockers and the training table. He was bothered by the fact that the two water bottles Frazier would use in the ring were already filled, three hours before the fight. Fennell dumped the contents into the sink, washed the bottles and personally refilled them. He kept them in his own hands until moments before the opening bell.

After Fennell pronounced the room safe, Coffey ordered all the cops to stand by the door while Frazier changed into his working clothes. "I could not believe it. We were as nervous as could be, but after he put on his boxing trunks and shoes, Frazier actually took a nap. He was the coolest man I ever met."

Later a fight commission doctor came into the dressing room to give Frazier a short prefight physical. The doctor turned out to be a bigger threat to the fight than the assassins in the shadows. Frazier had always suffered from high blood pressure, but that evening it was going through the roof.

"We were in the dressing room and the doctor was telling Durham that his man's blood pressure was way too high to allow him to fight. Frazier was sitting on the training table staring straight ahead, as intense as he had been the past four days. Durham bit on his cigar, then motioned the doctor into the shower area," Coffey remembers. "In less than a minute they came out with big smiles on their faces and the doctor told Frazier he would approve the medical forms. Behind closed doors Durham convinced him to do the right thing."

At 9:30 P.M. Durham told the fighter to finish dressing. In minutes Coffey and the others would have to lead him through the screaming crowd, down to the ring. Coffey remembers discussing the murder of Lee Harvey Oswald with the security team. "I wanted to remind them of how easily a gunman could slip through a crowd. If anything went wrong, even if something was thrown at us, I was prepared to cancel the fight—to tell the Garden to have them fight in the dressing room and I, Detective Third Grade Joe Coffey, would tell the world who won."

Then it was time. Coffey, Mullins, Trapani, Fennell, and Detective Eddie Wright, a veteran investigator of sports fixing and gambling, surrounded Frazier and Durham. Sparring partners, trainers, and Aquafreda and his Garden security formed an outer perimeter and in a wedge formation pressed through the packed arena and into the ring. High above them cops patrolled for snipers and all around detectives stared into the crowd, alert to any threatening gesture.

"When we got to the ring, I wished him luck and Frazier simply whispered, 'Thanks, man.' I thought that if he lost I would cry. Now I could only hope that if there was a sniper, he would miss," Coffey reflects.

For the next hour, the only threat Joe Frazier had to worry about was Muhammad Ali, and he handled that like the true champion he was. In one of the greatest heavyweight fights of all time, Frazier and Ali traded blow after blow, both proving they were worthy of a championship belt. Eventually, Frazier wore Ali down. In the eleventh round he decked him, breaking his jaw. And by the end of the fight Coffey and the others were sure their man had won.

The judges agreed. As soon as the decision was announced, the security team led Frazier away from the ring. The actor Burt Lancaster, working as a fight commentator that night, pushed his microphone in Frazier's face only to be knocked aside by a detective.

Frazier at this time was barely able to walk. He had taken a tremendous beating from Ali and he had fought the fifteen rounds with blood pressure at the bursting point. Coffey noticed a glaze in his eyes and, despite the roaring crowd, heard him say he didn't think he could make it back to the dressing room.

Without hesitation Coffey wrapped his arms around the sweat-soaked fighter and supported him as they pushed their way back to the dressing room. Halfway up the aisle, from the middle of the crowd, New York Mayor John Lindsay was pushing his way towards the champ to get his picture taken with the biggest name in sports. But in the crush Lindsay slipped and fell to the ground. That's when Eddie Wright's wallet, containing his badge and police identification card, was stolen. As Wright bent over to help the mayor, he felt a hand on his hip. But there was nothing he could do about it. By the time he got up, the pickpocket was gone. Eventually Wright was fined thirty days' pay for losing his badge.

Finally in the dressing room, Coffey deposited the exhausted fighter on the dressing table. Durham and his corner team worked over him, getting him out of the trunks, sponging him down, and putting on a sweat suit.

Coffey, the roar of the crowd still ringing in his ears, was flushed and breathing hard. "Frazier was in agony. I've been around presidents and actors and ballplayers, but I never saw anyone as tough or professional as Joe Frazier—he was remarkable that evening."

Technically the job was completed. Joe Frazier had made it through the fight alive, the only damage being done by Ali. But by this time the security force had grown so fond of Frazier that they all agreed to stay on until he was safely tucked away in bed.

Coffey had to practically carry the fighter back to the Pierre, and he personally laid him down on his bed in the suite. Frazier's family was gathered around him now, and the detectives began to slip quietly out of the bedroom.

As Coffey was about to close the door behind him, Frazier lifted his head from his pillow and called the big Irish cop to his side. "Joe, don't let your guys go yet. I've got some gifts for them," he said, his voice barely audible.

Coffey tried to tell him those things could wait until he felt better, but the heavyweight champion of the world insisted. Joe stayed as Durham brought over a box of souvenirs and Frazier, in agony, autographed pictures, scorecards, caps, and T-shirts for the DA's men. For Coffey he autographed a special plate, which was made to commemorate the fight, and a fight brochure. He wrote: "To Pat Coffey, you have a good man . . . don't forget it."

When he finished he practically passed out.

The next day, the plate and the brochure turned up at the Northside School, where little Joe Coffey was able to prove what his father had done.

The next time Frazier fought Ali at Madison Square Garden was January 28, 1974. Neither man was champion and there were no death threats. Joe Coffey and his partners handled the security as a moonlighting job for $500 a day.

As for Ruby Stein and Jiggs Forlano, the wiretap indicated they had lost heavy money on Ali. Eventually both were convicted of loan-sharking.

·V·

TERROR

Although no terrorist attack was ever carried out against Joe Frazier, it was clear that elements existed in the United States at that time that would find some motive for murder. Later in his career Joe Coffey came face to face with such factions.

Joe reported to uniform patrol in East Harlem's 25th Precinct in March 1973. He was quickly placed in the mix with the other precinct sergeants and charged with supervising the precinct's patrol officers, both on foot and in the worn-out green and white RMPs—radio motor patrol units.

Uniform patrol was the front line of police work. When the public thought of a police officer, the picture that most often came to their mind was of a tall Irish-looking young man in a deep blue, heavy woolen uniform with an uncomfortable-looking high collar. On the man's chest would be a gleaming silver badge in the shape of a shield. Joe Coffey fit that picture to a T, except that his badge was gold because of his rank and he had three light blue stripes on his arm.

It wasn't his first assignment in uniform. Directly out of the Police Academy, Joe was selected for duty in the elite Tactical Patrol Force (TPF). That was a unit of cops six feet tall or taller who were used as a reserve force for duty in especially troubled areas. During the campus disruptions of the sixties the TPF developed a reputation among students as storm troopers whose only mission was to bust the skulls of young people exercising their constitutional rights. It was while serving in the TPF that Coffey first met the future chief of detectives who would have a profound effect on his career, James Sullivan.

But uniform work was not the kind of police work he wanted to do. He looked at it as a necessary evil, a short detour from his upward path in the detective division. Each day as he buttoned the heavy winter blouse, before beginning his tour through one of the toughest neighborhoods in the city, he reminded himself of Frank Hogan's promise. He expected to spend only the minimum amount of time—six months—in the two-five before being transferred back to the Detective Division as a detective sergeant in the office of Queens District Attorney Thomas Mackell. The threats of William Aronwald, the federal prosecutor whom Joe had accused of foot-dragging in the Vatican case, to block his path to promotion did not enter his mind.

Shortly after he arrived in East Harlem similar threats came from another direction. One afternoon the radio in Coffey's patrol car barked an order for him to return to the station house. When he got there he found a lieutenant and a sergeant from the Internal Affairs Division—the unit that investigates corrupt cops—waiting to speak to him.

Sitting in the precinct commander's office, the two men from "downtown" offered Coffey the opportunity to join their elite unit. They explained that very few cops are given the chance to perform such important work. They said service in IAD was a quick route to promotion. If he accepted the offer he would be back in plainclothes fast. A a detective of his proven ability and honesty could make an outstanding reputation for himself.

Joe knew what kind of work Internal Affairs did. He knew it was essential to the running of a clean department. But it was not what he wanted to do.

"Look, Lieutenant," Coffey replied after the two men finished their recruiting pitch, "I already have a good reputation in the department. And I have a lot of friends. I couldn't do the job. I have to look at myself in the mirror when I shave every morning. Besides, I'm going back to the Detective Division shortly anyway."

The two IAD men were not accustomed to uniform cops working in dangerous precincts refusing their offer of a headquarters job with a high-profile career path.

"If you don't accept our offer you'll spend at least two years in that blue suit you're wearing," the lieutenant said.

"Thanks, but no thanks," Coffey responded, bringing the interview to a halt. He stood and carefully placed his cap with the gold braid on his head as he left the two gumshoes sitting in the precinct commander's office.

Coffey was proud of turning down the opportunity to get back to detective work by spying on his fellow cops. But when six months came and passed without a change in assignment, he began to wonder if he wasn't making too many enemies. Undoubtably the IAD guys had the clout to hold him back. There was also Aronwald, and when Queens DA Tom Mackell, who had indicated he would welcome Coffey, was indicted for corruption, the chance for transfer began to grow slimmer. A short time later Frank Hogan died of cancer, and Coffey saw his return to the Detective Division passing away.

While he waited, he had no choice but to keep pestering influential friends in the department and doing his duty as a patrol supervisor. That duty almost got him killed one cold night in January 1974.

132

It was a subfreezing morning. Joe was working the midnight to 8:00 A.M. shift. He and police officer Ralph Fico, who was driving, had been enjoying their brand-new patrol car. It was a 1974 Plymouth painted in the department's new colors, blue and white. Not only was it a pleasure to get genuine acceleration when the gas pedal was stepped on, but the car did not yet have the musty odor caused by constant use, shuttling of prisoners, and occasional duty as an ambulance when a victim did not have the time to wait for the paramedics. Best of all, the heater worked.

At a little after 3:00 A.M. Coffey ordered Fico to begin "coop" patrol. One of the duties of a patrol supervisor is to check out the nooks and crannies of the precinct where tired cops might go to catch a nap when they were supposed to be cruising their sectors.

It was a perfect night for "cooping." As usual the cold weather put a damper on street crime. The radio on the dash board, which normally squawked out commands constantly to the busy two-five, was quiet. The streets were cold and empty. It was difficult for cops on the overnight shift to stay awake on nights like that. But Coffey knew it was his job to make sure they did.

Fico headed for a coop on a small street adjacent to the Harlem River Drive. As they approached the spot, hidden from other streets by the approach to the drive and kept in constant darkness by the surrounding industrial buildings, Coffey noticed a car straddling the middle line of the two way street. It was not a police car.

He reached out to touch Fico's arm to signal him to slow down, but the driver too had already spotted the car and was lightly tapping the patrol car's brake.

"Stay behind him; don't go alongside," Coffey ordered. As they pulled to a stop the heads of four black men, two in the front and two in the back, were visible. The car was a late model Lincoln.

At this time the radical Black Panthers and their even

more violent offshoot, the Black Liberation Army, were carrying out a shooting war with police officers across the country. Cops in pairs had been ambushed and murdered in New York, and the BLA had even tried to attack the home of District Attorney Frank Hogan. The two cops who thwarted that attack were both critically wounded by machine gun fire. The assailants escaped.

With that on his mind Coffey was being very careful. He and Fico stayed about fifteen feet behind the Lincoln as Coffey radioed the license plate to headquarters. When Fico put the turret lights on, the Lincoln started slowly backing up. Coffey thought it might be pulling alongside. His hand went to the revolver on his hip.

Then in a sudden move the Lincoln backed into the patrol car. It hardly touched the front bumper before screeching forward again. It kept going, making a sharp right turn onto the entrance to the Harlem River Drive. Without waiting for orders, Fico pursued the Lincoln.

By the time they hit the drive, both cars were going 100 miles per hour. Coffey radioed headquarters to report the chase. He requested that units from the 32nd Precinct try to cut the Lincoln off at the next entrance to the drive, about three miles away. Other cars from the 25th, monitoring the radio calls, sped northward towards the drive. Coffey remembers thinking that his old RMP could not have kept up and being thankful for the new car.

With the Lincoln still well in front of them after about one minute of chasing, Coffey could see the flashing lights of the cars from the three-two spreading out across the roadway.

The driver of the Lincoln also saw them. He hit his brakes, and for a moment Joe thought his car was going to ram the suspects'. But before he came to a full stop, the driver of the Lincoln executed a fantastic U-turn onto the southbound roadway. When they spotted all the other police cars heading up the drive, the suspects decided to abandon their car. They skidded to a halt, almost adjacent to where Fico had braked, and jumped out of the Lincoln.

Coffey and Fico also jumped out of their car, and units were closing in from all sides. In desperation the four men from the Lincoln opened fire. Two had shotguns; the other two fired nine-millimeter automatic pistols.

Coffey, for the second and last time in his career as a police officer, fired three shots from his .38 caliber Smith & Wesson. Fico also returned fire.

As all the other police cars pulled up to the scene, the gunmen gave it up. They threw their weapons to the ground and surrendered to Coffey and Fico. No one had been wounded.

Later the gunmen confessed they were members of the Black Liberation Army and were waiting at the cooping spot to ambush a police car. Coffey and Fico both received medals for meritorious duty.

During the next year Joe settled into his patrol duties. The six months he expected to spend out of the Detective Division had come and passed. He did not give up hope, but realistically he knew it would be a tougher road than he had emotionally prepared for.

Then on January 26, 1975, one of the most outrageous acts of terror ever committed in the United States accomplished for him what Frank Hogan and Tom Mackell could not do.

At 1:25 P.M. that day a thunderous explosion ripped through a 100-year-old annex to the historic Fraunces Tavern in New York's Financial District. The tavern was the scene on December 4, 1783, of George Washington's farewell address to his officers.

Four people were killed and fifty others injured. One of the dead was decapitated.

The victims in the tavern restaurant and the second-floor dining room of the adjacent Anglers Club were thrown from their tables. For fifteen minutes, until help arrived, the three-story red brick building was a scene of terrifying screams amid flying debris, collapsed walls, and a fallen marble stairway. The force of the blast wrecked a truck parked outside the restaurant and shattered heavy plate-glass doors and windows in a New York Telephone Company building across the street.

Fifteen minutes after the blast, callers identifying themselves as members of Fuerzas Armadas de Liberación Nacional Puertorriquenda (FALN), a Puerto Rican revolutionary group, telephoned the Associated Press. They said, "This is FALN. At Bridge Street and Water Street, ten feet from the corner in a telephone booth, there's a communiqué there."

Police found a three-page document in which the FALN took all responsibility for the bombing. It went on to say that the FALN was the armed forces of Puerto Rican nationalists and that the bomb was in retaliation for the "CIA ordered bomb" that had killed three people in a restaurant in Mayagüez, Puerto Rico, two weeks earlier.

The revolutionary rhetoric went on to charge the United States with terrorizing and killing Puerto Ricans in order to stop them from seeking independence. It called for the release of political prisoners and said that a storm had been unleashed that "comfortable Yankis cannot escape."

It ended with the demand, "Free Puerto Rico right now."

The FALN was not unknown to the New York Police Department. Since the late sixties they had been setting off small explosive devices and making threatening telephone calls in the name of Puerto Rican independence. In late 1974 they seemed to be increasing their activities, first by setting off small bombs in Manhattan office buildings in October, which injured no one, then on December 11, they set a booby-trap bomb that blew up in the face of Police Officer Angel Poggi. It was the twenty-two-year-old cop's first night on duty. He lost his right eye in the explosion. Coffey and Fico were the first cops on the scene of that booby trap. Joe held Poggi in his arms, trying to stem the flow of blood from his head until another patrol car arrived and they were able to rush the rookie cop to a hospital.

The NYPD's Bureau of Special Services Intelligence was

having no luck in dealing with the FALN. They seemed incapable of developing useful information and were not able to identify its leaders or predict its movements. At one time they resorted to putting a rookie cop with no training directly into an undercover assignment. But it also was to no avail. With few Hispanics on the force and weak ties to the Hispanic communities, the police were desperate. The bombing of Fraunces Tavern, however, threw the problem into the public spotlight, and the NYPD was forced to react.

The day after the bombing, Police Headquarters sent out a call for all officers who might have a special ability to help in the top-priority investigation of the FALN. Joe Coffey's reputation as a wiretap and bugging expert, developed during his years in Hogan's office, overcame any intradepartmental resistence to bringing him back to the Detective Bureau. Before the week was over he was ordered to put away his sergeant's uniform and report to the Arson and Explosion Squad at Police Headquarters.

The department's quick fix, aimed at making it appear in the media that something constructive was going on, was to assign 150 cops to the investigation.

The first night that the new group assembled at headquarters, it was Detective Sergeant Joe Coffey's duty to assign them to the various leads that had been pouring in to the department's switchboard. Sitting at the supervisor's desk in the eleventh-floor offices of the Arson and Explosion Squad, he tried to make some sense of the mass of 150 cops squeezed in around him.

"There were tall cops, short cops, fat cops, skinny cops, Irish cops, Spanish cops, black cops, and just plain nondescript cops," Coffey recalls. Many had no other expertise other than that they spoke Spanish. Few had ever worked a major investigation.

He made a mental note of the nondescript types, knowing their value to undercover work. Two of that type were standing in the back of the room laughing and joking.

Thinking to himself that he had to establish his authority

and bring some order to the room, Coffey yelled out, "You two court jesters in the back, what are your names?"

Unintimidated by their new supervisor, they shot back, "Frank McDarby and Tom Kilduff from the Narcotics Division, Sarge."

Noting one was as tall as himself, Coffey took him on first. "You, the tall one, which jester are you?" he asked as the room fell silent.

"I'm McDarby, Sarge."

Feeling all eyes on him, Joe realized he had gone too far to turn back. He proceeded to load a list of orders on the Narcotics detective.

"McDarby, I want you to go to the medical examiner's office and pick up autopsy reports, then get the property vouchers for the victims' personal belongings, then stop at the bomb squad and get copies of their reports, and on your way back pick up coffee for anyone who wants it. I'll have a cup of tea."

There was dead silence in the room as all the eyes shifted to McDarby.

"Hey, Sarge," McDarby shot back, "do we have a long-handled broom in the office?"

Startled, Coffey asked why he wanted to know.

"So I can stick the broom up my ass and sweep the floor on the way out," McDarby replied.

At that point the 150 streetwise cops in the room waited for Coffey to drop the other shoe.

But despite the hard edge he was trying to display, Coffey broke up in laughter. "Go on. Get the fuck out of here," he told McDarby. The rest of the room also broke up, and a lifelong friendship was born between Joe Coffey and the nondescript detective from Narcotics.

No matter how happy he was to be back in the Detective Division, Joe Coffey found the two years he spent in the Arson and Explosion Squad to be the most frustrating and unrewarding of his career. Terrorism was an international problem. The worldwide attention paid to the Fraunces Tav-

138

ern and other FALN acts of terror caused the New York Police Department to move gingerly for fear of being second-guessed.

Radical groups like the FALN that operated across international borders were difficult for local police departments to infiltrate. They did not have undercover agents accustomed to dealing with foreign citizens. In the case of investigations of Hispanic groups, they had precious few cops who could even go undercover in the Barrio of East Harlem.

"The bosses of the Arson and Explosion Squad were not used to having people looking over their shoulders. They were used to running their own show and not having outsiders brought in for help. Fraunces Tavern changed that, and they did not like it," remembers Coffey.

"The green-eyed monster was always present when an outsider like myself, McDarby, or the others brought in to supplement the squad had an idea."

But Coffey had battled the green-eyed monster before and once again he threw himself into his new job with abandon. He soon developed the trust of a prominent member of the Puerto Rican community in New York. He was a person who, though sympathetic with some of the goals of the FALN, did not condone the kind of violence they were perpetrating.

The civic-minded citizen helped Coffey place an undercover agent named Jimmy Rodriguez into a pro-independence group which met in a storefront in East Harlem. On the surface the group appeared to be a collection of fringe players, people with an interest in independence for Puerto Rico but not the inclination to fight for it. But Coffey had an informant who indicated that the group's leadership were actually members of the secret war panel of the FALN. Jimmy Rodriguez was told to find out all he could about four people: René Rodriguez, Julio Rodriguez, Dylicia Pagan, and William Morales.

Coffey had worked with Detective Rodriguez once before. During the Vatican investigation he had followed an important lead to Argentina and proven himself to be an exceptional undercover agent.

The civic-minded citizen had passed on his suspicion to Coffey that René Rodriguez was dealing in guns. Coffey decided to have Jimmy Rodriguez pose as a Puerto Rican nationalist who wanted to buy some guns to conduct his own private war.

René Rodriguez was suspicious at first, but after several weeks of conniving, Jimmy finally convinced him to sell him some automatic weapons. After the transaction was completed, Coffey took the information to a judge to get permission for a wiretap on René Rodriguez's telephone.

The judge, impressed by the case Coffey was building, okayed the wiretap. But back at headquarters Coffey's bosses were beside themselves with anger. "They were pissed off that someone they perceived as an outsider brought in the first solid lead in the investigation," recalls Coffey. "There were two lieutenants and one sergeant who up to that point were the department's experts on terrorism. I could not believe it, but they actually went to their supervisor and suggested killing the wiretap idea. They argued I was an organized crime expert and knew nothing about terrorists."

The three "experts" made no secret of their argument against the wiretap. They expected Coffey to back off when word got around that the chief of the Arson and Explosion Squad was leaning towards taking their suggestion. But they knew little more about Joe Coffey than they did about the FALN.

Instead of backing off he went to visit his old friend from the Tactical Patrol Force, Jim Sullivan, who was the executive officer of the Detective Division.

"Sullivan wasn't convinced I really had the goods on the FALN, but he realized the department had no better lead at the time," Coffey says. So Sullivan agreed to argue in favor of the wiretaps with the chief of detectives and the supervisors in Arson and Explosion.

Sullivan was persuasive, and the wiretap was installed. It did not provide the success Coffey had hoped for. The FALN operatives proved to be highly skilled at disguising their intentions. They spoke only in code on the telephone. Transcripts of the first recorded conversations provided ammunition to the anti-Coffey factions that he should be sent back to chasing Mafia thugs, not trained subversives.

But Coffey's experience with wiretaps had taught him patience. No matter how much code or confusing conversation was recorded, he argued, some valuable information could be gleaned from the tap. He turned out to be right when, after hours of listening in on René Rodriguez, he and his team realized the Dylicia Pagan was the real message center used for the passing on of FALN orders. Up to that point Pagan was considered a dilettante, a young woman who was getting her kicks from hanging around with Puerto Rican desperadoes.

Coffey argued to expand the wiretap to Pagan's telephone. However, this time the "experts" won out and his plan was rebuffed. "All we've got out of Coffey's operation was a gun charge on René Rodriguez and a bunch of useless wiretapped conversations," they argued.

While bombings continued all over Manhattan, the supervisors of the Arson and Explosion Squad decided not to wiretap Pagan's telephone.

Instead they launched "Operation Watchdog" which entailed detectives riding around the city in taxicabs trying to catch the bombers in the act. The operation became a joke on the streets. Prostitutes, drug dealers, junkies, and Bowery bums quickly picked up on the tactic and began waving to the cops as they went by. "How you doin', officers?" became a police headquarters punchline.

In 1977 William Morales was arrested after he blew his own hands off while making a bomb in his Queens apartment. The ensuing investigation revealed that he was the mastermind behind all the FALN bombings and the master bomb maker. His girlfriend was the woman whose telephone the bosses of the Arson and Explosion Squad had refused to let Coffey tap two years earlier, Dylicia Pagan.

A few months after his arrest Morales escaped from the prison ward at Bellevue Hospital and fled to Mexico. On January 1, 1980, the FALN set off two bombs at police headquarters that left three cops seriously maimed.

Throughout 1975 the Arson and Explosion Squad detectives made little or no progress in their investigation of the Fraunces Tavern bombing. Then, two days before the end of the year, they were faced with a new threat and a catastrophe of even greater proportions.

At. 6:33 P.M. on Monday, December 29, 1975, a bomb exploded in a coin locker in the Trans World Airways baggage claim center at La Guardia Airport. Eleven people were killed and more than fifty-three were injured. The first thought of the detectives who rushed to the scene was that the FALN had struck again. But hours, then days, passed without the terrorist group's customary telephone call claiming responsibility. After three days department brass realized they had a new threat on their hands. A task force was formed to work out of a special office at the airport. Joe Coffey was taken off the Fraunces Tavern case and sent to La Guardia. Before the week was over more than 500 investigators, 300 from the FBI alone, were assigned to the case.

There was a bizarre development in the bombing which threw the investigators off the track for almost one year. Among the victims were a deep cover CIA agent who had been killed and an undercover FBI agent who had been seriously injured. In addition, Golda Meir, the prime minister of Israel, had walked through the terminal on the way to her plane about thirty minutes before the bomb detonated.

The only evidence recovered was small pieces of a timing device and a piece of a battery.

With no group taking responsibility for the act of terror, Coffey and the rest of the detectives assigned to the task force spent months looking into the backgrounds of the government agents to see if anything they were working on could have resulted in the attack. At the same time there was a general feeling that considering the constant pressure from terrorists that Israel was always feeling, the bomb was aimed at Meir and just went off too late.

One of the supervisors who gave Coffey so much trouble during the FALN investigation had once been involved in a bombing attributed to the Weather Underground. He insisted they be pursued in the La Guardia case, and Coffey was dispatched to Seattle, Washington, to track down a one-time campus radical. After two weeks of searching by Coffey and two agents from the Treasury Department's Alcohol, Tobacco and Firearms unit, the suspect could not be located. Coffey was ordered back to New York.

Thousands of investigative hours passed and no genuine leads were developed.

Then on September 10 another act of international terrorism was carried out that had a tremendous impact on Coffey's role in the La Guardia bombing and in his future with the Arson and Explosion Squad.

On that day five terrorists saying they were Croatian nationalists hijacked TWA Flight 355 from New York to Paris. One hour into the flight the pilot was ordered to radio New York that the hijackers had left a bomb in a locker at Grand Central Station. They said they would reveal the exact location of the bomb and how to disarm it if they were allowed to take the airplane to Yugoslavia.

The New York Police decided not to count on such an improbable occurrence. The Bomb Squad was sent to Grand Central to find the bomb and disarm it.

As the hijacked plane crossed the Atlantic, the New York cops searched dozens of lockers. After about thirty minutes of hunting they found the device and removed it.

Sergeant Terrence McTigue and Detective Brian Murray took the bomb to the police pistol range in a deserted area of the Bronx called Rodman's Neck. As they attempted to defuse the device it blew up in their faces. Brian

143

Murray was killed and Terry McTigue was scarred for life.

Meanwhile Flight 355 had landed in Paris. If it was to continue on to Yugoslavia it would have to be refueled. But the French police decided not to let it go. They issued an ultimatum to the terrorist leader Zvonco Busic. Although he claimed to have explosives aboard the aircraft, the police told him to surrender or they would attack the plane.

Busic later claimed he surrendered after he learned what happened to Murray and McTigue. But it turned out the explosives aboard the aircraft were fake.

Two days later on a Sunday, Busic, his wife Julienne, and the three other hijackers were returned to New York in the custody of FBI agents. They were taken to FBI headquarters and placed in separate interrogation rooms.

Joe Coffey and Frank McDarby were assigned to question the group about the Grand Central bomb.

"A female FBI agent and I went in to question Mrs. Busic, and McDarby and another agent were to question her husband, the ringleader," Coffey remembers. "Before McDarby went into the interrogation room, I reminded him to ask Busic about the La Guardia blast."

Coffey had suspected a link to the Croatian Nationalist Movement since he learned that on the same day of the La Guardia attack, December 29, a bomb was set off at the Yugoslavian diplomatic mission in Chicago. December 29 was a state holiday in Yugoslavia.

Coffey and the woman from the FBI got nothing from Mrs. Busic. She claimed she did not know of the hijack plans and did not know of any involvement her husband had in setting bombs.

McDarby had better luck. Busic, in tears, admitted placing the Grand Central bomb. McDarby asked him about the La Guardia blast. The tears increased as Busic bawled that he did not mean to hurt so many people. He admitted being at La Guardia thirty minutes before the blast.

McDarby stopped questioning and went to get Coffey. With an assistant district attorney in tow they returned to

Busic's interrogation room. McDarby resumed asking about La Guardia. Busic again began crying and saying he never wanted to hurt anyone.

"Just at that moment an FBI agent started knocking on the door saying he had to get Busic to court for arraignment or he would endanger the case," Coffey remembers. "McDarby kept pressing, but then the agent threatened to arrest us for obstruction of justice if he did not turn Busic over immediately. We had no choice, but we figured we'd get another crack at him, so we let the agent in."

The insistent FBI agent took Busic away, and he and the others were locked up in the Metropolitan Correction Center that evening.

By the next day, when Coffey and McDarby went back to continue the La Guardia line of questioning, both men had been on duty for thirty-six hours straight. They were ordered to go home and another team of detectives was sent in to question Busic. But Busic said he would only talk to the "cop with the blond mustache and beard." The description fit McDarby, but the case supervisors refused to call him back.

The next day, when Coffey and McDarby finally got back to Busic, the terrorist had retained an attorney who refused to let him speak to anyone about La Guardia.

Eventually Busic was sentenced to life in prison for the hijacking and the murder of Detective Brian Murray.

The frustration Coffey felt in being so close to solving the La Guardia case was greater even than he felt when he was turned down on the FALN wiretaps. He was not enjoying his work with the Arson Explosion Squad and yearned to get back to a unit where the level of frustration might be less.

Desperate, he increased his effort to get a transfer and finally got the word that he could report to the Queens Homicide Squad in January.

· VI ·

SAM

Bitter cold, below zero. The kind of day when radio
car cops find ways to linger at the scenes of indoor
crimes and detectives find a million reasons to hang out at
the squad room. Bad weather, it is said, is the cop's best
friend. It was Monday morning, January 31, 1977, and Coffey was on his way to his new assignment with the Queens
Homicide Squad.

Despite the weather and the general gloom of a Monday
morning, Coffey's spirits were high. For a cop his age, he
already had had an incredible number of challenging experi-
ences. He had tracked Mafia dons through Europe, protected the heavyweight champ of the world, and successfully
navigated the dangerous waters of international terrorism.
But until now he had never had the opportunity that every
serious detective yearns for. He had never been assigned to
solve a homicide—the most serious crime, the crime that
deals with the most basic of human evils, the taking of an-

other human's life. The assignment might not lead to much globe-trotting or to front-page headlines, but homicide was a choice assignment.

The day after word got around Police Headquarters that he was leaving the Arson and Explosion Squad, a reporter approached Joe in a restaurant and asked him if he was disappointed with his new assignment. Without hesitation Coffey responded, "Homicide is the best job." The detectives sitting at the table all nodded in agreement.

He had no idea as he walked into the borough headquarters to report for duty that he was about to step into a case that many in law enforcement and the press believe to be the biggest ever to have hit New York.

The Queens headquarters office did not exactly burst into cheers when Coffey arrived. Joe had many friends in the department and his work was highly respected. But he was also known as a sergeant who pushed himself around the clock and expected the same from his men. Coffey was welcomed coldly by the acting borough commander, George Weinert, who was filling in for the ill Dick Nicastro.

Weinert's attitude made it clear that while Joe Coffey might be a hotshot from One Police Plaza via the Manhattan DA's office and the Arson and Explosion Squad, he was the new kid on the block in Queens and homicide was what detective work was really about.

"We had a strange one over the weekend. A couple of kids were making out in their car in Forest Hills. Someone walked up and blew the girl away," Weinert said. He handed the file to Joe and told him he would be the supervising sergeant on the case. "Report to Joe Borrelli and see where he wants you to go with it," were Weinert's final words as Joe put on his heavy overcoat and headed out to the freezing streets of Forest Hills, one of the best neighborhoods in the city.

Knowing that he would be working under Captain Joe Borrelli, an old friend, was the first good news Coffey had that day. The two talked for about an hour before getting down to the gruesome work of finding out why someone would want to shoot to death a twenty-six-year-old Wall Street secretary named Christine Freund.

Christine was sitting with her boyfriend, John Diel, in his car near the Forest Hills train station. It was a popular make-out spot. At 12:30 A.M. on Sunday morning, a lone male fired three shots through the passenger-side window. Christine was hit twice in the face; Diel was not injured.

All that was known at the time was that the couple had spent the evening in Forest Hills. They went to a movie and then to a small restaurant on Queens Boulevard and were seen by passersby playfully sliding and falling on the ice-covered streets as they made their way back to the parked car.

Borrelli called in his squad commander, Lieutenant Bill Gorman, and his number one sergeant, Dick Conlon, to go over the case with Coffey. Joe was floating on air. He was in a room with three pros, the kind of cops he loved working with. He knew both Conlon and Gorman personally and by reputation. "This assignment will be a good one," he thought, "as long as I can work with guys like these."

It was decided that Joe would concentrate on the Freund case, supervising the detectives working the night tour, roughly 4 P.M. to midnight, while Gorman and Conlon would continue to run their shifts as usual, adding the Freund case to their already heavy caseloads. At this time New York City was at the height of its fiscal problems. For the past year the department had been operating with only about 1,000 detectives, about one-third the number there had been when Coffey first reported to DA Hogan's squad ten years before. Squad commanders like Gorman were hard-pressed to spread their resources around. A hard-working cop like Coffey was a valuable commodity, and by working the night shift he would be able to do the important follow-ups and second looks, the leg work that was increasingly falling through the cracks of the thinned-down Detective Division.

After the short meeting, Coffey and Detective Marlin Hopkins took a ride to the murder scene, where the car still was. Behind police lines, local residents were being interviewed by reporters doing second-day stories. The murder of a white Wall Street secretary who was killed while making out in a car parked on one of the finest streets in New York City was big news.

As the preliminary detective report indicated, the passenger-side window was shattered, glass covered the front seat, and there were blood stains all over the passenger area. Coffey tried to imagine the moment of death. He thought the young woman probably never knew what happened. Her companion, who ran through the streets screaming for help, would live with the nightmare forever.

Throughout his career Joe had been taught that a good detective must always keep the eventual court case in mind. Catching the criminal was the cop's job. Most police cases were considered closed once the perpetrator was identified. If the case was lost in court, or never even made it that far, as has happened to many of the terrorist cases, that was considered the fault of the prosecutor. But Coffey felt that if the detectives did their jobs properly, the prosecutors would have to be imbeciles not to be able to make the case. First on the list of doing things properly, was establishing and protecting the chain of evidence. Even if there was very little physical evidence it had to be safeguarded and examined from every possible angle.

So far, the only physical evidence that existed that might help catch the killer of Christine Freund was the two bullets removed from her head. Coffey traveled into Manhattan to the ballistics lab at the Police Academy, to see what the examination of those bullets could tell him about the killer.

The bullets were in the hands of a veteran ballistics expert named George Simmons. He was a man whom Joe had worked with on many occasions, and Simmons was glad to see him on the case. He needed a friendly face, because he had a frightening theory about the person who killed

Christine Freund. Simmons knew from experience that most detectives did not usually accept the theories of "tech" men like Simmons whom they considered eccentric geniuses out of touch with the mean streets, who lacked an understanding of the criminal mind and the instinct of the street cop.

Coffey was hardly through the laboratory door when Simmons spotted him and cried out, "Joe, I think we've got a psycho here."

"What do you mean, George?" Joe asked.

Simmons explained that the bullets taken from Christine Freund were a rare .44 caliber. He said it was a very unusual bullet to find but that in the past year or so they had been showing up in his lab with regularity, the first on July 29, 1976. It was taken from the body of an eighteen-year-old medical service technician named Donna Lauria. She had just returned from a New Rochelle discotheque and was sitting in a car with her girlfriend Jody Valente, age nineteen, in front of her apartment building in the Pelham Bay section of the Bronx. At about 1:00 A.M. a lone male fired two shots through the passenger side of the car, hitting Donna in the back and Jody in the thigh. Donna died instantly.

Simmons continued that in October 1976, a similar bullet was taken from the head of a twenty-year-old man named Carl DeNaro who was critically wounded while sitting in his car with his girlfriend, Rosemary Keenan, the daughter of a New York cop, in Bayside, Queens. Rosemary was not injured. Interestingly, DeNaro wore his hair long and may have looked like a woman from the rear.

On November 27, 1976, two more .44 caliber bullets were found. They were removed from Joanne Lomino, eighteen, and Donna DeMasi, seventeen. The two girls were sitting on a stoop in front of a house in Bellerose, Queens, at 12:30 A.M., when a man wearing army fatigues approached, mumbled some questions, and fired five shots into the car. Joanne was hit once in the back and was paralyzed from the waist down. Donna was struck in the neck but recovered.

Simmons had filed the proper reports and passed on his hunches, but there was no inclination on the part of the police department to link the cases. This was because all the bullets recovered so far were badly mutilated, having passed through glass, metal, and bone before arriving at Simmons's microscope. Psychos were bad news; a serial killer on the loose would panic the city! What detective commander would be courageous enough to announce such a possibility based on the theory of a tech man and a bunch of mutilated bullets?

Coffey was stunned by the information. First of all he knew something about .44 caliber bullets and the Charter Arms Bulldog handgun they were designed for. During his work against FALN and Croatian terrorists, Joe had met several agents of the Federal Aviation Administration. They were known as sky marshals because they were charged with guarding airplanes against skyjackings. Their standard weapon was the Charter Arms Bulldog. It weighed only eighteen ounces and was designed to fire the .44 caliber bullet at a slow velocity so that it would not exit the body of a skyjacker. A standard bullet coming out of a powerful gun at short range would almost certainly pass through a body and then might endanger the aircraft and its passengers by puncturing the skin of the fuselage and causing the plane to depressurize.

"George," he asked the white-haired ballistics expert, "do you believe these bullets were fired from the same gun?"

The response sent a chill down Coffey's spine.

"Joe, tell Borrelli it's the same gun."

"Sure, tell Borrelli it's the same gun," Coffey thought as he drove through frigid streets on the way back to his office. "Tell him there's a serial psycho on the loose in New York. That ought to make me some points with the boss."

As crime ridden as New York was during the seventies, a serial killer was one kind of criminal that seemed to have passed the city by. The closest Coffey could remember to anything like that particular horror was the "Mad Bomber" case of the early fifties, when a former Con Edison employee was seeking vengeance on his boss and setting bombs on the utility's property.

He had come into contact with professional hit men, drug dealers by the score, and the lowest of the street criminals. But a serial killer investigation, he figured, was a different kind of ballgame and he was not sure he wanted to throw the first pitch. He decided to let things sit for a day or two until he had a better handle on what the status of the other investigations was. "I really hoped someone would make an arrest and put this dark notion to bed," he remembers.

Coffey spent the next day making phone calls to the detectives working on the three previous cases that Simmons had theorized were linked to the Christine Freund investigation. At the same time other detectives from Borrelli's unit were questioning Christine's friends and family and her boyfriend, John Diel.

Coffey's phone calls did not produce much help. In all the cases there were sketches drawn from details provided by survivors and witnesses. But if there was one investigative tool that Coffey went out of his way to avoid, it was the sketch. His experience had taught him that a sketch often led a detective in the wrong direction. "When people witness a shooting they remember nothing but the flash and noise of the gun," he often told his younger partners. "Forget about their providing reliable descriptions."

In the Donna Lauria case, Bronx detectives had felt that there might be an organized crime tie-in. Lauria's father and a former boyfriend were said to have some mob connections, but after six months that lead had gone nowhere and no other lead had developed.

The other two cases prior to the Freund killing had produced even less of a solid lead than the mob possibility in the Lauria case. All the detectives Coffey spoke to agreed that the .44 caliber bullet was unusual. But without a well-preserved bullet that they could actually match to a gun, none of the detectives even wanted to speculate about the possibility of a serial psycho. Coffey, however, was beginning to feel there was no other choice, no other possible road to follow. When Borrelli's guys returned that evening with nothing solid to go on, he made up his mind to tell the captain the following day that he was buying into Simmons's theory.

Back in Levittown that evening Joe told Pat about the cases and what he was going to lay on Borrelli the next morning. She thought he was nuts. "When are you going to let someone else run the police department for a change?" she asked. But she knew that Joe would never let anything rest until it was settled. He had already forgotten how his ambition and impatience with the bureaucracy had lost him friends and cost him choice assignments. She was not anxious to see him involved in another assignment that would keep him away from home for days at a time. On this freezing night in January, though, neither Joe nor Pat Coffey could imagine how her fears would be realized.

True to his word, Coffey marched into Borrelli's office early in the morning on February 3, 1977, and told him he believed, based on the information from the ballistics unit and after telephone conversations with detectives in the Bronx and Queens, that two people had been killed and four wounded in four separate shootings since July 29, 1976, by the same gunman. He told Borrelli that he was convinced the killer was using a .44 caliber Charter Arms Bulldog and that unless some organized effort, at least borough wide, was made to catch him, he would definitely kill again.

This information did not exactly thrill Captain of Detectives Joseph Borrelli. He knew of Simmons's theory and he knew the facts of the case. He did not buy it. But he was too much of a pro and too good a manager to write off the idea without some advice. As Coffey lit his umpteenth cigarette of the day, Borrelli called Lieutenant Gorman and Sergeant Conlon into his office. Coffey went over the scenario again.

The three veteran detectives heard him out and from the looks on their faces he knew what they were thinking: "This guy is on the job three days and he's telling us we've got a serial killer on the loose and we had better do something about it." Coffey could also tell they agreed with him.

For a while, after he finished talking, it was colder in Borrelli's office than on the street. Then the captain broke the ice. He told the group that it might be a good idea for them to work the case as if a serial psycho was a strong possibility. He would circulate the idea to the proper authorities at Borough Command and downtown at Police Headquarters.

Coffey knew where his boss was coming from. The real detective in Borrelli knew that Coffey and Simmons were right and that someone had better start pursuing that lead soon. But Borrelli did not become an influential detective captain without knowing how to play office politics. Coffey thought, "Borrelli is covering his ass by passing the word upstairs but not chancing the embarrassment of the department by appearing to panic over something that might turn out to be a total fantasy." Coffey would never play the game that way. He was more willing, as he thought Borrelli should be, to suffer embarrassment in the name of saving the life of a potential victim.

Joe Coffey would never overcome his inability to play office politics. Though he would never regret maintaining that posture, his career would end in bitterness and frustration. Joe Borrelli would eventually become chief of detectives.

So a more or less informal task force was formed. About fifteen detectives and squad commanders in the Bronx and Queens were advised of the serial psycho theory and would share information that might prove a link between the killings—or as each of these hard-boiled cops hoped, disprove a link.

"There are times," Coffey says, "when a detective would rather be proven wrong. This was one of those times." But Joe Coffey, a devout Catholic, knew deep inside his police-officer soul that he was about to go one on one with the devil.

A tremendous sense of urgency began to invade the lives of the detectives who carried an almost secret knowledge. These men believed a serial psycho was lurking in the shadows and young women appeared to be his target. Coffey's sixteen-year-old daughter Kathleen was not much younger than the killer's victims; this is a thought Joe still carries with him.

For the next six weeks the investigation went nowhere. Borrelli's men, including Coffey, interviewed the Freund family over and over. They dug into John Diel's background, learning that he had had a relationship with another woman while romancing Christine. However, logically they did not identify him as Christine's killer and did not link him to the other cases that weighed so heavily on their minds.

The task force was stymied at 7:45 P.M. on March 8, 1977, when a twenty-year-old Barnard College student named Virginia Voskerichian was walking home from the Forest Hills subway station not far from where Christine Freund was parked with her boyfriend when she was killed.

As Virginia turned from the subway stairs and headed down Dartmouth Street in the direction of her family's small Tudor-style home a few blocks away, a lone male walked up to her with a gun in his hand. Instinctively, Virginia put her school textbook up in front of her face at almost the same instant the man fired one shot. The .44 caliber bullet ripped through the textbook and into Virginia's skull. The medical examiner would later report that the young woman was dead before she hit the ground.

Coffey was at home when Virginia was killed. Borrelli's office called and told him about the shooting. The detective on the phone said that it did not look like the serial m.o. but it might be a good idea for Joe to come to the scene. Joe was racing towards Queens in his 1975 Chevy before the receiver was settled in its cradle. Within forty-five minutes, he was in Forest Hills. Virginia Voskerichian had been dead about ninety minutes. Her brother, brought from their nearby house to identify the body, was at the scene.

Coffey was briefed by the detectives already there, and what he heard convinced him the psycho had struck again. He could not see how anyone could think otherwise. He also felt the good guys had gotten their first break in the case. He ordered the bullet to be rushed to the ballistics lab as soon as it was removed. "This time, I thought we would have a good bullet. I did not believe the book would have mutilated it to the point that we could not match it with one of the other .44's," Coffey remembers. Joe went to the morgue himself to make sure the bullet was handled properly—as evidence against a mad killer that was haunting his city.

In the meantime other detectives canvassed the neighborhood. There were many witnesses to this murder, and they all agreed on one interesting point: the killer did not run away from the scene as one might have imagined he would. Instead he walked calmly away toward the nearby Forest Hills Tennis Stadium, at the time home to the U.S. Open.

This information was consistent with descriptions of the killer leaving the scenes of the other murders in Coffey's notebook. Descriptions of the shooter as a white man wearing a ski cap, assuming a police- or military-type stance before he fired, also matched the earlier cases. It was circumstantial evidence to be sure, but enough to begin to convince even the most skeptical cops working the case that the serial theory was probably on the mark. "There will be no explaining this one away," Coffey thought.

This was the first of the serial murders committed on Joe's watch and he was glad for the opportunity to become totally immersed in the case from the beginning. He had been working up to this point with a savvy streetwise detective named Marlin Hopkins, and within two hours of the murder they went to the Voskerichian home. Going through the routine steps of a murder investigation, they spoke with the young student's family.

They learned a lot about Virginia. They learned she was born in Bulgaria in 1956. She was an A student, majoring in Russian languages. Her parents, Garo and Yolanda, immigrated to Queens when Virginia was ten years old. She had two older brothers and an older sister. She was a beautiful, popular, studious young woman, who promised to fulfill all the potential immigrant families yearn for. To the rest of her family she was an American, and they couldn't be prouder. This was all interesting information—heartbreaking considering the situation—but it offered Coffey and Davis not a hint of motive, not a whisper of a suspect.

"A goddamn, fucking psycho ruined a life like this," Coffey thought as he listened to the Voskerichian family struggle to explain why no one in the world would want to hurt Virginia.

The next day Queens Detective Commander Richard Nicastro ordered more detectives to be assigned to the Borrelli task force. Coffey requested that two old colleagues, George Moscardini and John O'Connell, be brought in. The three would spend many, many hours together over the next eight months.

They began by driving up to Barnard College, which is a part of Columbia University in upper Manhattan, for a look at Virginia's records and to interview students and faculty who had known her. On the way up the three talked about the slim chance that they would develop a useful lead. If this was a routine homicide, they reasoned, the trip to Barnard would almost certainly prove fruitful—a spurned lover, a jealous classmate, some ancient family feud maybe going back to Bulgaria. These were three detectives who could believe anything; they had seen it all. But in reality they understood they were practically wasting their time at the school. They would find no clues, no motive, no sign of passion that would lead them to this killer.

As Coffey walked the Columbia campus, which was stirring with the news of Virginia's murder, he thought again of his own daughter, Kathleen. His career to this point had not brought him into much contact with average people. He had spent most of his thirteen years on the force pursuing professional criminals—criminals who for the most part did not come into direct contact with John Q. Public. But this case was different. He could not shake the thought that his own daughter could have easily been the victim that Virginia Voskerichian became. As he spoke to the bright, pretty young students who went to class with Virginia he thanked God a thousand times that his daughter was alive, that the evil force that had invaded the Voskerichian family had so far avoided the Coffeys.

Joe, Moscardini, and O'Connell were sitting in a faculty lounge reviewing their notes when Coffey's beeper went off. All three shared the same thought. "Another murder." Coffey called his office back in Queens and was told that George Simmons wanted to talk to him. "Call Simmons at the lab" was the message.

Simmons was unusually excited when Coffey got through to him. It was good news. "Joe, the Voskerichian bullet matches the Donna Lauria. I'm sure of it. The same gun was used to kill both girls. I wanted to tell you first; now I'll spread the word through channels."

The three cops raced off the Columbia campus with siren screaming. They made the trip across Manhattan back to Queens in fifteen minutes.

By the time they arrived at Borrelli's office, he had gotten the news from Simmons. Borrelli began gathering his brain trust. Coffey remembers a high state of anxiety in the office. He felt some satisfaction in knowing, now, that he was right, but that feeling was overwhelmed by a sense that things were about to get out of control.

A new chief of detectives, John Keenan, was now in office. He, Nicastro, and Borrelli gathered to work out a strategy. Police Commissioner Michael Codd was brought up to speed, and Borrelli's small task force was immediately expanded, doubled in size from sixteen to thirty men. Lieutenant John Power from the Bronx and his men who were investigating the Lauria case were brought in. Power was one of the department's best officers, and Coffey was glad to see he would play an important role from here on in. Mayor Abe Beame was briefed, and because everyone agreed all this police activity was impossible to hide from the press, the department's deputy commissioner for public information, Francis McLaughlin, was given access to the entire operation.

One hundred cops were assigned for the weekends, Friday night to Sunday night, the times the killer seemed likely to hit. Coffey was ordered to command the weekend detail.

Two days after Virginia Voskerichian was gunned down on Dartmouth Street in Forest Hills, Commissioner Michael Codd—a tall career cop with the bearing of a paratroop general and a true love for the uniformed cop, whom he favored over detectives—held a press conference in the second-floor auditorium at One Police Plaza.

As is usually the case before a major press conference, the city's reporters had a strong inkling about the subject. Most of the press who covered the police regularly had already alerted their city editors that Codd was about to put forth a blockbuster—"something about a serial killer."

The reporters had underestimated what would occur. It was bigger than they could have imagined. The auditorium was packed wall to wall with print, radio, and television reporters and all their equipment. Coffey stood with his back to the exit door as Deputy Commissioner McLaughlin called the group to order.

Codd soon took over and for more than an hour explained to the media that a link had been established between the murders of Donna Lauria on July 7, 1976, and Virginia Voskerichian just two nights before. The link, he explained, was the .44 caliber bullet and the certainty, on the part of the department experts, that it was fired from a Charter Arms Bulldog. Codd explained there was also general agreement on the part of detectives assigned to both cases

159

that the same gun was used in three other attacks in the Bronx and Queens.

The reporters went nuts. This was an enormous story. Some recognized it to be the biggest story ever in New York—bigger than the gang wars of the thirties, bigger than the Mad Bomber of the early fifties, bigger than the blackout of the sixties. And they all wanted to know one thing. Almost as one voice they asked, "What is the police department doing to protect the young women of the city?"

Coffey smiled at that question. He knew Codd had little to offer. But valiantly the commissioner, who was never comfortable in these situations, described the "John Doe" warrant that had been issued based on descriptions of the killer given by witnesses to all five attacks as "a white male, twenty-five to thirty years old, six feet tall, medium build, and dark hair."

Codd explained how the killer seemed to use a military-style crouch when he fired and that he walked away from the scene, apparently to an unknown type of car parked nearby. He repeated that additional cops had been assigned to the case and ended the press conference with an appeal to the public for help.

The reporters were left to use their own sources to learn that all the victims, even Carl DeNaro, had long dark hair. They contacted victims' families and pumped Coffey and other detectives for any tidbit they could get. That evening's newscasts and the next day's papers described a city in fear and a police force searching in desperation for the kind of real clues or informants it would need to bring the killer to justice.

Things would only get worse.

By the weekend of April 17, 1977, Coffey's men had established a routine of stakeouts in unmarked cars that covered virtually every lovers' lane or darkened area near a disco or bar. In the Bronx, Sergeant Fred DeLuca whose regular assignment was with the Sex Crimes Unit, patrolled the service road of the Hutchinson River Parkway. It was a road that the killer could use as an escape from Queens into the North Bronx or Westchester. His patrol took him within blocks of where Donna Lauria was killed. In fact, DeLuca met the two detectives assigned to the Lauria case while on patrol that night and spent some time talking to them. But by 3:00 A.M. an uneventful tour of duty had passed and he checked out. Coffey, also having an uneventful evening, cruised Queens and spent a few hours clearing paperwork and answering telephones in the office. At about the same time DeLuca called it quits, Coffey left the office and went to a Chinese restaurant and bar with another cop for a winding-down drink before heading home. The two cops bemoaned the fact that almost 200 stakeouts that night had produced nothing.

At about 4:30 A.M. Joe arrived in Levittown. He was just in the door when the phone rang. It was a detective from Borrelli's office. "Joe, we've got a shooting in the Bronx that fits our boy." Fifteen minutes of 100-mile-per-hour driving brought Coffey to the murder site as the body of Valentina Suriani was being placed into the city van that would take her to the morgue. Her companion, Alexander Esau, was already in surgery at nearby Jacobi Hospital. He would not survive.

Valentina, age eighteen, and Alexander, twenty, were a beautiful young couple, deeply in love. They were not the kind of couple Hollywood makes movies about. They were from middle-class homes. Alexander was a tow-truck operator; Valentina dreamed of being an actress. They had spent the evening in Manhattan, seeing a movie in Times Square, then having dinner before heading home to the Bronx. These two kids reminded cops of their own youths.

They parked about 3:00 A.M., for a few private minutes, on the Hutchinson Parkway service road, just across from Valentina's apartment house. It was three blocks from the home of Donna Lauria and almost the exact spot where Sergeant Fred DeLuca had parked fifteen minutes earlier.

The engine had just been turned off when four shots

slammed through the windows of the 1968 Mercury Montego. The youngsters were each hit two times. Valentina died almost instantly; Alexander fought for his life for two hours at Jacobi before succumbing.

Coffey knew the m.o. fit the other .44 caliber cases, and he would not need the bullet to see that this time. But now there was a twist. One of the first cops at the scene had found an envelope in the street about fifteen feet from the car. It was addressed to Captain Joe Borrelli.

When he heard about the envelope, Coffey was immediately concerned that it would be mishandled. He passed orders to safeguard it: Watch for fingerprints and don't open it. That should be done by police lab technicians. By that time however, the envelope had gone through several sets of hands and cops' fingerprints were all over it.

Coffey knew the murder scene was in DeLuca's sector. He called the sergeant at home to ask if he had noticed anything. "Freddie broke down on the phone when I told him what had happened. He believed he was parked in that exact spot. But he didn't see anything," Coffey says.

This incident shattered Coffey. His plan to stake out likely areas and patrol the escape routes seemed to be on the mark, and this latest attack proved it. But he felt he was up against a killer who lived in the shadows, perhaps drawing strength from the energy of the cops who were hunting him.

He couldn't remember the last time he had sat down for a real meal. He hadn't seen one Levittown Little League game yet that year, and he had lost 20 pounds, falling to below 200 for the first time in his adult life. The spirits of Donna Lauria and Virginia Voskerichian haunted him, demanding action. Now he had to go to the morgue to examine the body of a beautiful eighteen-year-old girl whom he was supposed to have been protecting.

He lost his cool at the morgue. This is how Coffey remembers it: "I never liked going to the morgue in the first place. I never could get used to dead bodies, although I had seen plenty of them. Now, here was one of the most beautiful young girls I had ever seen, lying on the morgue table, just a thin sheet covering her.

"I found it hard to look at her. She was just two years older than Kathleen. She seemed so innocent. I wondered, 'How could this happen to such a child?' She was covered from head to toe with dried blood, hers and Alexander's. She had a gold bracelet on her wrist."

A morgue attendant approached the body with a knife. When he lifted the girl's arm, Coffey grabbed him. "What are you doing there. What are you doing?" he demanded.

The attendant said he was going to cut the jewelry off, as he always did. Coffey grabbed him by the neck, lifted him off his feet, and threw him against the morgue's white-tiled wall. The attendant screamed and groaned as he slumped to the floor. The room fell silent. Three other detectives standing around the table watched the scene, not reacting. Coffey gently removed the bracelet from Valentina's wrist and placed it in an evidence envelope. He turned and walked out, a new burst of adrenaline pumping through his exhausted body. A renewed determination pushed him behind the wheel of his car. He went to visit Fred DeLuca hoping he had seen something and hadn't realized it.

The next day the letter to Borrelli was opened at the department's Fingerprint Section. The first paragraph read:

Dear Captain Joseph Borrelli,
I am deeply hurt by your calling me a wemon [sic] hater [referring to Borrelli's remarks at the March 11 press conference]. I am not. But I am a monster.
I am the "Son of Sam." I am a little brat.

The letter went on with about 200 rambling, nonsensical phrases and ended with a warning:

I say good-bye and good night.
Police: Let me haunt you with these words:
I'll be back!
I'll be back!
To be interrpreted [sic]
As—bang, bang, bang, bank [sic], bang—ugh!

> *Yours in Murder,*
> *Mr. Monster*

Coffey was furious that the letter was mishandled, though as it turned out no useful fingerprints were lifted from it and it would not be valuable evidence in the event of a trial. However, it served another purpose in this case. In early June, the *Daily News* got hold of a copy of the letter. "Son of Sam" was born in the public's mind, and the case would be known by that title forever.

On April 19, as pressure from the media for police action mounted and precinct telephone lines around the city were choked with calls from frightened citizens, it was announced that the Queens task force would be expanded. Because of its high priority and the crossing of precinct and borough lines—and not incidentally because the case was now costing the city almost $100,000 a day—it would be headed by an inspector. Codd chose a mild-mannered detective with a reputation for supervising group efforts named Inspector Timothy J. Dowd.

The veteran group of cops who had been working the serial cases from the beginning resented the intrusion of Dowd, but they knew a headquarters heavyweight was needed. Borrelli may have felt pushed to the rear but admitted to colleagues that naming Dowd was a necessary move.

The group was named Task Force Omega with headquarters set up at the 109th Precinct in Flushing. Detectives from all over the city were now being assigned to the case during days, nights, and Coffey's weekend shift. Coffey adjusted his escape route surveillance with the additional tactic of shutting down all bridges and tunnels leading out of Queens as soon as word of another hit was broadcast on the police radios. Such a tactic required manpower. In the absence of physical evidence, manpower would play a large role in hunt for the .44 caliber killer, as the press was now calling the serial psycho.

Coffey continued planning based on his strong feeling that the killer lived either in the Bronx or Westchester. A decade later he cannot call that feeling any more than a hunch. But he was always a hunch player and had learned to trust his instinct.

For the handful of detectives like Joe, Gorman, Power, and Conlon, the efforts on the case were what police work was about. It was challenging, dangerous work, toward a worthwhile end. They found professional satisfaction in being assigned to such a case no matter how much pain it would cause them. A handful of cops from all over the city volunteered to join the Omega group for the same reasons. But for the most part, Coffey was disappointed in the attitudes of most of the cops ordered to report to Task Force Omega. He found them to be resentful and cynical about the assignment beyond reason.

"Most of the guys, and I had a relative and some close friends among the group, thought it was a bullshit assignment. They resented being taken from their own cases, cases they controlled, to be used as foot soldiers in a manhunt," Coffey says. "They just did not see it as work that would advance their careers or salaries. I never could understand that attitude and I guess they could never understand mine."

The task force was undoubtably a political maneuver to make the public believe the department had a handle on the case. Coffey did not really think it would help. He continued to believe the killer would be caught through old-fashioned police work or a lucky break. Almost one year after his first attack, the .44 caliber killer was still totally anonymous to his pursuers. He might as well have been a ghost. Recognizing all that, Joe resigned himself to being somewhat under the control of the bureaucracy he hated so much. "Whether I liked it or not, I got the help," Coffey says.

There was a feverish mood in the city about the case. Press conferences were held every day. Mayor Beame could not attend any type of function without being asked about the manhunt. Dark-haired young women were dying their hair blonde; long-haired girls were rushing for haircuts. Parents were stepping up their warnings about lovers' lanes. Reporters interviewed disco owners who feared the news of the killer would ruin their businesses, and psychics popped up who claimed they knew where and when the killer would strike next.

Coffey had no use for most of the help the public was offering, especially the psychics. One famous crystal ball reader who had worked with New Jersey police on several occasions showed up at the 109th Precinct one morning to offer her help. Coffey rudely dismissed her. The next day she ripped into "that Detective Sergeant Joe Coffey, who really doesn't want to solve this case," on a radio talk show. Joe was thankful most of his superiors agreed with his view of supernatural detective work.

While the task force detectives blanketed areas around lovers' lanes and other places young people might park in their cars and stopped any suspicious-looking man walking alone, they continued their patrols of escape routes. Work was also continued on the individual cases as if they were not connected. If any case could be solved alone and established as not having a link to the others, it could bury the thought of the .44 caliber killer.

The detectives traced all 28,000 Charter Arms Bulldogs manufactured by the Bridgeport, Connecticut, company, a complicated task that failed to lead to Son of Sam because the gun, it turned out, was purchased by a friend of the killer in Houston, Texas. Coffey assigned himself to do background checks on auxiliary cops in the precincts where the attacks occurred because of the military- or police-type shooting stance of the killer—another hunch.

Coffey's other specific assignment was to follow up on the "kites"—reports alleging a cop was guilty of a crime, usually just thrown up for grabs anonymously by another cop. During the course of the Son of Sam investigation Coffey received more than 300 "kites." Some were like the call from a patrol sergeant who suspected his police-officer driver. The driver had offered to fix the sergeant up with a willing woman in a pickup spot on Queens Boulevard known as the "Wrinkle Room" because of the advanced age of its female patrons.

"If he hangs out in places like that and the way he knows his way around the borough, I'm pretty sure it's him," offered the otherwise competent sergeant. Before hanging up the sergeant told Coffey he wanted credit for the call if the police officer was arrested but asked Coffey not to mention it to anyone if the tip did not pan out.

Another "kite" was from a priest in the Bronx who suspected one of his congregants. The suspect was a police officer who in recent months had taken to cursing at young women who walked down the aisle to take communion. "He called them whores and tramps," the priest said, "and all of a sudden he has been wearing a large gold cross."

Coffey took this one seriously and staked out the cop for a while. Eventually he decided that while this was one cop who needed help, he was not the .44 caliber killer.

It was a wild time in the 109 squad room, which now bristled with two or three telephones on every desk and piles of police forms waiting to be filed filling up every available corner. "We were getting calls around the clock. Wives were turning in their husbands; mothers turned in their sons; angry girlfriends were sure that their lovers were the killer and demanded that they be arrested and sent to the electric chair," Coffey remembers. "It may be hard to believe, but we checked into most of the calls. We had nothing else to go on."

Coffey was now working around the clock, seeing little of his family. As he left his house early one Saturday morning, Steven Coffey, eight years old and missing his father's attention, ran after him, a thin rope in his hand. "Daddy, use this rope to catch the guy, like Deputy Dog," the youngster yelled. "Deputy Dog" was one of his favorite television shows at the time. Coffey put the rope in his trunk, promising Steven he would use it if he needed it. The rope stayed there throughout the Son of Sam case.

Things were getting very rough on the nighttime streets of the Bronx and Queens. Coffey spread the word that he wanted people followed, questioned, frisked, and ordered to open their packages and cars, without warrants.

"I guess we kind of put the constitution on the back burner for a while," he concedes. His men began calling their procedures "Coffey's Martial Law." The public did not complain. "More often than not, after we explained what we were doing, the people thanked us."

It was around this time that the task force cops on Coffey's shift began doing their most dangerous work. Joe devised a plan to put cops in unmarked cars posing as young lovers making out. A local department store chain supplied a bunch of mannequins that were fitted with wigs. Coffey took the first shift himself.

Night after night detectives sat in their cars with mannequins or sometimes with other male detectives wearing wigs. They wore bulletproof vests and kept their regulation .38 caliber revolvers in their laps. Backup teams armed with shotguns kept watch from nearby cars and from behind bushes and trees. This was a desperation tactic. Police brass do not like putting officers in positions of such jeopardy, but there was nothing else to do.

"We thought we were going to have to catch this guy in the act," Coffey says. "We were ready to kill him. It seemed to be the only way the nightmare would end."

Fearing the brass would call off the decoy squad before someone got hurt, Coffey spoke to a friend in the Secret

Service and got the name of the company that made the bulletproof cars used to protect the president of the United States. He contacted the company, and they offered five cars free of charge if that would help catch "Son of Sam." When Coffey passed the offer to his superiors, he ran into the type of response he never learned to live with.

Headquarters told him that the department, still smarting from the corruption scandals of the seventies, could not accept the cars for free. But they thought it was a good idea and might be able to afford to buy one car. Eventually a blue bulletproof 1977 Chevrolet Monte Carlo was purchased for $5,000. It arrived in New York the day after Son of Sam, David Berkowitz, was captured.

More than two months had passed since the murders of Valentina Suriani and Alexander Esau, and detectives were pursuing one false lead after another. Joe spent days following a bus driver whose route passed almost directly by the crime scenes. Finally confronting the man, Coffey had to be physically restrained by John O'Connell when the bus driver began complaining that the cops had no right to bother him.

Tips to the police were being classified in three categories: priority one, priority two, and priority three.

Coffey and O'Connell spent a whole day checking out a tip that involved the television series "Starsky and Hutch." A caller to the task force made a convincing argument that an episode of the show paralleled the .44 caliber case. With nothing more pressing to follow up, the two seasoned detectives went to ABC network headquarters and in one marathon session reviewed every episode of the popular show. It was a waste of an afternoon.

Then Inspector Dowd got a hunch of his own. Every night on his way home from the Omega headquarters he passed a disco called Elephas on Northern Boulevard in Bayside, Queens. He talked to Coffey about beefing up the task force presence at the popular disco, which was in an area bordered by single-family homes on tree-lined streets. Coffey never doubted a cop's hunch and readily agreed to the adjustment even though he already had extra cops there, and he made sure to swing by the disco himself on every patrol. Other cops, behind his back, poked fun at Dowd's request. "It's the only disco he knows, so that's his big contribution," they murmured. At the same time they doubly admonished their own daughters to steer clear of the Elephas. "Even Inspector Dowd thinks the place is a target," they warned.

Bingo. In June, Dowd's hunch seemed prescient.

On June 26, 1977, Judy Placido, eighteen, and Sal Lupo, twenty, met for the first time at the Elephas Disco. Judy had gone there for an evening of dancing and drinking with two girlfriends from the Bronx. Sal introduced himself to Judy, and when her girlfriends left she decided to stay for another drink with Sal. He and his friend, a bouncer at the club, would drive her home later.

Sal and Judy really hit it off and after the last drink they walked to the car on 211th Street and 45th Road about a block away while Sal's bouncer friend helped close up. The young couple had talked about the Son of Sam cases and both admitted to being frightened about being on the dark streets at that hour, about 3:00 A.M. Sal let Judy in the passenger side and then ran around to the driver's side of the Cadillac to let himself in. They were hardly settled into their seats when the car exploded in a blast of noise and shattering glass. Four shots were fired. Lupo was hit in the arm, Judy Placido struck three times in the head, neck, and back. Doctors cannot explain why she did not die. But both survived the attack.

Leaving the scene, the shooter walked down Northern Boulevard. He was a lone man, wearing a ski hat, carrying a paper bag. Two detectives, assigned to the beefed-up patrol by Coffey, stopped him. They began to ask for identification when their hand-held walkie-talkie barked, "Shots fired, two down, 211th Street and 45th Road." Turning their back on the lone man, the two detectives ran to their unmarked car and sped to the scene. At the precinct house that night both men sobbed. Son of Sam had been in their hands and had walked away. It was not the only time that night that Coffey's team had the chance to nail the killer.

According to plan, the Triborough Bridge and Tunnel Authority, upon being notified of a "Code .44," forced all traffic crossing the Throgs Neck and Whitestone Bridges into one toll booth. On the Bronx side of the toll booth two women detectives were stationed. Their orders were to stop and search any lone male crossing into the Bronx following a "Code .44." Many weeks later, David Berkowitz would tell Joe Coffey that the two women detectives let him drive right through. He said his .44 caliber Charter Arms Bulldog was in a paper bag on the seat next to him.

At this point in his career, Joe had a low opinion of women's value in police work, feeling that other than as specific decoys or in undercover operations, they were about as useful as artists' sketches. He eventually approached the two women about Berkowitz's statement. "They told me they were too afraid to stop anyone that night. The tactic was perfect, but two policewomen, too scared stiff to do their duty, blew it," Coffey says. The sympathy he has for the two male detectives who walked away from Berkowitz does not carry over to their female counterparts. The difference? "The two guys made a mistake; they acted before they thought. The two women were cowards." Case closed.

In the same conversation with Berkowitz, Coffey learned that he too was within striking distance of the killer that night in Bayside. He and George Moscardini were on the Clearview Expressway service road heading away from the Throgs Neck Bridge deeper into Queens when the "Shots fired . . . 211th and 45th Road," squealed from their police radio.

Fifteen minutes earlier they had circled the Elephas, noticing the crowd was breaking up early for a Saturday night.

"Holy shit, that's him. We missed him," Coffey yelled as Moscardini raced to the next street to turn around so that they could head for the scene. Within a minute the "Code

.44" was broadcast over the detective band as units at the scene identified the m.o.

Coffey grabbed Moscardini's arm, almost causing him to ram a parked car. "I've got an idea, George," Joe screamed over the wail of the electronic siren. "Back up the service road toward the Northern Boulevard entrance ramp. If he's headed for the Bronx he'll get on there."

Coffey was right but too late. Berkowitz would eventually tell him that he saw a police car heading backward on the service road, but he was far in front of it heading for the bridge where the two women detectives would let him pass. Luck was on the killer's side.

Finally at the scene, Coffey remembers mayhem. Judy Placido had been taken to the hospital and Sal Lupo was wandering around in a frantic state, blood pouring from his arm. He apparently did not realize that he had been shot.

The newspaper columnist Jimmy Breslin, who had received a letter from Son of Sam, was there. Coffey, who usually admired Breslin's writing and had for many years maintained an excellent relationship with the city's tabloid reporters, resented Breslin's presence. "Headquarters, after he got the letter from Son of Sam, gave him total access to the investigation. Now here he was at the scene and, completely without basis in fact, going around telling people the killer was a priest. Breslin was making himself the story, and that sucked," Coffey said.

While he remained at the scene, Coffey dispatched Moscardini to Flushing Hospital to find out what the two victims might be able to add to the pitifully empty Son of Sam evidence container. Shortly after he arrived, Moscardini watched as the doctors removed a .44 caliber bullet from Sal Lupo's right forearm. The detective, who had become a second set of eyes and ears for Coffey, took the bullet and placed it in an envelope designed for just that kind of evidence. Lupo and Placido could not identify their assailant. It was another successful attack by a devil living in the shadows of the night.

"As the case built up and we continued without gathering evidence, it became increasingly apparent to us on the front lines that we would have to kill Son of Sam in order for any kind of justice to be dealt out," Coffey says. "Judging from the letters, he was clearly insane and we had no kind of court case." The overworked, undernourished criminal justice system had no way of dealing with the killer, but on the street cops were prepared to take him down. "If he came into our sight, he was dead," Coffey says.

These are unusually harsh words from a man who disliked firing his gun, even at the police range, but Son of Sam had taken over his life. As surely as the demonic killer had entered the lives of his victims, he had become a dominant force in the thoughts of the detectives charged with bringing him to justice. Barracks humor disappeared from the crowded headquarters squad room. Cops and reporters got into violent arguments. Marriages, already strained by the pressures of everyday police work, were now at the breaking point. Detectives had to be ordered to take their time off. Dowd, Borrelli, Power, Coffey, Gorman, and Conlon had to be pried from their desks and yanked from their patrol cars.

A great, fearful concept began to dominate their thoughts. The first anniversary of the murder of Donna Lauria, Son of Sam's first victim, was approaching. Would the demon create some special event to mark the date?

Everyone agreed he would. The only argument was over which day. The attack on Lauria was on July 29, a Saturday night. In 1977, July 29 would be a Friday. Coffey argued that the attack would come on July 30 or 31 because all his previous attacks, except the one on Voskerichian, occurred late Saturday night or early Sunday morning. It seemed a small thing to be arguing about—the Omega operation would be in force all weekend—but at that point everyone was grasping at straws.

In mid-July a Yonkers man named Sam Carr went to the 109th Precinct to complain about a neighbor named David Berkowitz who had been harassing his family. He thought

Berkowitz could be the Son of Sam killer. The information was classified priority two.

It did not go unnoticed in the press that the anniversary was approaching. The media, en masse, demanded answers to their questions about protecting their readers and viewers that weekend. It was then, Coffey believes, that Dowd made a serious mistake. The inspector revealed the bridge plan to the papers, letting the killer know how the police planned to catch him. "I was afraid that we had now driven him out of the Bronx and Queens, perhaps to Brooklyn or the suburbs, and those places were not involved in the task force. If he hit there, we might end up back at square one," Coffey says.

In the early morning hours of July 31, 1977, David Berkowitz, known to the city as Son of Sam, opened fire with his eighteen-ounce, .44 caliber Charter Arms Bulldog on a car containing Stacy Moskowitz, age twenty, and Robert Violante, also twenty. The couple was parked in a lovers' lane area off Shore Parkway in the Bay Ridge section of Brooklyn.

Stacy Moskowitz was mortally wounded. Robert Violante's eyes were shattered, leaving him legally blind.

Coffey, Moscardini, and O'Connell had cruised Queens Boulevard most of that evening. Dowd had ordered the Omega force to continue to concentrate on Queens. "He called the Elephas shooting right and that made him hard to argue with," says Coffey. So only the bridges that connected the Bronx and Queens were being covered. Brooklyn's highways were left to the one Omega car and the regular Highway Patrol units.

At 2:35 A.M., as they were riding past the West Side Tennis Club in Forest Hills, not far from where Christine Freund and Virginia Voskerichian were murdered, their radio barked with a report of a shooting at Bay 17th and Shore Road in Brooklyn. Coffey knew the area was a favorite parking spot. A follow-up report said to be on the lookout for a single gunman and that it might be a homicide.

Moscardini pulled up to a pay phone and Coffey called Omega Headquarters. He asked to speak to Dowd. He told his boss he wanted to respond to Brooklyn. Dowd said he doubted it would be their man but told Coffey to ride out anyway, because the sole Omega unit in Brooklyn had already gone off duty.

Moscardini broke all his personal driving records as he maneuvered down the Van Wyck Expressway and the Belt Parkway to the scene. This time, the scene was crawling with cops who had no inside knowledge of the Son of Sam case. They had not been included in the task force. All they knew was what they had read in the papers. So they had no special response planned. They reacted like it was just another murder.

But moments after he arrived, Coffey's worst fears were realized. "Son of Sam had left his calling card," Coffey says. "Right in the middle of the steering wheel of Robert Violante's car was a .44 caliber bullet."

But there were other forces at work against the demon that night, and though Joe could not know it at the time, Son of Sam's luck was beginning to run out. Stacy Moskowitz was to be his last victim.

Coffey sent Moscardini and O'Connell to the hospital where Stacy and Robert were fighting for survival, and he headed for the local precinct. The first thing he did when he got there was to call Dowd. The inspector would have to get in touch with Brooklyn Homicide brass and make them a part of the task force—fast. Coffey took no satisfaction in the fact that he was right about the date and about having tipped Sam off about the Queens bridges. He was emotionally drained, without a clue about where to go next in the investigation. So he turned to routine detective work and called in the two police officers who patrolled the sector in which the shooting occurred. He asked them a routine question, something all detectives ask local patrol officers: "Did you two guys issue any parking summonses tonight?" The theory was that a killer might have to park illegally to facilitate a quick getaway. The two cops answered, "No Sarge, we didn't write any tickets."

To this day Joe Coffey cannot understand why they answered that way, because about four days later, rechecking every possible area for clues, detectives Ed Blaise and Ed O'Sullivan discovered that a summons for parking at a fire hydrant had been given out that evening for a 1977 Ford Galaxie, registered to a David Berkowitz of 35 Pine Street, Yonkers, New York.

"I can only imagine that the two uniformed cops were covering their asses. Both had had problems with Internal Affairs, and I think they were afraid of being called on the carpet for missing a killer wandering in their sector," theorizes Coffey more than a decade later. For their part, the two cops told superiors they were caught up in the excitement of the evening and couldn't even remembering dropping the summonses into the box at the precinct reserved for that purpose.

At any rate, events now began to unfold quickly, and Joe and the men of the Omega Task Force were pretty much left out of them. The detectives of Brooklyn's 10th Homicide Zone seized the Moscowitz-Violante attack and ran with it. Although the department's Intelligence Division was in touch with the Yonkers Police Department about a strange, single man named Berkowitz who was threatening and tormenting his neighbors and although the report filed at the 109th Precinct by Sam Carr about Berkowitz's being a likely suspect was working its way to the top of the pile, it was the guys from the 10th Homicide Zone who ran Son of Sam to the ground.

They were instinctively bothered by the information the summons issued to Berkowitz contained. It was written at 2:05 A.M., minutes before the shooting, and they could not understand what a man with a Jewish-sounding name was doing parked illegally in that heavily Italian neighborhood in the middle of the night.

On the morning of August 10, 1977, detectives Ed Zigo

and John Longo went to the Pine Street address to interview Berkowitz. When they arrived they saw his car parked in front of the building and looked inside. What they saw made their hearts stop. Behind the front seat was an army duffel bag with the name D. Berkowitz stenciled on it. Sticking out of the top was undoubtably a machine gun.

The two detectives called their office back in Coney Island and were told to take no action. Zigo was ordered to head to Yonkers Police Headquarters and get a search warrant for the car. The Omega force was notified of the find, and Chief of Detectives Keenan, Inspector Dowd, and Borrelli, guessing that they had their man, drove to Yonkers Police Headquarters to coordinate the capture.

By 7:30 that evening Pine Street was crawling with New York City detectives. Local residents, seeing something was going on, came out in beach chairs to view the action. At 10:00 P.M., David Berkowitz, a postal worker from the Bronx, left the building at 35 Pine Street and headed for his cream-colored 1977 Ford Galaxie. Zigo was still not back with the arrest warrant, and the cops did not want to move without it. On the other hand they were not going to let Berkowitz drive away.

So as David Berkowitz opened his front door and threw a paper bag containing a .44 caliber Charter Arms Bulldog on the front seat, Longo and Detective John Falotico, who had been sent up by the 10th, aimed their .38 caliber detective specials at his head and put him under arrest.

As police legend has it, Falotico ordered Berkowitz to freeze and the suspect murmured, "You've got me."

"Who do I have?" Falotico is said to have asked.

"You've got the Son of Sam."

The most vicious killer in New York's history was taken into custody without a struggle. As he was driven into Yonkers Police Headquarters, he had a childlike smile on his face. The smile would become as much a trademark as the .44 caliber bullet.

Joe Coffey was at home when Berkowitz was arrested. A

call from Keenan's office ordered him to go to One Police Plaza, where Berkowitz was to be brought for questioning. Coffey would lead the questioning because he was the only detective familiar with every aspect of the case. He was, after all, the only one who had thought they were dealing with a serial killer from his first day on the job in Queens, when he was sent to Station Plaza in Forest Hills to investigate the murder of Christine Freund.

Berkowitz and a police bodyguard were alone in an interrogation room when Coffey and Sergeant Dick Conlon entered to question him. "I was filled with rage when I went in that room. This was a man I was prepared to kill, a man I thought I hated," remembers Coffey.

"But after a few minutes I actually began to feel sorry for him. He was a vegetable. He had this pitiful smile on his face and he never blinked.

"But his mind was sharp. He walked us through every case, every shooting. He remembered the smallest details, like what color coat the victim was wearing. He told us that two cops had stopped him on the Willis Avenue Bridge in the Bronx after he shot Stacy Moskowitz, but they, like others before them, let him go. He told me how he saw me on the highway the night of the Elephas shooting. He said he didn't care about our plans on the bridges or anything else. He said that demons told him where and when to kill and that the orders were given to him by Sam Carr's dog.

"He also said he was an auxiliary cop in the 45th Precinct, the precinct where he killed Donna Lauria. Remember I had assigned myself to check out auxiliaries in those precincts in the Bronx and Queens where attacks took place. For some reason I never made it to the Bronx. I stopped after background checks in Queens did not pan out."

Coffey spent two hours with Berkowitz and came out feeling sorry for him. After the session Coffey went to a makeshift bar set up and paid for by Mayor Beame in the chief of detectives' office.

Following the interrogation Coffey led a motorcade of cars to the 84th Precinct, where Berkowitz was booked for the murder of Stacy Moskowitz and the attempted murder of Robert Violante. The precinct was in chaos, with cops, reporters, and photographers all fighting for a look at Son of Sam. Coffey remembers having to stop Deputy Commissioner McLaughlin from punching an overly aggressive photographer. Finally, he found a quiet phone and called Pat to tell her it was all over.

Joe believes that had Berkowitz not pleaded guilty but gone to trial, either pleading insanity or innocence, he might have beaten the case. Following the arrest, the criminal justice system behaved like Keystone Kops. District attorneys argued about who would prosecute, detectives who had little or nothing to do with the Son of Sam murders negotiated with Hollywood producers, and reporters wrote books in a weekend.

For a month the men of Omega force could not buy a drink in Queens. They were the toast of the city and were eventually rewarded. Twenty-five who played a role in the case were promoted. Dowd was raised to deputy chief and Borrelli, starting on his path to chief of detectives, was raised to deputy inspector. Because a sergeant cannot normally be promoted to lieutenant without taking a civil service test, Joe Coffey was provided with a loophole in that rule. This allowed him to receive lieutenant's pay, about a $5,000-a-year raise. Power, Conlon, Moscardini, O'Connell, and Marlin Hopkins, who had played a crucial role in the beginning of the manhunt, were also rewarded with promotions and raises.

There was a lot of infighting over who would get promotions. The mayor wanted the task force men rewarded. Commissioner Codd, who had little love for detectives, insisted uniformed cops also be included in the rewards. The two police officers who could not remember giving the ticket to Berkowitz's car were promoted to detectives.

Coffey has few regrets about the way the manhunt for Son

of Sam was handled. Given the fact that the killer was in-sane, there was probably no deductive way to figure out his next move. Catching him in the act still seemed like the best course of action.

After the commotion died down, Joe went to the 45th Pre-cinct to see what he might have found if he continued his auxiliary background checks. Nothing in the file would have indicated Berkowitz was a suspect. In fact, Coffey's attitude might have been just the opposite. In Berkowitz's file was a letter of commendation from Police Commissioner Michael Codd, praising Berkowitz's volunteer work. Joe Coffey was ordered to destroy the letter.

Detective Sergeant Joseph Coffey.

Joseph Coffey, Sr. and Margaret Coffey.

Frankie DePaula and Joe leave DA Hogan's office. Shortly thereafter DePaula was rubbed out because the mob thought he was an informant. He wasn't. (N.Y. *Post*)

Joe relates the events leading up to the cracking of the Ladenhauf case.

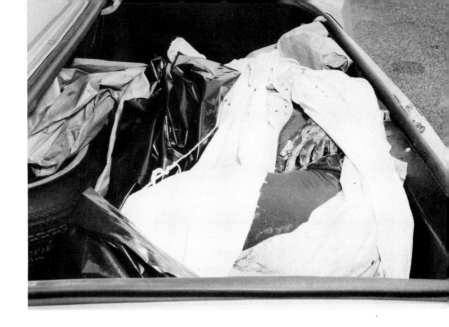

Leo Ladenhauf's body as found in the trunk of his car at LaGuardia Airport.

Carmine Galante after lunch at Joe and Mary's, July 12, 1979. Galante's murder was believed to be a mob hit.

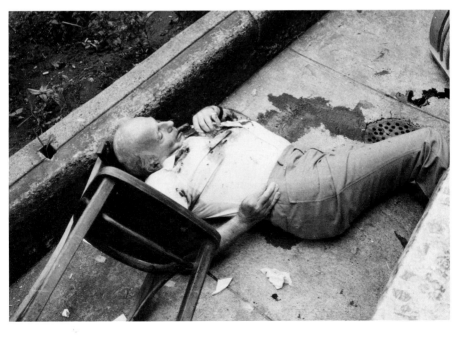

Joe Coffey and Chief of Detectives James Sullivan (seated). Assistant Chief of Detectives Frank Sullivan and the Coffey Gang.

Joe Coffey, Police Commissioner Robert McGuire, and Detective Larry Mullins (from left to right).

Monsignor Paul Marcinkus escaped Coffey's dragnet during the "Vatican Connection" case. Marcinkus received immunity from prosecution from the Italian government. (AP/Wide World Photos)

Italian financier Michele Sindona behind the bars of the defendant's cage in a courtroom in Milan. Sindona, who was imprisoned for his involvement in the "Vatican Connection" case, was later murdered while in jail. (AP/Wide World Photos)

Guns recovered from the mob as a result of "Operation Clyde." Kenny "The Rat" O'Donnell was the informant who set up the operation.

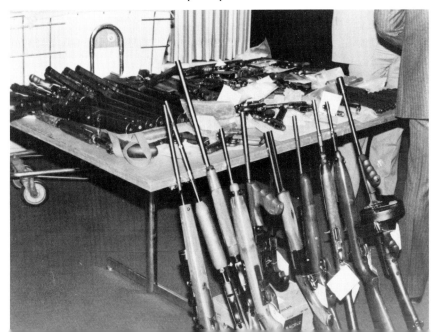

Rudolph Guliana, the man who had the guts to take on the don's of New York's five families. Joe's participation in the Ruling Commission case capped his career. (AP/Wide World Photos)

Frank (Funzi) Tieri, reputed boss of the Vito Genovese crime family, being taken from FBI headquarters in 1973. He entertained Joe on the porch of his house. (UPI/Bettmann)

The Son of Sam Task Force Omega. Joe served as supervisor. Captain Joe Borelli is on Joe's left. To the right of Joe is Task Force Commander Timothy Dowd.

David Berkowitz a.k.a. Son of Sam. (AP/Wide World Photos)

Joe served as a perimeter guard for Nancy Reagan and was asked to dance by the First Lady. He said, "Yes" and the Secret Service had a fit. (AP/Wide World Photos)

Pope John Paul II at Yankee Stadium in October 1979. Joe keeps a watchful eye. (Doug Malin)

Joe escorting Joe Frazier back to his dressing room after the first fight with Ali, March 1971.

John Gotti, reputed successor of Paul Castellano as Godfather, has been arrested by Joe Coffey three times. (AP/Wide World Photos)

· VII ·
THE
RAT
SQUAD

During the winter of 1982, when the Coffey Gang was in the fourth year of its original thirty-day assignment, the U.S. Attorney's Office for the Southern District of New York was involved in an investigation of a stolen car ring. The ring had a distinctive specialty: it stole luxury cars and shipped them to the Middle East where they were resold on the black market at enormous profit.

The federal investigation into this operation was pointing increasingly towards the involvement of New York's Mafia families in the racket. The Gambino family, specifically, controlled the locations where most of the Mercedes Benzes, BMWs, Jaguars, and Cadillacs were stolen, including the parking lot at Kennedy Airport and the surrounding streets, as well as the garages of Howard Beach, Queens.

After some minor alterations to serial numbers and maybe a fast paint job, the cars were driven to ports in Brooklyn and New Jersey, deposited on freighters, and shipped to the Middle East.

When it became clear to the investigators that the Gambinos were behind the scheme, U.S. Attorney John Martin called New York Police Commissioner Robert McGuire and requested the help of his specialized units.

After huddling with Chief of the Organized Crime Control Bureau Dan Courtney, McGuire agreed to the assignment of Lieutenant Jack Ferguson to supervise detectives from the Auto Crime Unit who would be assigned to the U.S. Attorney's Office.

It was also agreed that because of a number of homicides apparently attributed to the car theft ring, Joe Coffey would set up shop at Martin's office, in a smaller building a short walk across the plaza from Police Headquarters. Another expert detective who was being assigned to the new operation was Ken McCabe. He had spent much of his career chasing the Mafia in Brooklyn and was an expert on the Gambinos.

The highly regarded assistant U.S. attorney Walter Mack, chief of the federal Organized Crime Strike Force, was put in charge of the expanded unit.

Joe was elated about the prospect of working with such an elite team. He had followed the stolen car ring investigation as best he could without official involvement. He suspected the ring was the work of the Gambino family and thought it might provide a route to bring down Paul Castellano. As usual, he was thinking big. He knew he could clear several homicides with information already compiled by Mack and his men.

He was also happy about the chance to once again work with Ferguson, whom Joe considered one of the best men working in the New York Police Department. The two had shared a couple of cases two years earlier that had almost cost an undercover agent his life and had come close to ending Joe Coffey's career in disgrace.

It began in February 1980, when Joe got a call from two

detectives who had worked under him on the Son of Sam case. They said they had a present for him and set up a meeting for later that evening.

Joe had learned by now never to attend any kind of meeting, even with two cops he knew and had no reason not to trust, without a member of his team with him. So with a new member of the Coffey Gang, Sergeant Harry Sakin, in tow, Coffey met detectives Ron Marsenison and Richey Paul at a restaurant called T.T.'s Cellar in midtown. It was a favorite watering hole of FBI agents assigned to New York.

Coffey and Sakin arrived first and took a table near the back of the restaurant. Coffey hoped he did not run into any federal agents he knew. He had little regard for the agency, agreeing with the New York cops' definition of their acronym as "Famous But Incompetent."

"It's not that the bureau wasn't capable of good work. Their record proves they were. But most local cops did not like working with them," Coffey says. "We used to say streets were named after the FBI—One Way. They took all they could get from us and offered very little in return."

Joe still harbored resentment of the bureau's foot-dragging in the Vatican case, and around this time he was reliving that experience as the primary source for a book on the subject. As years passed he grew more and more convinced that if the FBI had been more aggressive, Archbishop Marcinkus would not have escaped justice.

When Marsenison and Paul showed up they had a seedy, nervous-looking man with them. He was the kind of character veteran cops look at and classify as a "criminal type."

The detectives noticed the look of displeasure on the faces of sergeants Coffey and Sakin, who did not like unscheduled appointments with "criminal types." In response to the greeting, Paul agreed to sit alone at the table with the unknown guest while Marsenison took Coffey and Sakin to the bar to explain what was going down.

"Look fellas, don't get the wrong idea. I think you're going to like this guy," Marsenison told the two sergeants.

"His name is Kenny O'Donnell and he's been a reliable informant for us and the Bronx DA's office for years. He's very wired into the wiseguys."

Coffey and Sakin had the same thought. "If he's so good, why are you giving him to us?" they asked simultaneously.

Marsenison explained that O'Donnell had been living in Florida after helping the Bronx DA make a big case. But his money had run out and he was looking for some action. O'Donnell was one of those people who thrived by living on the edge of death. He was currently involved with some Brooklyn wiseguys and was willing to rat them out. He had some information Marsenison thought Coffey's gang could use.

Coffey and Sakin both trusted Marsenison, and they agreed to return to the table to interview O'Donnell.

"I remember that as I sat down O'Donnell even *looked* like a rat. From that moment on I always referred to him as Kenny the Rat," recalls Coffey.

Back at the table Marsenison introduced O'Donnell to Coffey and Sakin. No hands were offered in greeting. For a second or two there was a cold silence. Joe Coffey had little respect for informants and the message his eyes delivered made that clear to O'Donnell.

O'Donnell was nothing if not streetwise. He realized that if he did not break the ice, Coffey and Sakin might sit there all night and not say anything. With a nervous stutter he offered: "I—I can give you some of the top—some of the top wiseguys in the city."

"Who and what for?" Joe responded, judging O'Donnell to be a scam artist looking for a meal ticket.

His hand shaking as he lifted a scotch on the rocks to his lips, O'Donnell mumbled the names of several mob loan sharks. The men were well known to both Coffey and Sakin.

"We figured the Rat was into shylocks and wanted us to pay them off for him in return for some information that might or might not be important," Coffey says. "That was not an unusual arrangement to have with a stool pigeon, but

I was interested in hit men, not shylocks. I told him we weren't in the habit of buying a pig in a poke and would not reach for the department's wallet for every asshole who comes along with a good story."

O'Donnell began whining. "Please, Sergeant Coffey. I swear I'm telling the truth. Give me a lie detector test."

Joe had learned over the years that most professional stoolies can beat the lie detector because they are such practiced liars. To himself he thought, "I'll give this guy a lie detector test when we go back to the rubber hose in the interrogation room."

He had a better test in mind—the kind of test listed only in the textbook of Coffey's Martial Law. "Here's what we'll do," he told Kenny the Rat. "I want you to wear a wire and go up against one of the top mobsters in the Bonanno family and prove by actual conversation with him that you were shylocked by him."

"I'll do it. No problem," O'Donnell quickly agreed. A second later, when Coffey told him who the target would be, he was sorry.

"I want you to meet Al Embarrato and have a conversation with him that verifies what you have told us."

Embarrato, who was also known as Al Walker, was one of the most vicious loan sharks in the city. His patience with a nonpaying customer ran out much faster than other loan sharks', and his methods of collecting were distinguished by their brutality.

But to everyone's surprise O'Donnell pulled his weight. He set up a meeting, the time and place chosen by Embarrato. It was high noon on the street in front of the Veterans Administration Hospital in Bay Ridge, Brooklyn.

O'Donnell had borrowed money from the shylock in the past and wanted to borrow again. Standing on the street corner he asked Embarrato for $2,500. Embarrato did not hesitate. He reached into his pocket for the large roll of cash he always carried and peeled off twenty-five hundred-dollar bills, the standard small change of the Mafia.

The wire O'Donnell was wearing recorded the following exchange:

O'Donnell: I appreciate this, Al. Thanks for meeting me.
Embarrato: What's a friend for?
O'Donnell: I could have met you downtown if you wanted.
Embarrato: No, this is good. There's no eyes here that I don't know.
O'Donnell: Twenty-five is good if it's all right with you. I don't want to put you out.
Embarrato: The only way you put me out is if I don't see you every Friday with the juice. Then I put you out [laughs].
O'Donnell: You can count on me, Al. I ain't no deadbeat. You can ask anybody.
Embarrato: I already did. I want to see you every week. No exceptions. You capice?
O'Donnell: Anthony vouched for me with you.
Embarrato: See you next Friday.
O'Donnell: Thanks. Thanks, Al.

Embarrato's part of the conversation, all recorded on O'Donnell's wire, was eventually enough to put his loan-sharking crew out of business.

A few days later O'Donnell called Coffey and told him he could deliver into his hands a major gunrunner operating in Queens. Based on his success with Embarrato, Coffey agreed to set up an operation.

The target was a wiseguy named John Santora, a Colombo crime family soldier who earned his living by hijacking shipments from Kennedy Airport and selling the stolen goods to the highest bidders. Sometimes the goods were guns being shipped to legitimate dealers.

Coffey agreed to go after Santora as a means of breaking into the larger problem of the pilferage at Kennedy. Wearing a wire, O'Donnell paid $300 to Santora for a handgun. The same day, now knowing the possibility of nailing Santora and his associates was real and knowing a gun-buying operation would eventually strain the NYPD's resources, Coffey called Joe Kelly, the Group Supervisor in New York for the Alcohol, Tobacco and Firearms Division of the Treasury Department.

O'Donnell also had made contact with another gun dealer who said he could provide silencer-equipped machine guns. Each would cost $1,350. There was no way the NYPD, which was always strapped for money to spend on undercover assignments, was going to put up that kind of money, but Kelly, at ATF, agreed to split the cost for the purchase of ten such machine guns.

The Coffey Gang had passed on a great deal of information to Kelly during their investigation of the Irish Mafia, and Kelly had not forgotten those days. For the next few months O'Donnell led the Coffey Gang, now supplemented by the federal agent and his contacts, into all the dark alleys ruled by the Mafia. Coffey was building cases for units throughout the police department. Narcotics, vice, robbery, and his own homicide detectives were all profiting from the fearless work of Kenny the Rat. Joe realized that the number of cases being originated by O'Donnell was becoming more than his unit could coordinate alone.

He decided to call in another old friend and trusted ally, Lieutenant Jack Ferguson, commanding officer of the NYPD Investigative and Analysis Unit of the Organized Crime Control Bureau. Ferguson was the only other officer in the department who, like Coffey, reported directly to a three-star chief. Ferguson's boss was Dan Courtney, head of OCCB. Like Joe, Ferguson also spent almost as much time fighting off the green-eyed monster as chasing crooks.

Courtney agreed to have his men enter the case. Their knowledge and experience in dealing with all levels of organized crime was invaluable. They could quickly analyze O'Donnell's tips and help him decide in which direction to move.

Beginning in October 1980, Kenny the Rat started testi-

fying before a grand jury in Brooklyn about the information
he and two undercover agents, whom he had helped place
in the mob, had been gathering. The testimony was being
used to prepare the indictments that would support a major
roundup of highly placed mob figures. The project was
dubbed "Operation Clyde."

Joe Coffey and the undercover agents—Joe Lemondola, a
New York detective, and Dominick Polifrone, a U.S. treasury agent—also gave lengthy and detailed testimony to the
grand jury.

A few days after the grand jury began hearing the testimony, Joe and Jack Ferguson were having a drink in a gin
mill near Police Headquarters. Joe's beeper went off. He
called the Coffey Gang's office and was told an FBI agent
out on Long Island named Larry Sweeney urgently needed
to talk to him.

Within minutes Coffey got Sweeney on the phone. "Joe,
do you have an informant named Kenny testifying for you
right now?" Sweeney asked.

"How do you know that?" Coffey, instantly alarmed, shot
back.

The agent explained that he had an extremely high-level
informant of his own who was told by a mob friend about
an inside source who was keeping him apprised of something called Operation Clyde. Sweeney knew enough about
Operation Clyde to figure Joe was involved in it.

"They're waiting for this guy Kenny to show up at Anthony Spero's club. They've dug a grave for him in the basement," Sweeney said.

Coffey's sense of alarm increased. Spero was a loan shark
O'Donnell was currently trying to nail. Joe knew the Rat
was going to Spero's club that evening.

"Sweeney, you've got to help us identify that source,"
Coffey said, fighting to keep his composure and trying not
to reveal his surprise that an FBI agent was making such
an effort to help a local cop.

"Look, you don't have to tell me how important it is. I'll do all I can," the agent said.

Joe registered in the back of his mind that he owed Sweeney one as he slammed the receiver down and dialed the number where he knew O'Donnell could be warned. Frank McDarby and John Meyer were babysitting the informant in a house on the grounds of a state mental facility on Long Island. The Coffey Gang, which had used the safe house many times, called it 10 Downing Street. Joe prayed the three had not yet left for Spero's.

McDarby answered the telephone. "Frank, get the Rat out of there fast," Joe barked. "I don't even want to know where you bring him. Just go for deep cover *now*."

Without waiting for a response from McDarby, Joe hung up and went back to the bar to get Ferguson. Together they returned to the telephone and called Joe Kelly. They told him to bring the two undercover agents in from the cold. Next they called Chief of Detectives Jim Sullivan and Chief of the Organized Crime Control Bureau Dan Courtney and briefed them on the problem. Two undercover agents were in peril.

After the call to Courtney the two cops stood around the pay phone for thirty minutes. Joe chain-smoked. When the telephone rang, Joe grabbed the receiver. It was good news. Kelly's office reported that the two undercovers had been contacted and had fled to safety. A few minutes later the phone rang again. This time it was McDarby saying O'Donnell had been taken to an apartment on Governors Island, the Coast Guard base in the middle of New York Harbor. He would be safe there until Operation Clyde wound up.

That crisis over, Coffey and Ferguson turned their attention to the dangerous source of the leak. They reasoned it had to be coming from the Brooklyn district attorney's office, which had entered the investigation to prepare the case for the grand jury. Coffey called the chief of the DA's Rackets Bureau and the assistant DA who was handling the case. He asked them to meet him at Police Headquarters pronto.

The two attorneys were briefed on everything except where Coffey learned of the leak.

Three hours after their first conversation, Sweeney once again contacted Joe. This time he was able to tell him who the leak was. "My man says it's an assistant district attorney in Brooklyn," Sweeney said.

Coffey immediately called the two attorneys who had just left the meeting at Police Headquarters. He told them to meet him and Ferguson in a bar in Queens. It was a place Joe often used for high-security meetings. He knew the owner would provide him with a private back room and would watch his back.

An air of doom hung over the back room as Coffey and Ferguson told the Rackets Bureau chief and the young assistant DA what FBI agent Sweeney had revealed.

"I knew it. I knew it," the assistant blurted out before Coffey even finished.

With tears welling up in his eyes, he told the three men about another young assistant district attorney he carpooled with. He verified how the other man was always pumping him for information about the case. He wondered why he was so interested, but he never thought he might have such an evil motive.

The three veteran investigators soothed the younger man, telling him that he could not have known what was going on but that it should be a lesson to play everything close to the vest. All agreed the facts should be reported to the special state prosecutor for corruption. Coffey and Ferguson also decided to wind up the investigation as quickly as possible, as Kenny the Rat's cover was surely blown.

The next day, with the encouragement of the special prosecutor, a trap was set for the traitorous assistant DA. The young assistant who was feeling so guilty was given the chance to redeem himself. Coffey and Ferguson gave him a phony story about an impending indictment of a top mob boss to plant with his friend the next time they carpooled.

He would wear a wire to record the fact that he passed on the indictment information.

Within twenty-four hours Sweeney was told of the phony indictment by his informant. He, in turn, passed on the good news to Coffey and Ferguson.

With that accomplished, the special prosecutor agreed to go after the crooked assistant DA. As much as he wanted to personally strangle the traitor, Joe decided to put the incident out of his mind until he had completed Operation Clyde.

Finally, on the evening of November 1, 1980, a force of 150 agents and NYPD detectives was gathered in the auditorium of Police Headquarters. They were there to take part in a unique operation built almost solely on the information supplied to the NYPD and Joe Kelly's ATF agent by Kenny "the Rat" O'Donnell and analyzed by Ferguson and Coffey. The force was turned out to track down and arrest fifty Mafia figures as part of Operation Clyde.

Before the night was over they had knocked in doors to private social clubs, raided gambling parlors, and served warrants at the homes of suspects. By the next morning all fifty wiseguys, members of the Colombo, Genovese, Bonanno, and Gambino families, were locked up on charges ranging from criminal possession of stolen property to drug dealing to selling machine guns equipped with silencers. Kelly ended up laying out more than $50,000 in ATF funds to help create the traps.

Not a shot was fired or a punch thrown in anger by the arrested suspects. In the mob's usual style when apprehended by an honest cop, they went peacefully and relied on their capos and lawyers to get them out of jail on bail as soon as possible.

Kenny the Rat was the only person connected to the operation who was physically injured at all. He did not like being cooped up in the Governors Island apartment while all the action was taking place across the bay. He began whining to McDarby and Meyer that he wanted to take the ferry to Manhattan for a little nightlife. Several times he started for the door only to be stopped in his tracks by an icy stare from McDarby. But the Rat was nothing if not persistent. The two cops later told Coffey that the only way they could keep him quietly in the apartment was to knock him out. On his umpteenth try for the door O'Donnell was stopped by a left hook from Meyer.

The next morning as the hoods arrested in the "Godfather Roundup," as the press was calling Operation Clyde, were being arraigned, Kenny "the Rat" O'Donnell was spirited off Governors Island by U.S. marshals and placed in the Federal Witness Protection Program.

Joe was relieved Kenny was tucked safely away in the federal program. He reluctantly had to admit he had grown to like the informant since their first meeting. Usually he held all informants in disdain, but O'Donnell was the best he ever met and there was a certain likability in his eagerness to please and take on the most dangerous cases.

He was at his desk, surrounded by paperwork, about two days after the operation when he got a call from his old friend in Internal Affairs, Richard Condon.

Condon, who would one day become police commissioner, was at the time assigned as chief investigator for the special prosecutor. He was working on the case of the assistant DA who almost blew Operation Clyde. He did not call with good news.

He told Joe that the Brooklyn district attorney, Eugene Gold, who five years later would be charged with being a child molester and would move out of the country in disgrace, informed the corrupt assistant about the investigation against him before charges could be brought.

The assistant denied everything, and Gold was standing behind him.

"Joe, we want you and Ferguson to question the kid before we decide whether or not it is worthwhile to continue," Condon said.

The next day the two cops questioned the young assistant

for three hours. They grilled him as they would a Mafia hit man, saying they had a tape of him being told about the phony indictment. They told him they had a highly placed mafioso who had given him up.

In spite of the gathered evidence and the hostility of Coffey and Ferguson, the young man, knowing how the criminal justice system worked and how to beat it, denied everything. The next day they were informed that the case against the assistant DA would not be prosecuted. His career was over, but he would not face criminal charges. Coffey and Ferguson were livid over the decision.

"If that had been a cop they would have cut his balls off. It was a matter of a bunch of lawyers taking care of their own," he remembers feeling.

Together he and Ferguson tried to get the police department's Internal Affairs Division (IAD) to pick up the case. But their persistence began to backfire. "We were pushing so hard the IAD guys began to think we were trying to hide our own guilt. They began to investigate *us*. At that point Jack and I let it go. An assistant district attorney almost got two undercover cops and a trusted informant killed, and he got away with it," Coffey says.

That was not the end of the troubles heaped upon them by the ubiquitous Kenny "the Rat" O'Donnell.

More came when a lawyer for a small-time shylock named Ciro Perrone whom O'Donnell had helped nail told a television reporter that O'Donnell had committed dozens of stickups while working as a police informant.

The reporter, without checking with the police department, went with the story and added the lawyer's implication that the Coffey Gang was sharing in the proceeds from the robberies.

The report gave ammunition to the many enemies Joe Coffey had within the police department who wanted to build a case for corruption against him. All the jealous bureaucrats and less skilled detectives envious of his close relationship with the chief of detectives used the news story to push Internal Affairs to go after him.

Deputy Inspector Roy Richter, a straightforward, by-the-book police officer, was assigned to look into the possibility that the news report was correct. Coffey knew Richter. He liked and respected him. He also knew that he was the kind of cop who conducted a thorough investigation and would not hesitate to nail any corrupt cop.

At their first face-to-face confrontation Richter was prepared to take on the Coffey Gang. "Joe, this O'Donnell fellow committed twenty-six armed robberies while working for you," Richter said. His information came from the mob lawyer who first went to the television reporter.

"Inspector," Coffey responded, "if you did your homework instead of relying on a reporter's misinformation and a bunch of jealous cocksuckers in this job, you would know that I got that information first myself, from O'Donnell."

Coffey explained that when he had first brought O'Donnell to the grand jury, he made him reveal all his past crimes. O'Donnell admitted twenty-six robberies in 1976 and 1977, long before Joe met him in T.T.'s Cellar.

"In fact, Inspector," Coffey went on, "I assigned Detective Jerry Maroney to accompany O'Donnell to all the robbery locations and tell the local precincts that the stickup man had been identified and they could clear the cases. I also told all the prosecutors involved in Operation Clyde about the possibility that O'Donnell was implicated in those robberies. I never tried to cover up a thing and I never made an illegal penny from this job."

Richter was taken aback by Coffey's defense. Joe Coffey was surely the most careful detective he had ever come across. Still, as Coffey remembers it, Richter thought he had an ace up his sleeve. He said he knew for sure that O'Donnell had committed a house robbery during the period he was working for Coffey.

Again Joe was prepared. "I know all about that also. The

morning he did it, O'Donnell called me and confessed. He said he had to do it to maintain his cover."

A smile crossed Richter's face. "That's not good enough, Joe. How can we believe O'Donnell about that?" he said.

The smile on Joe's face was bigger and lasted longer as he replied, "I guess you don't know about the tape." The morning after the house robbery, Coffey and McDarby met O'Donnell for breakfast. They had him confess to the incident on tape, including the part about trying to get in touch with the cops before the robbery. This was a fact verified by the log in the chief of detectives' office, where calls to the Coffey Gang were listed.

When Coffey finished his explanation Richter looked up from his notebook. Deliberately he placed his pen inside his jacket pocket. "Joe, I always knew you were extremely competent and possessed a high degree of integrity, but I must say I'm impressed. Consider this matter closed," he said as he snapped his notebook shut and offered his hand.

That was a narrow escape from disgrace for Joe. His enemies in the department were greatly disappointed by IAD's failure to nail him. One detective with one too many drinks in him told McDarby, "That son of a bitch always lands on his feet, but if he wasn't Sullivan's boy he'd be gone."

"Looking back on Operation Clyde I realize the best thing that came out of it, not including the locking up of fifty hoodlums, was my relationship with Jack Ferguson," Coffey says. "So of course I was thrilled that he would be a part of Walter Mack's strike force against the stolen car ring. The first day Ferguson, McCabe and I met in Mack's office and spent more than an hour rehashing the stories about Kenny the Rat and how the green-eyed monster got Richter to come after us."

Soon Walter Mack laid out his battle plan. Ferguson would concentrate on analyzing all the auto ring information so far gathered and try to link it up with either ongoing investigations or previously gathered evidence that could be used to begin a prosecution. McCabe, with his vast knowledge of everything involving organized crime, would seek some previously overlooked or not obvious areas the federal prosecutors could pursue. The Coffey Gang would run down every homicide lead developed by the entire strike force.

It soon became obvious to the team that one hood could be the link to the success of their case. His name was Vito Arena and he was known, especially to McCabe and Coffey, as a three-hundred pound slob of a stickup man and car stripper. Coffey suspected he might also be a hit man. He was unique among mafiosi in the fact that he made no secret of his homosexuality. He was a member of the crew of Roy DeMeo, a top earner in the Gambino family who reported to capo Nino Gaggi. Gaggi, a confidante of "Big Paulie" Castellano himself, and DeMeo were major-league mobsters.

A great deal of the accumulated evidence against the luxury car theft ring pointed to Arena. His name was consistently heard on wiretaps. Informants pointed to him as DeMeo's enforcer. Even two cops who were sent to Kuwait to detail the delivery of the stolen cars heard tales of a "gay hit man" who made sure there was no double cross. It was clear to the strike force members that Arena had knowledge of and had participated in both ends of the stolen car operation. He stole them, he helped ship them to Kuwait, and he eliminated anyone who got in the way.

Coffey desperately wanted to put some pressure on Arena as quickly as possible. He, McCabe, and Ferguson wanted to use Arena as a link to DeMeo and Gaggi, arguing they could continue the chain all the way to the capo di tutti capi, Paul Castellano.

The only problem was that Arena was at that time on the run. There were warrants out for him in connection with armed robberies, and he had skipped town. He was on the lam with his lover, a pathetic two-bit criminal named Joey Lee.

As Joe and his gang spread out in their search for Arena, they realized that he was a feared killer. No one would help at all. As unlikely as it seemed, the 300-pound slob seemed to have vanished. Coffey began to consider the possibility that he may have even been hit on orders from DeMeo because of the heat he was bringing down on the crew.

Then, on a Saturday night in November 1982, the gang ran into a stroke of luck, one that would have a profound impact on the Mafia in New York.

It occurred when an off-duty detective named Steve Marks, who usually worked in Brooklyn, stopped with his wife at a Long Island Chinese restaurant for a late night dinner. As he sat at the table he noticed an enormous man and a smaller unkempt younger man engaged in conversation at the counter.

The detective realized the two men were the wanted Vito Arena and Joe Lee. Prudently, Marks told his wife to remain at the table while he went to the restaurant's pay phone. He called Suffolk County police and asked for backup. Vito Arena was not the type of criminal to try to take down by yourself in a restaurant full of people including your wife.

The Suffolk County Police Department also responded professionally and prudently. As uniformed cops in patrol cars ringed the place, two plainclothes detectives came to help the Brooklyn cop. Arena never realized what was happening before a snub-nosed .38 was placed in the nape of his neck and a handcuff was on one wrist.

Within an hour after the call for backup, Arena and Lee were behind bars. The next day they were in the Brooklyn House of Detention on armed robbery charges.

The strike force was itching to get their hands on Arena, but they had no official reason, at the time, to take him in custody. Their investigation had not yet reached the indictment stage, and they had nothing but circumstantial evidence against Arena and nothing at all against Joey Lee.

By that time the gay hit man had a lawyer who made it clear the feds were not to speak to his client. "I knew we would make Arena roll over if we could just get a chance to talk to him. If we could get him to start talking, no lawyer would even bother taking his case," Joe recalls.

So Coffey, Frank McDarby, and Jack Ferguson and some of his auto crime detectives made a midnight trip to the Brooklyn House of Detention. With the help of a contact in the New York Department of Corrections they signed Arena out and brought him to Walter Mack's office in lower Manhattan.

Arena may have looked like a big dumb slob to most of society but he was wise to the ways of the underworld. He knew what Coffey wanted from him, and he knew he was in a position to deal.

"By that time we were convinced Arena would bring us to Roy DeMeo and Nino Gaggi, and the prospect of Castellano still was real, so we were ready to give the guy almost anything he wanted—even a free ride on the warrants against him," Coffey remembers.

"What do you want in exchange for cooperation?" Joe asked the hit man.

"Then he made our day; I realized we were on our way to a major victory against the mob."

"All I want is to be put in the same cell with my lover Joey," Arena responded.

The tough bunch of cops standing in a semicircle around the thug were at first stunned. Then they began giggling like school kids. Finally they cracked up. They laughed until tears ran down their faces. Not only at the vision of the enormous, hulking goon asking for his sad-faced, scraggly lover but also out of relief. Arena could have made things difficult for them. He knew that and they knew that. They all realized that they were on their way to a big score.

When Walter Mack arrived, the group had just gotten hold of themselves. They told him of Arena's request, and he quickly gave the okay. The interrogation of Vito Arena and the downfall of Paul Castellano began in earnest.

"We knew we had to move fast before the Brooklyn detectives realized we had our hands on their man. So I got to question him first. Homicide was the most serious crime to nail him with. I got right to the point and told him I wanted to hear about a murder he had committed. Right away he gave us a perfect case. A murder connected to auto crime," Coffey recalls.

Arena's first homicide story was about the time he killed a fringe player named Joe Scorney who owned a body shop on Glenwood Road in the Flatbush section of Brooklyn. The shop was often used to strip stolen cars for parts or repaint them and change the identification numbers for resale. But Arena said his boss, Roy DeMeo, thought Scorney was stripping some of their profits for himself. He told Arena to put a permanent halt to the larceny.

Arena said he and another enforcer named Richie DiNome walked into the shop and asked Scorney if they could speak to him in the back room. As Scorney walked in front of them, Arena took out his .25 caliber pistol and shot the auto body repairman in the back. Scorney was a big, strong man and the force of the bullet only knocked him to his knees.

"He turned around and screamed at me, 'What the fuck are you doing?'" Arena told Coffey, as a tape recorder captured every gory detail.

"I'm killing you, motherfucker!" Arena said he yelled back as he shot Scorney a second time, killing him with a bullet in the head.

Coffey wanted more. He wanted physical evidence. "What did you do with the body?" he asked.

Arena continued his story as he gobbled down huge amounts of pizza and hamburgers.

"We stuffed him in a 55-gallon drum. But his head kept sticking out, so DiNome took a shovel and chopped his head off. We put it next to the body and then filled up drum with cement," Arena said.

Noticing the puzzlement on the faces of the surrounding cops and obviously enjoying all the attention and free food, Arena explained that it was easy to chop someone's head off.

"The head comes right off," he said. "The hardest part of the body to cut off is the arm. It's hell to cut through the elbow area," he offered.

Arena continued that he and DiNome lugged the now heavy oil drum out to a pier in Shirley, Long Island, and dumped it in the Great South Bay.

The following day Coffey took a contingent of detectives to the exact spot. Scuba divers were sent under the water to search for the barrel.

On their first dive they found eight 55-gallon drums and a piece of bone they believed was human. They checked each barrel. Choosing the heaviest one as their target, they ordered a tow truck and lifted it from the water.

The drum was taken to the office of the Suffolk County medical examiner, where detectives using a hammer and chisel broke through the cement to discover the body of Joe Scorney. His head was still jammed in next to his shoulder just where Arena said he placed it.

"Vito Arena was the most despicable character I ever met. But he sure did the people of New York a service, once he started singing," says Coffey.

Day after day, Coffey sat feeding Arena french fries and pizza, and the hit man sang his songs. He loved to give details of how he cut bodies up, explaining how he once cut a man's testicles off and laughed as they rolled across the room, "like two white marbles."

He told the cops about a house in Brooklyn where victims were brought to be executed and dismembered. It was a house of horrors, and hardly a day would go by without a poor soul being brought in to be murdered by the sadists who were part of Roy DeMeo's crew. DeMeo, Arena said, would even drink the victims' blood.

Arena related that although he had nothing personally to do with it, he knew that Paul Castellano's own son-in-law, Frankie Amato, was executed in that house. The disappearance of Amato was indeed a mystery to organized crime watchers at the time. Eventually Arena gave Walter Mack's strike force information on twenty-five murders.

In August 1983, while Arena was singing his song, Richie DiNome, the killer who had stuffed Joe Scorney's head into the barrel, was the victim of a shotgun attack outside his house on Staten Island. He was shot because DeMeo mistakenly believed he was cooperating with Coffey. Miraculously he survived, spending six months in the hospital and at home recovering. All that time Arena continued to eat and sing, sing and eat. In February 1984, when he was fully recovered, Richie DiNome was ambushed again. This time he died.

The second attack had a profound effect on DiNome's brother Freddie, a thug who often worked as Roy DeMeo's chauffeur. Freddie thought that because his brother had survived the first attack, DeMeo would let him off the hook. He misread the Mafia code of "honor." In revenge he contacted Ferguson and Coffey and said he wanted to make a deal. It was agreed that if he cooperated he would be placed in the Witness Protection Program.

"I found a great irony in all this," Coffey states. "For decades people thought the Mafia survived because its members refused to cooperate with authorities. That was always true of the higher echelons, and until Joe Valachi opened the door on La Cosa Nostra in 1963, it was even true of the low-level guys. Now here I was running a Rat Squad with Vito Arena and Freddie DiNome, and they were doing great damage to the Mafia."

Freddie DiNome turned out to be as important to Coffey and Ferguson as Arena. He told Ferguson about how he performed the driving duties for DeMeo. He said he would often take his boss to Castellano's home, where he would drop off hundreds of thousands of dollars from the auto-theft, gambling, and loan-sharking rackets the Nino Gaggi crew was running.

He reported that once a week he would drive DeMeo to the corner of 57th Street and Eleventh Avenue in Manhattan, where he would meet a representative of the Westies. The Westie would hand over a paper bag filled with money—tribute the Irish thugs had to pay to Castellano in order to be allowed to operate their own illicit businesses.

DiNome said the money would sometimes be passed in the entrance of the building that occupied that corner—the building that contained the New York headquarters of the Drug Enforcement Administration.

Coffey realized that DiNome directly connected the activities of the Gambino family to the Westies. That was something he had been trying to prove for years, since he had arrested Jimmy McElroy for the murder of Billy Walker. Then DiNome recounted a murder that Arena had mentioned and that Coffey wanted desperately to solve. He told about the night he and several other members of the DeMeo crew hid in the house of horrors in Brooklyn. As an aside he mentioned that the house was owned by a low-level soldier named Joe Gugliamo, something Arena did not know.

The night he was referring to, the target was told to come to the house to assist in the murder of another man. But as soon as the target came through the door, DeMeo stabbed him in the heart with an ice pick and dragged him to the bathtub. The blood was drained from his body, with DeMeo pausing to taste it, and then the victim was cut into pieces, which were stuffed into a green plastic garbage bag. The bag was taken to Coney Island and, in the shadow of a broken-down pier, dumped into the Atlantic Ocean. DiNome said the murder was directly ordered by Paul Castellano. The victim was his son-in-law Frank Amato. He was murdered because "Big Paulie" believed Amato's womanizing was the cause of his daughter's miscarriage.

For his valuable singing, Freddie DiNome was granted his wish to enter the Witness Protection Program. Eighteen months later he was ordered to meet Ken McCabe in a motel in San Antonio, Texas, to help prepare a murder case. When McCabe arrived, he found the canary hanged from a pipe in the bathroom. He was evidently a victim of his own autoerotic sexual deviation.

Vito Arena also got his wish. He and Joey Lee lived happily under the protection of the Witness Protection Program, until March 1991, when Vito was killed trying to hold up a Houston supermarket.

About one year after their first meeting in Mack's office the strike force was turning up the heat on the Gambino family. Roy DeMeo was one of the first victims as the various capos began to panic. On January 10, 1983, DeMeo, the street leader of the Nino Gaggi crew, was murdered himself because it was believed he was singing to the feds. Not long after De-Meo's demise, Mafia hood Joseph Gugliamo, owner of the house of horrors, apparently met a similar fate for a similar reason. He disappeared off the face of the earth.

There was a lot going on, but Joe was worried that once again he was going to see a big fish slip through the net. Nailing Gaggi was not going to be hard. A jury would see him and his crew for what they were—thugs willing to murder to achieve their goals. DeMeo was dead, but the sadist was just a follower anyway. Joe wanted to see Castellano take the fall. Freddie DiNome's information provided a direct link to Castellano and the operations of Gaggi and the DeMeo crew. He described how the dirty money got into the godfather's hands. He even told of a murder carried out directly on Castellano's orders.

It was long shot to nail Castellano on a case built primarily on information provided by informants. The U.S. attorney for the Southern District of New York, John Martin, would have to get the clout of Washington behind him to even try. "Frankly," Coffey recalls, "I don't think John Martin would have done it. But we caught a big break."

Around the time Vito Arena was running out of murders to sing about, Martin resigned. President Ronald Reagan picked as his replacement a Justice Department lawyer named Rudolph Giuliani.

"Giuliani's appointment gave us reason to cheer," remembers Coffey. "He had a reputation as a doer. We all believed he was the one who could help us tie all the loose strings of the strike force together. We knew we had a gem who would find a way to nail Castellano in the homicide of his son-in-law and tie him in with Gaggi's stolen car ring."

Coffey was right. When Giuliani heard what Walter Mack, Coffey, and Ferguson had to offer, he agreed to pursue a RICO case—Racketeer Influenced and Corrupt Organization—which would argue that Castellano ran the Gambino crime family as a racketeering enterprise responsible for twenty-five murders, hundreds of car thefts, and a host of other crimes. It was an unusual route to take to nail a godfather, but Giuliani had confidence it would succeed.

"The evidence was all from informants like Vito Arena and Freddie DiNome," Coffey states. "It took courage for Giuliani to go to Washington and fight for the okay to go after Castellano. If he lost the trial, the Justice Department would have egg on its face. I wish someone had fought to go after Archbishop Marcinkus in 1972 the way Giuliani went after Castellano."

When word got around among the power brokers that Giuliani was going to make a move against Castellano, Roy Cohn, the lawyer with a reputation of being able to fix anything, paid a visit to the U.S. Attorney's Office.

As it was related to Coffey, Cohn had a private meeting with Giuliani and Walter Mack. He told them that he was there on behalf of his client, a legitimate businessman named Paul Castellano. "Mr. Castellano," Cohn said, "does not steal cars."

"You can tell your client that we are not accusing him of stealing cars," Mack responded. "We are accusing him of garnering the receipts of stolen cars."

"It was true," says Coffey, "that Castellano never got his hands dirty. Even when he was an up-and-coming mafioso working for his brother-in-law, Carlo Gambino, he was always the brain. But he made millions of dollars by figuring out how to make other people suffer."

On March 30, 1984, Castellano and twenty other Mafia figures were indicted by a federal grand jury in Manhattan. The fifty-one-count indictment charged them with operating a racketeering enterprise responsible for twenty-five murders, auto theft, loan-sharking, extortion, other thefts, fraud, prostitution, and drug trafficking. The cooperation of Vito Arena and Freddie DiNome provided the vital link that connected Castellano and his crime family to crimes dating back to 1973.

The investigative reports of Coffey, McCabe, and Ferguson were translated into court papers that explained that Anthony Frank "Nino" Gaggi was the capo of a crew which reported to Paul "Big Paulie" Castellano. Next in the chain of command was Roy DeMeo, who, until he was murdered, oversaw the day-to-day operations of the crew and reported to Gaggi. Their raison d'être was to generate income for Castellano.

The government was prepared to prove that they protected their criminal enterprises through murder and the bribery of jurors. On one bloody day, March 17, 1979, members of the Gaggi crew were accused of killing five drug-dealing rivals.

Most bone chilling of all, perhaps, was the charge of conspiracy to murder Frank Amato, Castellano's son-in-law. Castellano gave the order to Gaggi to kill his daughter's husband following her miscarriage because he believed the young man was fooling around with other women.

When the story of the RICO case broke in the local newspapers, Murray Weiss, a reporter for the New York *Daily News*, received a call from "a friend of Big Paulie." "Mr. Castellano is really pissed off that you wrote that part about Frankie Amato. You didn't need to do it," the caller said. There was no mention of Mr. Castellano's being the slightest bit annoyed about the other murder, drug, and weapons charges detailed in Weiss's story.

The morning the indictments were announced, Paul Castellano went to the office of his defense attorney James LaRossa. A phone call was made, and it was arranged for Joe Coffey and Ken McCabe to go there to arrest the godfather.

It was short drive from the U.S. Attorney's Office at One St. Andrew's Plaza to LaRossa's office in the shadow of City

Hall. The two cops had rushed excitedly to their unmarked car parked alongside the building. About two blocks into their trip they stopped for a red light.

While sitting at that street corner it slowly dawned on Joe what he was about to do. The youngster who more than forty years before had made a promise to himself to go after the men who tried to kill his father was about to arrest the most powerful mafioso in the world.

Paul "Big Paulie" Castellano may have considered himself a peaceful businessman. He may have lived in a mansion in a part of Staten Island shared by corporate executives and retired judges; he may have read *The Wall Street Journal* every day; but to Rudy Giuliani, Joe Coffey, Walter Mack, Jack Ferguson, Ken McCabe, Frank McDarby, John McGlynn, and the rest of the men who served in one capacity or another in the Coffey Gang over the years, Paul Castellano was a murdering sleazeball. As far as they were concerned he was about to get his *Wall Street Journal* in the library of a federal prison.

Standing in LaRossa's office waiting for the capo di tutti capi and his lawyer to join them for the ride back to the 1st Precinct, where "Big Paulie" would be booked the same way all the hookers and addicts who worked for him were, Coffey felt like he was in another world looking down on the scene. It was the greatest triumph of his career. Castellano had no Vatican walls to hide behind. He had no strange voices in the night to blame for his willingness to kill. His allies were not found among international espionage agents.

Instead Joe had Vito Arena and other slimeballs like Kenny "the Rat" O'Donnell lined up to bring "Big Paulie" down. Waiting in the wings were legions of young button men and middle-aged capos hoping their godfather would stick by the code of silence he so ruthlessly enforced over the years. If he did not, they were more than willing to take him out as he took out the capos and soldiers who threatened his own evil empire.

There was a very businesslike atmosphere as Coffey

placed handcuffs on the sixty-eight-year-old godfather. "I guess we both had a measure of respect for each other. Paulie wasn't an idiot. He asked me how Pat was, making it clear to everyone in the room we knew each other," Joe remembers. "Once you understand that Italian mob guys live only to make money it's easier to deal with them. Of course they think the only smart cops are the corrupt cops. So I don't think Paulie thought I was very smart. Of course he was the one who was in handcuffs."

As the four men walked through the lobby of LaRossa's office building, a newspaper photographer jumped from behind a column and snapped their picture.

Coffey, who was always accused of being a publicity hound, immediately defended himself to LaRossa. "Don't look at me, I didn't call them," he said.

"I know you didn't," LaRossa answered. "I did. Where could I buy publicity like this?"

The arrest of Paul Castellano was big news. The newspapers were filled with accounts of what Giuliani was going to prove. The luxury car ring, the Kuwait connection, the homicides, the murder of Castellano's own son-in-law all were stories the tabloids fought for. The picture of Joe leading the godfather to justice made the front pages.

Eventually there would be two trials growing out of Giuliani's fifty-one-count indictment, but none of the big three would ever be convicted.

DeMeo was killed on Castellano's orders because it was believed he was cooperating with Coffey and Ferguson. Nino Gaggi died of a heart attack in the midst of his second trial on the charges, and Paul "Big Paulie" Castellano was gunned down outside Sparks Steak House in midtown Manhattan December 16, 1985, in the middle of his trial in Federal Court. The Coffey Gang was not too disappointed that the mobsters died before convictions in a court of law. "They got the ultimate sentence," says Joe.

• VIII •

THE
RULING
COMMISSION

U.S. Attorney Rudy Giuliani's success in connecting
Castellano to the evil doings of the Roy DeMeo crew
through use of the RICO statute sent shock waves through
both sides of the criminal justice community.

Mob lawyers realized they had a courageous and innova-
tive new adversary in the U.S. Attorney's Office. They advised their clients that it would be much more difficult to
beat the conspiracy charges than individual murder or extortion raps. Not since Al Capone was sent away for tax evasion had the mob been forced to deal with a new twist in
society's favor.

On the other hand, prosecutors all over the country began
taking a different look at their ongoing investigations. The
idea of linking a small-time drug dealer to his capo or don
appealed as much to a sheriff's deputy in Montana as it did
to an assistant district attorney in Los Angeles.

In New York in late 1983, while indictments were still

being prepared in the auto crime case, Ron Goldstock, Director, New York State Organized Crime Task Force, figured out the way to use RICO to hit a grand-slam home run against La Cosa Nostra. Earlier in his career he had helped draft the federal RICO laws.

Goldstock was the assistant district attorney in Manhattan who, ten years earlier, had listened to Joe Coffey's first breathless report from Munich on the Vatican case. The two remained close friends throughout their careers. Joe often passed on important intelligence information to the Organized Crime Task Force.

A few weeks after the auto crime indictments were officially brought against Castellano, Gaggi, and DeMeo, Goldstock visited Giuliani's office in St. Andrew's Plaza.

With Coffey and Walter Mack in the room he stepped to the blackboard across from Giuliani's desk.

"Ron was very serious. He looked Giuliani right in the eye as he held a piece of chalk near the blackboard. He said he thought he had a way to bring down New York's five Mafia dons including Castellano in one vast RICO indictment," Coffey remembers.

Goldstock drew a circle representing a wheel on the blackboard. In the middle he drew the hub. He said the group should consider the hub to be a black 1982 Jaguar owned by Salvatore Avellino, Jr., whom Joe Coffey knew to be the chauffeur of Antonio "Tony Ducks" Corallo, godfather of the Lucchese crime family.

Next, Goldstock drew one spoke off the hub stopping at the perimeter of the circle. He said they should consider that spot the home of Paul Castellano. In reality, Coffey knew, it was a $2 million mansion on Staten Island called by its neighbors the "White House."

Then Goldstock drew another spoke from the hub to the perimeter of the circle. This spot he called the Palma Boys Social Club in East Harlem.

"At that point a thunderbolt came out of the sky and hit me between the eyes," Coffey says. "Goldstock was diagraming the three bugging operations in place at that time. His own unit had a bug in Avellino's Jaguar. The Famous But Incompetent feds had bugs in the kitchen of Castellano's mansion and in the ceiling of the Palma Boys Social Club, which was the headquarters of 'Fat Tony' Salerno, godfather of the Genovese family."

As Coffey began mulling over what all that gathered intelligence could produce, Goldstock put the finishing touches on his crude diagram. He told them to consider the perimeter of the circle to be the Ruling Commission.

The commission, organized crime experts knew, was the board of directors of La Cosa Nostra. It was composed of nine powerful gangsters including the five bosses of New York's crime families. Created in 1931 as a means of bringing a debilitating gang war to an end, its original members included such notorious hoodlums as Charles "Charlie Lucky" Luciano, Carlo Gambino, Albert "The Earthquake" Anastasia, Joseph Profaci, Thomas "Tommy Brown" Lucchese and Joseph "Joe Bananas" Bonanno.

Caught in the middle of a gang war that was not only destroying their private armies but also eating into their profits, the dons of the thirties realized they made money only when they were at peace. The commission was established as a sort of League of Nations where disputes could be ironed out without bloodshed. Unlike the League of Nations however, the commission often made rulings that resulted in the execution of troublemakers. The commission was a government within a government. It was so much like a legitimate government that its rules sometimes called for the taking of the life of a member.

At the time Goldstock was drawing circles on Giuliani's blackboard, the Ruling Commission was headed by capo di tutti capi Paul Castellano. The other members were Castellano's right-hand man, the underboss of the Gambino family, Aniello "O'Neill" Dellacroce; Genovese boss Salerno; Corallo; his Lucchese family underboss, Salvatore "Tom Mix" Santoro; Consigliere Christopher "Christy Tick"

Furnari; the Colombo family acting boss Gennaro "Jerry Lang" Langella and one of his soldiers, Ralph Scopo (who despite his low rank held a significant position); and Bonanno family boss Philip "Rusty" Rastelli, the man who ordered the murder of Carmine Galante from his cell in the Metropolitan Correction Center.

All this was known to law enforcement, and separate investigations were constantly being pursued against all the individual characters.

But on that day in Giuliani's office, Goldstock proposed to use the RICO statute to go after all of them in one vast case to prove they cooperated in a criminal enterprise which used extortion, murder, and labor racketeering to achieve its illicit goals.

Goldstock said the key to the entire case was the Jaguar tapes, more than one thousand hours of conversation between Avellino and mob leaders including Corallo recorded as they drove through the New York metropolitan area conducting the business of the Lucchese family.

Installing the bug in the first place was a remarkable piece of work performed by investigators from Goldstock's task force. For months, in the winter and spring of 1983, they followed the Jaguar, waiting for the opportunity to carry out a carefully rehearsed plan.

Then on a windy rainy night, as Avellino attended an affair at a restaurant in Huntington, Long Island, two task force members took up position outside the entrance while two others broke into the car.

Investigator Richard Tennien sat in the back of the Jaguar with a walkie-talkie, alert for word from the lookouts that Avellino was returning to the parking lot, while a task force technician removed the map light from its socket and placed a tiny transmitter behind it. Then, as he had practiced it on a similar car, the technician replaced the map light. In less than two minutes the device was installed. When they asked court permission to install the bug in the Jaguar, state attorneys argued it would be invaluable to their investigation of La Cosa Nostra. Years later Goldstock described the information it provided over an eighteen-month period as the best evidence he had ever heard in more than twenty years in law enforcement.

The Jaguar tapes contained many references by Corallo to the Ruling Commission. As Goldstock's men trailed the black car every day from Oyster Bay, Long Island, where Avellino would pick his boss up at his house, to construction sites and mob hangouts in Brooklyn and Queens, they recorded detailed explanations of the mob's control of the concrete industry. The tapes in Castellano's house and the Palma Boys Social Club also provided much evidence of extortion and labor racketeering.

One conversation between Avellino and Corallo even mentioned the fact that Giuliani had added six new investigators to his strike force. "He'd better do better than that; we added six ourselves last night," Avellino joked.

Other recordings revealed that different construction unions were considered under the control of individual mob bosses. "That one is Paul Castellano's union" was heard on one tape. On another tape a new Mafia recruit's intellect is challenged. "Does this guy really understand La Cosa Nostra?" Corallo asked. At the Palma Boys "Fat Tony" Salerno was overheard saying how much he admired a trusted capo but "I told him at least eighty times he can't sit on the commission."

One conversation in the Jaguar has become folklore among organized crime cops. Avellino was paranoid about being followed. He knew at least three law enforcement agencies were always after him and he prided himself on being able to lose their tails. One day he said to Corallo, "If they were able to follow us today, they're geniuses." Of course Goldstock's men were able to stay close enough to pick up the secret transmission.

Over the next few days, after the meeting at the blackboard, Goldstock laid all this out for Giuliani and Ken Walton, Assistant Director of the FBI in New York. All were comfortable with the fact that they could nail the commission for extortion and labor racketeering. What they needed to add to the mix was a commission-sanctioned murder. A homicide, they reasoned, would get a jury's attention and reinforce the image of the Mafia as a band of ruthless killers.

Joe Coffey was asked to suggest a case that might fit into the bigger picture. He did not have to think long. On his mind for the past four years had been the rubout of Carmine Galante. He remembered the surveillance tapes of the Indelicatos embracing Aniello Dellacroce outside the Ravenite Social Club. He said he would make that case for the Ruling Commission indictments.

Coffey's assignment to the U.S. Attorney's Office was on thin ice at that time. Robert McGuire was no longer police commissioner. Jim Sullivan was no longer chief of detectives. The new commissioner, Benjamin Ward, and the new chief of detectives, Richard Nicastro, did not share their predecessors' opinion of Joe's work.

His relationship with both men was strained, and he'd had run-ins with both at other times in his career. At one point Giuliani had to intercede through the mayor's office to keep Coffey assigned to his office during the auto crime case. Now it was again suggested that he be kept on until Goldstock's theory was played out.

Joe was too wise to the ways of intradepartmental politics to believe his special assignment or the Coffey Gang was going to survive the changes on the top floor of One Police Plaza. He decided to retire. In February 1984 Joe was approached by James Harmon, Executive Director of the President's Commission on Organized Crime, and asked to join the Washington-based unit as an investigator. He faced the certainty of a lessening of his stature in the NYPD with McGuire and Sullivan gone. In addition, his three children were approaching college age, and he needed to find a way to increase his income. He filed the necessary papers to make him eligible for retirement in July 1984.

He was elated to have the chance to help make the Ruling Commission case before he left. "I thought it would be a fabulous way to end my career with the NYPD. To bring down the commission would be the icing on the cake as far as I was concerned."

Coffey quickly threw his energies into the efforts of the strike force, which was now being headed by an assistant U.S. attorney named Barbara Jones, whom Giuliani had chosen to replace Walter Mack.

Ken McCabe agreed with Coffey's assessment that the murder of Carmine Galante in 1979 was a perfect example of a hit sanctioned by the Ruling Commission. If they could explain that to a jury, they could prove that the commission was guilty of homicide.

Joe remembered his initial investigation of the murder. He knew that the secret surveillance tapes shot by Detective John Gurnee, which showed "Sonny Red" and his son Bruno Indelicato embracing Aniello Dellacroce outside the Ravenite Social Club thirty-five minutes after Galante was hit, was proof positive of commission involvement.

Dellacroce, the Gambino underboss, sat on the commission. The Indelicatos were Bonanno family soldiers. Under normal circumstances Dellacroce would not have anything to do with them. What was needed was some way of proving through physical evidence that the Indelicatos were present at Joe and Mary's Restaurant in Ridgewood when Galante was shotgunned to death. The first time the Coffey Gang investigated that murder they were unable to come up with that physical evidence.

Coffey and McCabe went back to Joe and Mary's. They sat at the same backyard table where Galante, Leonardo Coppolla, and Guiseppe Turano had on that warm day, July 12, 1979. They had a glass of wine and discussed the clear motive for the murder—the argument at the time within the Bonanno family over Galante's desire to deal directly in drug smuggling and selling.

They knew that tapes from the Palma Boys Social Club

indicated that commission members "Fat Tony" Salerno and Paul Castellano as well as Galante's own godfather, Phil Rastelli, were concerned that Galante was out of control—what they called a "cowboy"—and needed to be brought down. They also knew that capos from the Bonanno and Gambino families visited Rastelli in jail the day before the hit and the day after.

A conversation between "Tony Ducks" Corallo and Sal Avellino recorded as they cruised in their Jaguar three years after Galante's murder proved how concerned the Mafia was about their involvement in drug dealing. On the tape, Corallo explained how federal prosecutors were able to get all the money they needed from their bosses in Washington for investigations of drug dealing. He told Avellino that the way to get the feds off their backs was to get out of the drug business.

Coffey and McCabe spent days going over the steps of the original investigators. In their minds they recreated the scene, imagining Galante, Coppolla, and Guiseppe Turano being blown out of their chairs and into the tomato garden behind their table. They wondered how John Turano was lucky enough to escape with a serious but not fatal wound. They knew he could probably help with descriptions of the hit men, but they knew he would not.

They recalled that two other men at the table, close friends of Galante's, Baldo Amato and Cesare Bonventre, were not sitting down when the hit men entered the backyard. That was a typical Mafia setup. There was no doubt that Amato and Bonventre picked the time and place for lunch that day and passed the information on to the hit men. That was standard operating procedure for the hit of a high-ranking mafioso. It was the same way Jimmy Hoffa's stepson arranged for his meeting with "Sally Balls" Briguglio in a Detroit parking lot. It was the same way "Sally Balls" was led to his own death by his mentor, Tony Provenzano, and his friend, Matty Ianiello.

They went out to the street and reinterviewed the witnesses who saw the hit men enter the restaurant and then escape in the Oldsmobile. They remembered that fingerprints lifted from the getaway car, which was found a few blocks away, had not matched any in their files.

The failure to match the fingerprints had been nagging Coffey for years, as he recalled the attitudes of the lab technicians and the precinct detectives on the case. To them it was a waste of time to even check for prints. It was the old "vermin killing vermin" philosophy that until the advent of the Coffey Gang had let so many Mafia murders go unsolved.

The two detectives decided to ask the police lab to check those fingerprints again. This time Coffey and McCabe would stand over their shoulders, representing the weight of the U.S. Attorney for the Southern District of New York, the same office that had just indicted "Big Paulie" Castellano for fifty-one crimes.

This time the fingerprint men did their work. Matches came back that placed Bruno Indelicato and a Bonanno soldier named Santo Giordano in the getaway car.

With renewed confidence, Coffey and McCabe put together a report saying that "Sonny Red" and his son Bruno Indelicato and Santo Giordano had killed Carmine Galante, Leonardo Coppolla, and Guiseppe Turano and wounded John Turano. The report said that the hit had been set up by Cesare Bonventre and Baldo Amato and sanctioned by the Ruling Commission. For proof, they would present the fingerprints, the visitors records for the Metropolitan Correctional Center where Rastelli met with the capos, the eyewitness description of the getaway car, and, most damning of all when properly explained to a jury, the tapes showing Dellacroce embracing the Indelicatos.

Circumstantially their case would be boosted by the fact that "Sonny Red" Indelicato and Cesare Bonventre had been murdered, Bruno Indelicato had narrowly escaped an attempted hit, and Santo Giordano had died in a mysterious plane crash. "Again, that was a classic Mafia scenario. The executioners rarely outlive their targets by much, and close associates are always used to set up someone of Galante's level," Coffey told Goldstock.

All their information was turned over to the strike force by early July, while Joe Coffey made plans to leave the NYPD and move to Washington.

Two days before his scheduled retirement, Joe got a call from James Harmon. Harmon said that the President's Commission on Organized Crime was expecting a cutback in funds and that they were not in a position to move forward with hiring Joe as planned. He thought things would ease up by fall and that Joe was still in their plans.

"I remember being disappointed by Harmon's call on the one hand, but on the other I was glad I would be around as the case continued against the Ruling Commission. I thought being involved with that would be the perfect way to end my career. I did not doubt Harmon's explanation for the delay," Coffey recalls. Instead he adjusted his retirement request until October.

In September Harmon called again. He told Joe that the presidential commission was about to lose its subpoena powers and that without that weapon a guy of Joe's caliber would be wasted.

"Again, I had no reason to doubt Harmon, and it looked like the Ruling Commission case was going down in early 1985, so I really was happy to put off retirement again," Joe says.

He decided to take up a standing offer to go to work for an old friend. He told Ron Goldstock that after the commission indictments he would accept his offer to be principal investigator of the New York State Organized Crime Task Force.

Over the next four months the strike force office was a madhouse. FBI agents, Coffey, McCabe, and a platoon of assistant U.S. attorneys met regularly to fit together the pieces of the Ruling Commission indictment they hoped to announce in late February.

Giuliani; the FBI's Ken Walton; Barbara Jones, who was heading the strike force; and the NYPD's Ward and Nicastro were cooperating on a level never before seen. Their agency rivalries and jealousies were put on the back burner for the sake of the biggest case ever made against the Mafia.

On February 26, 1985, the FBI handed out assignments to its agents to arrest Anthony "Fat Tony" Salerno, Paul Castellano, Antonio "Tony Ducks" Corallo, Philip "Rusty" Rastelli, Gennaro "Jerry Lang" Langella, Aniello Dellacroce, Salvatore Santoro, Christopher Furnari, and Ralph Scopo.

Joe Coffey was not sent out to make any arrests. "I did not expect my friends in the FBI to do me any favors. I was happy enough to wait at headquarters to monitor their progress. I tried just to concentrate on the importance of what was going on."

All the targeted mafiosi surrendered without a fight or an attempt to flee. It was part of their code. Joe Coffey heard it many times: "Find me, fuck me, just don't flake me." As long as they did not believe they were being "flaked," or framed, wiseguys, especially on the higher levels, did not resist arrest.

Later that day at a press conference, U.S. Attorney General William French Smith—with Rudolph Giuliani sitting on one side and FBI Director William Webster on the other, and with Ben Ward, Ken Walton, and Dick Nicastro all in view of the dozens of still and video cameras—announced that a federal grand jury in Manhattan had indicted the Ruling Commission. Smith described it as the ruling council of the Mafia's five families in New York and other American cities. Joe Coffey stood in the rear of the group as the announcement was made.

The fifteen-count indictment charged nine defendants—the five bosses or acting bosses of the New York families and four other high-ranking family members—with participating in the decisions and activities of the commission.

The commission, it was explained, regulated the relationships among Mafia families, including criminal activities ranging from loan-sharking and gambling to drug trafficking and labor racketeering. It carried on a multimillion-dollar extortion scheme, described as "the Club," which controlled the concrete industry.

The commission also authorized murders, specifically the killing of Carmine Galante and three capos in the Bonanno family who had carried out the murder.

"The commission press conference was the biggest circus I ever saw, even bigger than the Son of Sam one. Everyone was looking for a piece of the pie, and I thought there was enough credit to go around. For me it was the pinnacle of my career. I was happy to be a part of it," Coffey remembers.

Later that day Joe was called by the department's deputy commissioner for public information, Alice McGillion. She asked him if he would appear on a local television news show to help explain the meaning of the Ruling Commission indictments.

"The deputy commissioner thought it would be good to reinforce the public's impression of the role the NYPD had played in the case. It was to let people know we were still the experts when it came to fighting the Mafia. I told her I would do the show if it was okay with Barbara Jones," Coffey says. Jones told Coffey she had no objection as long as he talked in generalities about the Mafia and not about the specifics of their case.

"I did the program at about 5:30 in the evening and everything went well. The station had prepared a map of the Mafia in America, and the discussion was very general. The reporter understood I could not reveal details of the investigation at that point," Coffey recalls.

"I wasn't back in my office five minutes before Chief of Detectives Nicastro called. He ripped into me for going on the show. He said it was like my having my own press conference after the department's. I explained that my appearance had been cleared by both Commissioner McGillion and Barbara Jones.

"Nicastro made it very clear to me that he was mad and was going to hold it against me. I knew where the chief was coming from. I was Jim Sullivan's boy. Any glory I brought upon the department reflected on Sullivan and McGuire, not on Nicastro, who had his own image to protect. He had screwed me before, when he took me out of Homicide and sent me to Robbery after the Son of Sam case. I think he believed I was anti-Italian. Anyway, I sensed my glory days in the NYPD were over. I told Nicastro to go fuck himself."

The following day, February 27, 1985, Joe Coffey reported to the department's personnel division that he wanted to retire as soon as possible. It was arranged that his final day on the force would be March 20, 1985.

"That last day was a Wednesday and, despite some feelings of bitterness, I was really elated. My colleagues knew about the crucial role I played in the auto crime and the commission indictments, and everyone was patting me on the back. Reporters who were familiar with my work were quoting me, and I realized I really was an expert on organized crime. I loved it," Joe says.

For the last time that evening Joe looked around his office at One Police Plaza. The Coffey Gang was gone, most of the guys reassigned to new units. He stood for a few minutes at a corner window with a great view of the Brooklyn Bridge and lower Manhattan. He thought about a newspaper article that day which said the commission case would end like any other Mafia trial—light sentences and younger men moving into the capo roles. He thought that was probably true, except the part about the light sentences. The godfathers would probably draw at least twenty-five years.

Back at his desk he put some personal items in his briefcase, pausing for a moment to study the plastic cube with the .44 caliber bullet suspended in its center.

He decided to leave the sign behind his desk, the one with the line from Pogo, "We have met the enemy . . . and they is us," for the next guy. He always did seem to have more problems with the good guys than the bad guys, he thought.

That evening he took Pat to dinner. They planned a vacation and talked about how much Joe would enjoy working with Ron Goldstock.

Two days later Joe was guest of honor at a party thrown for him by Giuliani. It was very unusual for the feds to give a party for a local lawman and for a moment or two, as he entered the Ocean Club near City Hall, Joe wondered why he was chosen for the honor. But the thought quickly passed as Coffey was surrounded by almost every cop, federal or local, he had ever known. More than three hundred friends jammed the club, and there was a television news crew from WABC TV, where Joe's daughter, Kathleen, was working as an assistant to the news director.

Barbara Jones served as the emcee, and she struggled to get the raucous crowd to order. Joe had high regard for her. He was continually impressed by her ability to keep the commission investigation on the right track. He thought Walter Mack could have done at least as well, but Walter, like himself, was a victim of politics.

Jones made a short speech about how much she valued working with Coffey and then, in a room dominated by federal agents, including Giuliani and Ken Walton, she said that New York detectives were the best she had ever worked with and that Joe Coffey was the best of the best.

It was a rare compliment and a courageous thing for an assistant U.S. attorney who relied on the FBI for investigative manpower to say.

"Out of all the honors and pats on the back I received that night, Barbara Jones's words continue to mean the most to me," Joe says.

Giuliani spoke next and presented a plaque to Joe. His remarks were so lavish and glowing that once again that evening Joe wondered about the motive for the party. As soon as he finished speaking, Giuliani excused himself. He was riding a wave of publicity that painted him as the great-est crime buster since Elliot Ness, and he had to leave for another speaking engagement. Eventually the image born from the two RICO cases would define his run for mayor of New York City, which he was to lose by a narrow margin.

One after another Barbara Jones introduced representa-tives of law enforcement agencies Joe had worked with. They included friends from the Treasury Department and its Alcohol, Tobacco and Firearms Division; the Customs Ser-vice; the IRS; Drug Enforcement Administration, the NYPD's Organized Crime Control Bureau and Detectives' Endowment Association; the New York State Organized Crime Task Force, where Joe would soon be working; and the Federal Bureau of Investigation.

An FBI agent, Art Ruffles, was the final speaker. He was the lead agent assigned to the commission investigation. Like the speakers before him, he praised Joe as a modern-day Sherlock Holmes who was also a great guy and could really hold his liquor. But unlike the others, when he was finished speaking, he did not call Joe to the podium to ac-cept a plaque as a token of his agency's appreciation.

As the agent stepped down, his boss, Ken Walton, mo-tioned to him to come to his table. He had to pass Coffey to get there. When Ruffles went by, he leaned over and whispered into Joe's ear, "You got no plaque because of that damn book." He was referring to *The Vatican Connection* by Richard Hammer. It detailed Joe's pursuit of Vincent Rizzo and implied that the FBI had refused to follow leads into the Vatican that were developed by Joe Coffey. By the time of Joe's retirement, the book was an international best seller.

A few tables away Walton was clearly displeased with his agent. "It was because of the book and that other thing," Ruffles was heard saying.

2   Walton had the last word. "Make sure he gets a plaque,"
2 he barked at Ruffles.
2   Then it was Joe's turn to speak. When Barbara Jones

called him to the podium, the Ocean Club erupted in waves of applause and cheers. For five minutes Joe tried to begin his hastily prepared farewell speech. Twice he started to talk, only to be drowned out as the cheering and applause grew louder. By that time several gallons of booze had been consumed by the well-wishers. Quiet appreciation of his carefully chosen words was not on the menu that evening. The third time Joe tried to speak two burly detectives went to the podium and lifted him off his feet. There were tears running down his eyes as the two cops carried him to the bar. They had heard enough speeches for one night.

At the bar Ken Walton approached Joe. Coffey admired Walton's dedication and his willingness to buck bureaucracy. As much as he feuded with the FBI, he always tried to maintain a good relationship with Walton.

Walton offered an apology for not having a plaque. Coffey said he was sure it was just an oversight. "Forget about it," he said. He would not let the FBI ruin that night for him. "During the party I had come to terms with my retirement. I had reached the pinnacle of my career. There was nothing left for me to do in the NYPD," Coffey says.

The following Monday, Joe, a civilian for the first time in twenty years, joined Frank McDarby for a trip to Houston. One of the original members of the Coffey Gang, Frank had retired a few months before Joe and was making a good living doing private detective work. Joe agreed to help him out on an investigation in Texas.

McDarby's client was a huge real estate investment firm. The president of the company could not understand why his Houston office was not producing more sales. He was also suspicious that some of the cash that went through the office was being pilfered, and he was certain many expense accounts were phony.

Posing as potential clients, Coffey and McDarby realized after only one trip to the office what the problem was. Their experience on the streets of New York had prepared them well. They immediately spotted the signs of heavy cocaine use among the Houston staff. That would account for the decrease in productivity and the missing cash. It was also a motive for doctoring expense accounts as a means of getting cash for drugs.

The two ex-cops turned private eyes were a little disappointed that they found the problem so quickly. They were each being paid $500 a day, which was almost a full week's pay in Joe's last years with the NYPD. When they reported back to New York, they were relieved that the client asked them to stay on to do a complete report on who they thought the ringleader in the office might be and who the drug connection was. They eventually spent two lucrative weeks in Houston.

Back in Levittown Joe and Pat found themselves with more time together than they had in the past twenty years. They decided to go to Florida for their first vacation ever.

Joe's brother Tom owned a condominium near Boca Raton, and for two weeks Joe and Pat happily relaxed there. He was happy to see that the Florida newspapers were reporting on the Ruling Commission case. Giuliani and the New York cops were looking like heroes all over the country.

Joe was truly rested when he and Pat returned to Levittown two weeks later. Life had been easy for the past month. The demons of David Berkowitz, Archbishop Marcinkus, and the oddball collection of Mafia killers and informants were behind him, put to rest for the time being. The green-eyed monster was also at rest. His enemies within the police department could rejoice at his retirement. He was at peace with himself and anxious for a fresh start with a new boss.

The first morning home Joe drove to the local bakery for fresh rolls for breakfast and stopped at the post office, where his mail was being held while he was away.

A short time later he sat at the kitchen table going through the junk mail that had accumulated when he spotted a thick envelope from the New York Telephone Company.

"Pat, I thought you paid all the bills before we left for

Florida," he yelled to his wife, who was in the laundry room busy with the clothes left in a heap by Steven and Joseph III.

Before she could answer, Joe had the envelope open. Immediately he knew what he was looking at, and his freshly tanned face turned ashen. The telephone company was notifying the Coffeys that the U.S. Attorney for the Southern District of New York had subpoenaed a copy of the phone numbers called from the Coffey residence for the past eighteen months. Copies of Kathleen Coffey's calls were also being provided. The letter mentioned the name of the assistant U.S. attorney in charge of the investigation. Joe knew the man was the head of the anticorruption unit.

Joe Coffey was very familiar with the paperwork in his hands. It was a common practice while investigating a criminal suspect to try to find out whom he was calling from his private residence. This method was used when there was not enough cause to get an okay for a wiretap. The telephone company was required by law to provide the information to the police. The law also stipulated that the customer must be notified when the investigation was completed. Many mobsters sent to prison by the Coffey Gang had at one time or another opened similar notifications at their kitchen tables.

When Pat came in from the laundry room, she was frightened by the look on her husband's face. She noticed the telephone company letter crumpled in his fist. "Are you all right?" she asked, fearing he may have had a heart attack.

Moments of silence passed. After what seemed like an eternity Joe said, "I'm all right. I just can't believe it."

Pat poured a cup of coffee for herself and made tea for Joe as he explained what the letter from the phone company meant.

"Who wanted these records?" Pat asked.

"The FBI."

"The FBI? Weren't you just working with them?"

"Don't remind me. I was just trying to forget it," Joe answered, as he reached for the wall phone.

"Don't get excited, Joe. Why don't you call Giuliani? You always said you could trust him," Pat implored.

That's who Joe was calling. He dialed his old office number and asked to speak to Giuliani. A secretary told him the U.S. attorney was not in. Coffey then asked for Barbara Jones. He was told she also was not in. "Then get Walter Mack on the phone," Joe demanded.

The call was transferred to Mack's office. Coffey did not even give his old friend a chance to say hello. As the phone was picked up, Joe said, "Walter, it's Joe Coffey."

But Walter Mack was used to unexpected confrontations and he tried to give himself some thinking time. "Joe, how have you been? What's the matter? You can't stay away from the office?" he said.

Joe also knew how to play that game. He was not about to be put off by small talk while Mack figured out his story.

"Walter, stop the bullshit. Why have my telephone records been examined? Why was I the subject of an official investigation by the Justice Department?"

Mack knew it was time to deal with the issue. But he tried once more to avoid it. "Listen Joe, forget it. It's over. It meant nothing."

"Walter, I haven't gone senile in a month. Don't tell me it's nothing. I'm coming over to see Rudy." Then he slammed the phone down on his friend.

Driving as if he still had a light and siren on his car, Joe made it into the city in about thirty minutes, and during the trip he grew even angrier. He realized he must have been passed over for the job on Jim Harmon's presidential commission because at the time he was supposed to be hired, he was under investigation by Giuliani. While he was chasing the Ruling Commission of the Mafia, his colleagues were chasing him. He knew from his own experience that they must have even been tailing him as he drove around pursuing homicide suspects.

Coffey parked in the space reserved for U.S. marshals and barged past the lobby receptionist up to Walter Mack's office.

Again Mack asked Joe not to push. "Forget it Joe, please let it go," he said.

"Are you kidding? You think I can let something like *this* go?"

"Joe, we had no choice. Last year—July of '84—the FBI informed us that a reference to you was picked up on the bug in the Palma Boys Social Club. We had to check it out."

"That's bullshit. What kind of tape? What was on some bullshit tape?" Joe demanded.

"I'm sorry, I can't tell you that," Mack responded.

"Fuck you. What do you mean you can't tell me that? It's bullshit and you know it. Get Rudy and Barbara Jones in here."

"Joe, they are not around today. Please let this thing drop. You have some powerful enemies over there. We understand you feel betrayed," Mack said. "But believe me," he continued, "we aren't proud of what we had to do. We were working with you every day. We were taking everything you had to offer and all along we knew this day would come. We knew the FBI would have to clear you and we knew you would find out about the investigation. If it were me, you would have had to do the same thing."

Joe knew Mack was right. The Famous But Incompetents left them no choice. Now he understood why Giuliani threw the party for him and why Barbara Jones spoke so glowingly. Now he knew what "the other thing" was that Art Ruffles mumbled to Ken Walton one month earlier at the Ocean Club.

Once more Joe asked Mack to reveal the specifics of the tape. He wanted to know what was on it that could make everyone so suspicious of him.

"Joe, the only thing I can say is you made some powerful enemies along the way," Mack said.

"Yeah, I guess you're right. But it's a bitch when you think you're on the same side," Joe sneered.

With that Mack turned his palms towards Joe and said, "It's a tough game, Joe, on both sides."

That signaled the end of the meeting. Mack rose and escorted Coffey from the office. On the way out Mack asked when Joe was going to start working for Ron Goldstock. "Not soon enough," he replied. The two shook hands as Joe left the building.

About a month after he began working for Goldstock, Joe learned that the son of an old friend, Detective Ron Cadieux, who worked the Castellano case, had been killed in a motorcycle accident. Joe attended the funeral on Long Island and saw many of his former colleagues there. After the services he and Ken McCabe were talking in the parking lot when they saw FBI agent Art Ruffles and Walter Mack.

As Ruffles walked past, McCabe turned to Joe and said, "I couldn't believe the feds chased that Palma Boys thing."

"You know about that?" Joe said. "Tell me about it."

"I thought you knew. Didn't you get it from Walter Mack?" McCabe responded.

"No way. He wouldn't give me shit. Nothing but bullshit. I don't know *what* the tapes said."

McCabe told him. There were actually two references to Joe Coffey on the tapes, and both times a Genovese capo named Tony Rabito referred to the fact that Joe Coffey was with him and that he could handle Coffey.

"You've got to be kidding. You know who Rabito was talking about?" Joe said to McCabe.

McCabe did know. Everyone involved in organized crime investigations in New York knew that there was a half-assed hood in the Bonanno family named Joe Coffey. They knew that he was a two-bit mob guy who ran errands for Rabito. Because he was half Italian and half Irish he could never become a "made" member of the Mafia and he was always looked upon with suspicion by the other soldiers. Rabito was constantly in the position of defending him, and it was a running joke among the NYPD that Joe Coffey's namesake was a gofer for the mob.

"The FBI insisted on pursuing the lead," McCabe said. They wouldn't take no for an answer."

Coffey looked across the parking lot toward Ruffles, obviously furious. Ruffles noticed Coffey's glare. He walked towards Joe and said, "Calm down, I've got your plaque in my car."

"Stick the plaque up your ass," Coffey snapped back, as McCabe worked his way between the two crime fighters.

The incident once again renewed Joe's anger, and he vowed never to trust an FBI agent again.

His bitterness began to grow, and he became more and more sarcastic whenever the subject of a joint investigation with the FBI came up. In November 1985, Joe's friends from the NYPD threw a party for him at Antuns, the popular catering hall in Queens. Two hundred people showed up to honor the man who was responsible for solving eighty-two Mafia homicides. It was an interesting collection of people. There were friends from Joe's old neighborhood, under the El on Third Avenue, some of whom had walked on the other side of the law and served time in prison. His father, having lived to see his son avenge him, was there with some of his friends, labor racketeers of the thirties and forties.

There were gifts for Pat and Kathleen and more speeches and plaques. Even Art Ruffles had the nerve to get up to make a speech. This time he called Joe to the podium. Finally he handed him the plaque that he had been carrying around for nine months.

"Joe, we're sorry about what happened. Sometimes we go after the good guys," he said as the place exploded in an outpouring of loving applause and admiration.

· IX ·
THE
NEW
GANG

In the middle of May 1985 Joe Coffey reported to work at the office of the New York State Organized Crime Task Force. He felt a tangle of emotions as he drove up the Bronx River Parkway to White Plains, the suburban city twenty miles north of New York where the OCTF was headquartered.

This "city kid" felt a little uncomfortable on the tree-lined streets of White Plains. It was an affluent city where Bloomingdale's, Neiman Marcus, and Saks Fifth Avenue operated stores. It had no Little Italy or Chinatown. Instead of the hustlers and scam artists Joe was used to walking past on the way to One Police Plaza, the streets were filled with suburban housewives and small-town businessmen.

He also struggled with the bitterness he continued to feel over the treatment he received in his final days with the police department. He did not want his anger to get in the way of new relationships. Of course the parties and the

230

awards brought warm, happy memories, but he still relived the moment he opened that letter from the telephone company, and he continued to be uneasy about how two-faced he thought Giuliani was. In a sense he had much more respect for Dick Nicastro, who replaced Jim Sullivan as chief of detectives, and Benjamin Ward, who replaced Bob McGuire as police commissioner. He thought neither man liked him very much. They were understandably concerned that his loyalty would remain with their predecessors, and they did not disguise their feelings.

Coffey took some satisfaction in the fact that Nicastro, an excellent detective with a genius for coordinating large-scale investigations, continued the Organized Crime Task Force. But most of the original gang, like McDarby, McGlynn, O'Connell, and Maroney, were retired or transferred. Joe unabashedly felt that it was his desire to chase the Mafia that had been the driving force behind the success of the task force.

An official police department memorandum written by Coffey on January 11, 1983, regarding the accomplishments of the Organized Crime Task Force reported that the unit was responsible for the indictment and arrest of more than 100 members of organized crime enterprises, going on to state that the Coffey Gang directly solved fifty-two organized crime homicides.

The memorandum concludes that "prior to the formation of this Task Force . . . it was felt by some people in law enforcement that the successful investigation of gangland slayings was impossible because of certain myths perpetuated through the years. It has been shown by this group of police officers that nothing could be further from the truth."

At the time of the report, the cases had been closed in the murders of Leo Ladenhauf, Pasquale Macchiarole, Mauro Agnello, Michael Spillane, Louis Milo, William Walker, Dennis Curley, John Earle, Joseph Gallo, Irving Miller, Janice Drake, Augie Carfano, Willie Alston, John Manfredonia, Alphonse Indelicato, Dominick Trinchera, Philip

Giacone, Salvatore Briguglio, John Quinn, Sherry Golden, John Alagna, Joseph Vescovi, William Maselli, Joseph Scorney, and Patrick Dowd. These were all notorious cases covered by the media.

Coffey was welcomed warmly in his new office. He knew many of the investigators from joint operations dating back to the early 1970s when he was working in District Attorney Hogan's office in Manhattan. In those days the state Organized Crime Task Force was not taken too seriously by other law enforcement agencies. It was considered an office created in order to pay off political favors by providing jobs for cops from around the state who were on the last leg of their careers.

"The task force was a political toy until Governor Hugh Carey appointed Ron Goldstock to head it in 1981," says Coffey.

Goldstock was a prosecutor with a reputation as being eager to chase down powerful organized crime figures and capable of doing so. When he worked as an assistant district attorney in Manhattan, under Frank Hogan, he was considered the office organized crime expert. Later, while a law professor at Cornell, he helped draft the RICO (Racketeering Influence and Criminal Organization) laws that were used to indict Paul Castellano in the auto crime and murder case and then to nail the rest of the godfathers in the Ruling Commission case. Castellano had not been brought to trial yet on either of those indictments when Joe reported to White Plains. Not only had Joe Coffey been a principal investigator in those cases, but his relationship with Goldstock dated all the way back to the Vatican affair and the investigations of the Jiggs Forlano and Ruby Stein loan-sharking and gambling rings.

When Goldstock took over the task force he refused to be part of a "political toy." He began to assemble a cast of first-class investigators with backgrounds in pursuing organized crime. By 1985 when Coffey came aboard, it was the only unit in the state, except for the gang Coffey had assembled in the NYPD, with the specific mission of investigating organized crime. With Goldstock's expert leadership and investigators like the ones who planted the bug in Sal Avellino's Jaguar, the task force made itself a significant part of organized crime cases from Buffalo to Brooklyn.

Joe was determined to start fresh. No cynicism, no sarcasm would find its way out of his mouth. Sitting with Goldstock that first morning on the new job, he was filled in on the major investigation the task force had going at the time. They were deeply engaged in trying to prove that organized crime controlled the carpenters' union in New York City. The reason it cost 40 percent more to build something in New York than anywhere else in the country, Goldstock theorized, was that tribute had to be paid to the Mafia on almost every construction and renovation site in the five boroughs. The first indictments against Castellano, which included charges that the Gambino family operated a "club" that extorted construction companies and extracted a "tax" on everything from demolition contracts to laborers' jobs, barely touched the surface of the overall problem. Coffey was assigned as the coordinator of the construction industry investigation.

He would be working with Eddie Wright, another old friend from Hogan's office. Wright was the detective whose badge was stolen fourteen years earlier as he helped lead Joe Frazier from the ring the night Coffey and the guys from the DA's office protected the heavyweight against death threats.

Coffey quickly caught up on old times with Wright, and was beginning to feel at home once again. Goldstock had given him a new gang to work with, and these guys knew what they were doing. He had known for years that the Mafia controlled New York's construction industry. "Maybe," Coffey thought, "I can still hurt them, even if my office is twenty miles outside the city limits."

Wright had some good news right away. He explained that one of the task force's expert lock pickers had broken into the Bergin Hunt and Fish Club in Howard Beach,

Queens, and a "bug" had been installed in the ceiling.

Throughout his career Coffey marveled at the work of the cops who were better burglars than the mob. They consistently were able to break into and enter Mafia sanctuaries, even the kitchen of Paul Castellano's mansion, to place bugs. The bug in Jimmy's Lounge was crucial to the Vatican case, the bug in the Jaguar had become a legendary feat, and the one in the Palma Boys Social Club had almost cost Coffey his own career. He liked to tell reporters about how cheap the Mafia was. They never had twenty-four-hour security on the hangouts and never spent money on burglar alarms.

The Bergin Hunt and Fish Club, not incidentally, was the headquarters of a Gambino capo named John Gotti who was thought to be behind the mob's efforts to take control of unions with heavy membership among plumbers and carpenters.

By the end of 1985, Joe was busy with major investigations into Carpenter's Local Union No. 257 on East 25th Street in Manhattan, which had a predominantly Italian membership, and No. 608 on West 51st Street, the heart of Westie territory, which had predominantly Irish membership.

He continued to maintain an interest in the two major indictments against Castellano and the rest of the godfathers. Giuliani's office was busy preparing for trials, and Joe was often called into Manhattan to consult with the assistant U.S. attorneys. So his fears of being banished to the suburbs were pretty much behind him. He was spending as much time in the Dirty Apple as he always had.

One day in November he ran into Castellano in Foley Square near the Federal Court House. By this time the law man and the godfather had developed a kind of mutual respect. Castellano asked Joe how his family was. Joe answered politely while thinking to himself about how Castellano had ordered the murder of his own son-in-law.

The thing Joe remembered most from the conversation

was Castellano's complaining that he could not go to dinner in the area around the court house. The surrounding blocks, which bordered the area known as Little Italy, home to many capos and soldiers of the Gambino and Genovese families, contained a few of New York's best Italian restaurants. Castellano was embarrassed that the owners of the restaurants would not take his money. They treated him like some kind of godfather or something, not like the millionaire meat wholesaler he and his lawyer, James LaRossa, said he was. He told Coffey he was starting to use the uptown steak houses for his dinner meetings. There they were used to millionaires and celebrities and everyone got a check. Joe left the meeting wondering how "Big Paulie" would like the food in the Big House.

On December 2, 1985, Aniello "O'Neill" Dellacroce died of cancer at the age of seventy-two. When Joe heard about the death the next day he was disappointed that the underboss of the Gambino family, indicted as part of the Ruling Commission, had not lived to face the charges in court. He would rather see old capos die in prison.

For more than fifty years Dellacroce worked as a Mafia soldier. He rose through the ranks to capo and finally underboss. He was greatly responsible for helping La Cosa Nostra evolve from a loosely knit collection of Sicilian immigrant gangsters running illegal booze to speakeasies to the $50 billion a year hidden government Rudy Giuliani charged it was in 1985.

Before Carlo Gambino, the one-time henchman of Lucky Luciano, died in 1976 he declared that his place as don of the family that bore his name would be taken by his brother-in-law and cousin Paul Castellano. Because the Gambino family was the largest and most powerful in America, with hundreds of gunmen among its assets, its don was automatically the capo di tutti capi—the ruler of all the mafiosi in America.

The naming of Castellano angered quite a few of the long-time Gambino associates who had toiled many dangerous and evil hours for Don Carlo. They had hoped Dellacroce, the loyal underboss, would be handed the mantle of leadership. The general opinion of Castellano was that he was selfish, greedy, and not as smart as he liked people to believe. Dellacroce, they argued, was the real brains of the family. He deserved the top spot.

There was much agitation for Dellacroce to reorganize the family by having Castellano hit. His associates suggested taking by force what godfather Carlo Gambino had denied him. But Dellacroce was an old-style mafioso. He would not think of going against the wishes of his godfather. He argued with his loyal henchmen and won. In the end they listened to him. In effect he was the man who really ran the family anyway, and that would not change. "Big Paulie" needed him, and all would prosper if they just stayed cool.

Castellano did nothing over the next eight years to improve his status with the mobsters who worked for him. But they did prosper as Dellacroce continued to be the criminal mastermind Carlo Gambino had put his trust in for so many years.

But no matter how much he relied on him, "Big Paulie" always resented Dellacroce's authority and influence in the Gambino family. When the underboss died, the godfather decided not to go to his wake. He told his counselors that he was afraid it would bring too much attention to the family because he was being followed by a host of agents from several different law enforcement offices at the time.

Following Dellacroce's wake, law enforcement officials believe, Castellano contacted Jimmy "Jimmy Brown" Fialla, the long-time chauffeur of Carlo Gambino, who was a man trusted by all factions within the Gambino family. He told Fialla he would like to sit down with Dellacroce's son Armand to offer his condolences in private and suggested that Fialla set up a dinner meeting at Spark's Steak House.

The meeting was set for December 16, 1985. At about 6:00 P.M. Castellano and his driver-bodyguard Thomas Billotti pulled up outside the restaurant on East 46th Street.

As the two men got out of their car, eight gunmen who had been hiding in the shadows of nearby doorways approached from all directions.

It is unlikely Castellano and Billotti ever realized what happened. The killers opened fire. "Big Paulie" was halfway out of the car when the hail of small-caliber bullets tore into his chest and head. He was dead before he hit the gutter. Billotti actually made it to the street but never had a chance to protect his boss. The bodyguard died without doing his duty. The killers fled into the night. They would have to deal with forces that were sure to rise up against them, the same way the killers of Carmine Galante never lived to enjoy their rewards.

When he heard the news about Castellano, Coffey traveled to the scene of the crime. Art Ruffles from the FBI was there. So was Dick Nicastro, supervising the work of his detectives. Most of the talk was about how Castellano was probably better off. He would have hated dying in prison. There was also a lot of talk about John Gotti.

Reporters covering the assassination reasoned that Castellano was hit because he would not stand up to the pressure of the two trials he was facing. His mob colleagues were afraid he would sing, the columnists said, while law enforcement sources were quoted as saying that Gotti, the don headquartered at the Bergin Hunt and Fish Club, had ordered the hit so that he could take over the Gambino family before Castellano either went to jail or rolled over for the law to protect himself. Joe Coffey saw it a little differently: "Dellacroce was the only reason Castellano was alive to that day. When he died, Castellano lost his protection. There was no one else, especially not John Gotti, who was going to protect the Mafia code. No one else cared who Carlo Gambino chose as his successor. It was a sanctioned hit. The commission—'Fat Tony,' 'Tony Ducks,' Jerry Langella, and the rest—all approved it. It may be the last classic sanctioned hit in mob history. The way the Mafia in New York handled its own disputes changed forever the day Dellacroce died. There are no longer any ties to the original dons and godfathers—the guys who understood the importance of a commission. More and more families are letting their own in-fighting get in the way of making money." John Gotti, in contrast, was a cowboy. He wrote his own rules as he needed them.

A year earlier the murder of Castellano would have become the Coffey Gang's number one priority. But Joe was no longer concerned with solving only homicides. He took notes and gathered all the intelligence he could but basically filed it away for future use. Joe would continue to concentrate on the mob-influenced unions. Of course he would be happy if there were a tie-in somehow to the assassination of the capo di tutti capi, and he would not be surprised if there were one.

Over the next few months the bugs in the two carpenters' union locals in Manhattan convinced Goldstock and Coffey that it was time to press the investigation harder. The key figure, the man the tapes seemed to indicate was the liaison between the unions and the mobs that were controlling them, was John O'Connor, the business agent of Local 608, the "Irish" local on West 51st Street and Broadway. O'Connor's duties as business agent were much the same as those performed by "Sally Balls" Briguglio for Tony Provenzano. "We believed at the time," Coffey says, "that O'Connor was the bag man for the union's president, Pascal McGuiness. He visited the construction sites, made the threats, and picked up the money." McGuinness was acquitted after a trial in the Summer of 1991.

The decision was made to bring O'Connor into the White Plains office for questioning. However, because Coffey hoped to turn the business agent and convince him to rat on the mob to save his own skin, he set up a simple but effective plan to get O'Connor to the office without anyone's noticing.

O'Connor was an early riser, who usually left his home in the Putnam County town of Brewster a little after 5:00 A.M. in order to make the one-hour drive into Manhattan in time to get to the union hall when the members were arriving looking for work.

On the morning of May 5, 1986, a New York State Police patrol car was positioned on the southbound shoulder of Route 684 about five miles outside Brewster. When the waiting trooper saw O'Connor pass, he followed for a short time. Then the trooper flashed his turret lights and sounded a short blast on his siren.

O'Connor pulled over immediately, and the trooper pulled up behind. As if he was about to issue a traffic ticket, the trooper approached O'Connor. When he got to the driver's side window he issued an unusual order. "Mr. O'Connor," the trooper said, "please follow me. We're going to the offices of the New York State Organized Crime Task Force in White Plains."

Without objection, O'Connor followed the cruiser down Route 684 about twenty miles to Coffey's office.

Coffey was waiting at his desk for the union man. O'Connor seemed a little stunned by the sudden developments. He knew he was not under arrest but obviously wondered just what was going down.

"Mr. O'Connor," Joe began, "I do not want you to say anything. I do not want you to answer any questions. You have the right to remain silent. Anything you say or do may be used against you. There is something I want you to hear."

For the next three minutes Coffey played a tape recorded by an undercover agent. On it, the agent was heard offering a bribe and O'connor was heard accepting it.

When the tape ended Joe continued, "We have enough on this tape and others to send you to prison for many years. But we also know that you have more to fear from the mob than from us. We've heard them repeatedly refer to you in less than flattering terms. They are not happy with the way you run your local. They think you are ripping them off. Today is Tuesday. I'll give you until Friday to make up your mind. Join our team or you will be indicted. If you don't come aboard, we will prosecute you. What the Mafia decides to do about you is up to them."

By 7:30 A.M. O'Connor was at his desk at Local 608. It did not seem possible that anyone knew he had been talking with Joe Coffey. The first thing he did when he arrived was call a priest he knew on Staten Island. He explained to the priest that he was under great pressure. He said he needed counseling and prayers. The priest agreed to meet O'Connor for lunch the following day.

On May 7, 1986, at 6:30 in the morning, almost exactly twenty-four hours after being pulled off the road by the New York State trooper in Westchester, John O'Connor was shot five times in the back and buttocks as he entered the offices of Local 608. He was rushed to St. Clare's Hospital by a city ambulance crew. When he arrived, his condition was listed as serious but not life threatening.

"There was panic in White Plains when we heard about the shooting," Coffey remembers. "It certainly appeared it was connected to our pulling O'Connor off the road. It looked like either we had a leak in our office, which would have been a disaster, or O'Connor himself told someone about meeting me, which would have been stupid. But instinctively I felt there had to be another reason. The shooting had to be a coincidence."

The office was in chaos. Investigators telephoned their mob sources. A hurried strategy session was in progress. The shooting incident could destroy years of work, and it would almost certainly scare O'Connor into not cooperating if he thought there was a leak in the task force.

It was Eddie Wright, Coffey's old friend from the DA's office and the Frazier fight, who saved the day. Amid the chaos he walked into Joe's office with a tape casette in hand.

"Joe," he said, "I think I know what's going on with this O'Connor thing. Listen to this."

240 He played a recording made from the bug in the Bergin Hunt and Fish Club on February 7, 1986. On the tape John Gotti is allegedly talking about John O'Connor.

In preparing a case against Gotti in 1990, the Manhattan district attorney charged that Gotti was recorded saying, "Find out who this guy O'Connor is. We're gonna bust him up . . . we'll murder him."

When the tape ended, Wright shared some other intelligence gleaned from the Bergin operation. He and Coffey were able to put together a scenario that explained the shooting.

It was O'Connor's responsibility, on behalf of his union, to pressure money from the owners of the Bankers and Brokers Restaurant in the Wall Street district. The restaurant was owned by the Gambino family. The money, usually in the form of a secret tax tacked on the charges for work performed by members of Local 608, was supposed to go to O'Connor's boss, the local's president, Pascal McGuiness.

However, it was the conclusion of Wright's investigation that O'Connor was holding out on McGuiness. To retaliate against O'Connor, McGuiness ordered O'Connor and three thugs to break into the Bankers and Brokers and trash it. They did about thirty thousand dollars' worth of damage. As McGuiness expected, the action made Gotti furious. He believed Local 608 was supposed to protect his restaurant, and he knew O'Connor was being paid to make sure thugs did not break in.

"The tapes and the other information made it clear to us that Gotti was up to his neck in this shooting and in the operations of the carpenters' union," Coffey remembers.

Five days after the shooting, Coffey and Special Investigator Jim Killeen, who had also worked on the Ruling Commission case, went to St. Clare's Hospital to see O'Connor.

A nun was stationed outside the door of the intensive care unit where the labor racketeer was being cared for. She told O'Connor that Coffey and Killeen wanted to speak to him.

O'Connor's wife, who was sitting in the hallway, appeared to be on the verge of a breakdown.

"Mr. O'Connor will only speak to Mr. Coffey," the nun said when she came out of the room.

Joe went into the room. He stood at O'Connor's bedside for a few moments. Then O'Connor spoke softly. "Joe, who did this to me?" the wounded man asked.

"John, you know who did this. I told you there was trouble waiting for you."

At that point Joe remembers O'Connor began shaking, convulsing to the point that Joe was afraid he was dying. He called the nurse. As he was being cared for, O'Connor said he would accept Coffey's offer. He would cooperate.

"For eighteen months we continued to gather tapes and listen to O'Connor. He gave us plenty of information on the Irish mobsters, including McGuiness, but he would never say a word against Gotti or any other mafioso. He was just too afraid."

On a Wednesday night in February 1988 the decision was made to arrest John Gotti for assault and conspiracy including the charge he had contracted Jimmy Coonan and the Westies to shoot O'Connor. Detectives were stationed at several different locations where the capo was likely to show up.

Coffey took up position down the block from the Ravenite Social Club on Mulberry Street in Little Italy. Wednesday was "Capo Night" at the club, when the highest-level hoodlums of the Gambino family could come to pay their respects and talk business with the godfather. Coffey was sure that before the night was over Gotti would show up to hold court.

In fact Gotti was already inside when Joe, a sergeant, and two detectives from DA Morgenthau's office pulled their unmarked car to the curb.

At 6:00 P.M. they saw Gotti and a capo named Jackie Giordano leave the club. When the godfather wanted to speak privately to one of his court without fear of being bugged, he would take the capo for a walk around the block. Carlo Gambino did it, Paul Castellano did it, Aniello Dellacroce did it, and that evening John Gotti did it.

The detectives' car followed the two hoodlums down the street. Two blocks away from the Ravenite, at the corner of Lafayette and Prince Streets, Coffey, who was driving, cut the two men off as they began to cross the intersection. With guns drawn the lawmen bolted from the car.

"Stop right there," Coffey ordered Gotti. "Turn around and put your hands on the wall."

Gotti had heard those words before and knew what to do. Without protest he spread his arms and legs. Giordano, who was not being arrested, quietly slipped away. He ran back to the Ravenite to alert everyone and make sure Gotti's lawyer, Bruce Cutler, was called.

With a small crowd standing around and backup cars pulling up to the scene, Joe Coffey expertly ran his hands up and down John Gotti's arms and legs. He frisked him according to the book, patting the inside of his jacket to see if Gotti was wearing a shoulder holster. Then he ran his hands across Gotti's waist to see if he had a holster on his hip. He did not expect to find a gun. Hoodlums of John Gotti's stature usually did not carry weapons. So he was surprised when he felt something large and metallic in the front of Gotti's belt.

"Are you wearing a gun, you cocksucker?" Joe snarled. Gotti did not answer right away and Joe began to raise his fist. One of the DA's men, afraid he would be witnessing a display of Coffey's Martial Law, cautioned Joe to take it easy.

"It's only my belt buckle," Gotti finally offered. Joe backed off. He took Gotti's right arm and twisted it behind his back. Then he did the same with the left. From his own waistband he took a pair of handcuffs and placed them on Gotti's wrists.

For the time being there were no thoughts of subpoenaed telephone records, no images of crooked priests escaping justice, no green-eyed monster dogging his steps. There were no young girls on the autopsy table and no nightmarish image of a father being gunned down in the entrance to his

243

own home. For the time being Joe Coffey was once again in control of his world. He had another godfather in handcuffs.

Over the years Joe had learned to take satisfaction in the fact that he did his job well, though he knew he had little control over the twists and turns of the criminal justice system. He learned to cope with his frustration by not dwelling on past cases. As quickly as he could after putting one case to bed, he liked to turn his attention to another.

John Gotti beat the rap in the O'Connor case. It was the second major case in which he was acquitted, and the tabloids began calling him the "Teflon Don." But Joe knew the hoodlum's luck could not last forever, and his job in the state's Organized Crime Task Force offered a much broader world of crime to explore.

In January 1991 the task force issued a report which stated that New York State's construction industry was so controlled by organized crime that it was virtually impossible for an honest man to do business. The corruption resulted in New York prices being almost 50 percent higher than those in other parts of the country.

Joe Coffey was the coordinator of the team of detectives from the city, state, and federal governments whose work the report was based on. He continues in that job today. There is plenty of work ahead.

.